Dr. Nathaniel Tuckerman True (1812-1887)

THE HISTORY OF BETHEL, MAINE

Dr. Nathaniel Tuckerman True

Edited with an Introduction
by Randall H. Bennett

HERITAGE BOOKS
2016

HERITAGE BOOKS
AN IMPRINT OF HERITAGE BOOKS, INC.

Books, CDs, and more—Worldwide

For our listing of thousands of titles see our website
at
www.HeritageBooks.com

Published 2016 by
HERITAGE BOOKS, INC.
Publishing Division
5810 Ruatan Street
Berwyn Heights, Md. 20740

Copyright © 1994 Randall H. Bennett

All rights reserved. No part of this book may be reproduced or transmitted in any form or by any means, electronic or mechanical, including photocopying, recording or by any information storage and retrieval system without written permission from the author, except for the inclusion of brief quotations in a review.

International Standard Book Numbers
Paperbound: 978-1-55613-932-1
Clothbound: 978-0-7884-5963-4

Introduction

The productive years in the life of Dr. Nathaniel Tuckerman True (1812-1887) were a propitious time for antiquarian efforts. Indeed, much of what we know today of Bethel's beginnings is in large part the result of a thirty-year period when True's awareness of the importance of local history spawned several major contributions to the historiography of western Maine.

A manuscript letter about Bethel history written by James Grover for William Williamson's *History of Maine* (1832), and the Segar narrative of the 1781 Indian Raid published in 1825, were the only visible antecedents of Dr. True's first literary work, the "History of Bethel," printed in serial form in the town's first newspaper, *The Bethel Courier*, between 1859 and 1861, and reprinted herein with editorial revisions. True shared with other "patrician" historians, mainly professional people who viewed their literary achievements as an avocation, a concern for thorough research, meticulous transcription, and fair and accurate reporting. On the local level he readily exchanged ideas with such Maine notables as William Willis and Edward Elwell of Portland, Thomas Moulton of Porter, David Noyes of Norway, and George Whitefield Chapman of Gilead. On a broader basis, his writing appears to indicate admiration and emulation of the works of Francis Parkman and Henry Adams.

A Pownal, Maine, native born in 1812 and trained at Bowdoin College for a medical career, True soon became absorbed with "matters foreign to the sick room," and in balancing an interest in research and writing with that of medicine, chose teaching as a profession. Nevertheless, during his terms as principal of the Academy at Monmouth (1837-46) and that at Bethel (1848-61), one finds frequent mention of his labors in botany, mineralogy, geology, and chemistry, as well as his dedication to agricultural societies (he helped found Maine's first "Farmer's Club" at Bethel in 1853).

Joseph Williamson's voluminous *Bibliography of the State of Maine* (1896) provides an indication of the range of Dr. True's writings, but the list is anything but exhaustive. His promotion and eventual documentation of the "antiquarian supper" at Bethel in 1855 was no doubt one of his first published articles. Thereafter, they appear extensively in the *Oxford Democrat*, the *Portland Transcript*, the *Lewiston Journal*, the *Bethel Courier*, and other Maine papers of the day.

Beyond the newspaper essays, True's pen produced innumerable articles for scholarly journals. Some, such as his "New Localities of Minerals in Maine" (1863) and "Grooved Boulders in Bethel, Me." (1862), both printed in the *Proceedings of the Portland Society of Natural Histo-*

ry, combined scientific inquiry with historical investigation. True's frequent mention of Bethel's unique geological and geographic features undoubtedly succeeded in promoting the town, which by the 1850s had become a major stopping-off point in the White Mountain region.

As an active member of the Maine Historical Society and a corresponding member of that in Wisconsin, Dr. True had access to a wealth of archival material, as well as published records of other towns and states. Between 1877 and 1884, while he was the head of schools at Bethel and Litchfield, Maine, and Gorham and Milan, New Hampshire, he contributed over a dozen articles to the recently-reprinted periodical *Old Times In North Yarmouth, Maine*. Besides giving us some clues as to his genealogical background in the Yarmouth area, the Doctor recalled his school days at North Yarmouth Academy in the 1830s, describing himself as "a raw, country lad, dressed in homespun." On a more humorous note, his comments on boarding-house life provide certain insights: "We cooked food when compelled to do so from sheer hunger, and washed the dishes from pure necessity, the safe rule being to do so when we could not well decide what was in them last." True's biographical sketch of Ezekiel Holmes (he succeeded Holmes as Editor of the *Maine Farmer* from 1865-69) and his "History of the Press of Oxford County" in Griffin's *The Press of Maine* (1871) also stand out as important contributions in the field of historical writing.

Like some of his Maine contemporaries, Dr. N. T. True was probably less an interpreter of history, than a recorder of it. Notwithstanding, the massive bulk of his original 102 chapter "History of Bethel" is seen today as one of the earliest and most significant efforts of its type to appear in print in Maine before the Civil War. Included in this important study is information on land grants, the settlement of the upper Androscoggin valley, town meetings, church history, biography, and the famous "Last Indian Raid" of 1781. Of his attempt at preserving Bethel's past, True wrote in 1862:

> [These sketches] were written under great disadvantages, and especially amid a pressure of other duties. No claim, whatever, is presented on the score of literary merit. His great object has been to embody the facts in his possession as far as possible, and leave them for the use of the future historian. It was well that these facts were collected before the death of the first settlers. Ten years later, and most of the early history of the town would have been irrecoverably lost.

Not surprisingly, many of True's findings later made their way into William B. Lapham's *History of Bethel* (1891), though the latter borrows freely from the earlier work without direct citations. In addition, a good portion of True's writings on Bethel, especially those relating to the local Indians, were not included in the 1891 volume, and are thus published here for the first time in book form.

In editing Dr. True's "History of Bethel," I have had access to a copy annotated by the author himself over a century ago. This fact enabled me to correct typographical errors in spelling and dating with a higher degree of accuracy than might otherwise have been possible. Where needed for clarity's sake, I have modernized capitalization and punctuation, and have removed sentences that were clearly repetitious. To improve the organization and readability of True's manuscript, I have combined or re-ordered many of his original chapters, re-titling most, and reducing their number drastically. While it is important to recognize that some of True's statements, particularly those regarding the origins of certain place names, have since been corrected, his theories retain value for those studying the times during which he wrote. To enhance True's text, a number of period illustrations, published through the courtesy of the Bethel Historical Society, Inc., have been added.

It is significant to emphasize that the largest area of Dr. True's interest, and one on which he was most widely known and acclaimed, was the Maine Indian. In fact, the first thirty-five chapters of his "History of Bethel" were devoted to accounts of the Ossipee, Pequawket and Anasagunticook tribes with special attention paid to the Indian language and its English translation. Among his contributions on the subject for periodicals were "Names and Location of Tribes on the Androscoggin" (*Historical Magazine*, 1864), "Collation of Geographical Names in the Algonkin Language" (*Essex Institute Historical Collections*, 1866), and "The Indians" (*Old Times*, 1879). The story is told that his great collection of unpublished Indian manuscripts was sold to an archives after his death in 1887. Perhaps, in time, some of these writings will also be "re-discovered."

Commemorative motives prompted Dr. True to accept the role of orator at numerous historical celebrations, many of which were in Oxford County, Maine. On August 20, 1863, he spoke at the Fryeburg Centennial. In 1867 he was present and delivered an address at the marking of Mollockett's grave in Andover. When the 1874 Bethel Centennial occurred (centered around his Broad Street home), he prepared a lengthy speech which subsequently appeared in printed form. One year later, he participated in the Waterford Centennial. During the 1881 Indian Raid Centennial, he gave a stirring oration before a gathering in Bethel's Kimball Park. If the municipalities failed to publish his protracted lectures, Dr. True usually saw to it that local newspapers did.

Second only to his "History of Bethel" in volume was True's 1882 "History of Gorham, N.H." published in successive issues of the *Gorham Mountaineer*. True's remarks served to encourage further study on the topic, and letters he received were quickly inserted into the text. His researches on Gorham were later utilized in the *History of Coos County, N.H.* (1888).

Throughout his life, Dr. True's concern with history was always to commemorate, to preserve, to collect, and to record. Speaking at a reunion of his former students held at Bethel in 1884, True noted, "For fifty-two years...I have never known what it was to have a well-rested brain." Today's historians, amateur and professional, can be grateful for True's efforts to capture an important slice of northern New England's past before it disappeared forever.

Randall H. Bennett
Curator of Collections
Bethel Historical Society, Inc.

TABLE OF CONTENTS

Preface	ix
Chapter 1 - Sudbury Canada Grant	1
Chapter 2 - Joseph Twitchell	5
Chapter 3 - Proprietors and Surveys	8
Chapter 4 - Early Settlers	11
Chapter 5 - Indians and the 1781 Raid	26
Chapter 6 - Molly Ockett	67
Chapter 7 - Matalluck	71
Chapter 8 - Other Indians of Note	75
Chapter 9 - Block Houses	77
Chapter 10 - Plantation Record	79
Chapter 11 - 1785 Freshet	81
Chapter 12 - Notable Residents	83
Chapter 13 - Hunting	95
Chapter 14 - Act of Incorporation	97
Chapter 15 - Ecclesiastical History	101
Chapter 16 - Physicians	117
Chapter 17 - Lawyers	163
Chapter 18 - Ministers	167
Chapter 19 - Education	182
Chapter 20 - Revolutionary Soldiers	188
Chapter 21 - Resident Proprietors in Lower Parish	190
Chapter 22 - Politics	191
Chapter 23 - Village of Bethel Hill	194
Chapter 24 - Geology, Natural History and Botany	196
Index	203

LIST OF ILLUSTRATIONS

Dr. Nathaniel Tuckerman True (1812-1887) .... frontispiece
The Bethel Courier, with one of Dr. True's local
   history columns on the left x
Site of Eleazer Twitchell's saw mill on Mill Brook 6
Original plan of Bethel (Sudbury, Canada), 1760's 10
"Captain" Eleazer Twitchell and wife, Matha Mason 18
Map of Sudbury, Canada (Bethel), c. 1780 22
Map of Maine Indian tribal lands with Bethel shown
   on the upper Androscoggin River 26
Map of 1781 Indian Raid of Sudbury, Canada 50
Middle Intervale Meetinghouse, 1816 114
Dr. Timothy Carter's "Brick-end House," 1816,
   Middle Intervale 118
Dr. Moses Mason 120
Dr. John Grover 120
William Frye 164
Rev. Daniel Gould 168
First Gould Academy Building, 1836 184
Map of Bethel Hill Village, 1858 194
Swift/Wiley Block, Main Street, Bethel Hill 194
Dr. Moses Mason's House, 1813 194
Atlantic & St. Lawrence Railroad Station
   (later Grand Trunk) 194
Map of the Town of Bethel, 1858 198

Preface

I suppose it to be necessary for me to write a Preface to my present undertaking, in which shall be set forth the reasons that have prompted me to commence, and, as far as possible, carry through a work fraught with no pecuniary advantage whatever. The only explanation I have is that which may be given to many other things of a public nature -- somebody must do it, or it will not be done.

The materials for a History of the Town have been accumulating on my hands for several years. Many of them, and among them some of the most interesting and important, were obtained from the oldest settlers who are now dead. We have but few records save those in the memory of men advanced in life; and unless they are transferred to writing, will soon be lost forever.

Among the living, to whom I am especially indebted, should be mentioned first, HON. MOSES MASON, who had previously collected much valuable information, and whom I really ought to regard as a co-laborer with me. Without his assistance and encouragement, I could hardly have dared to commence this work in arranging the material already selected. I am also under especial obligations to DEA. GEORGE W. CHAPMAN, who has been familiar with the history of the town nearly 70 years. Mr. Joseph Twitchell, the second person born in town, has also furnished much assistance. Jedediah Burbank, Esq., and Mr. John A. Twitchell, have rendered valuable service from time to time.

Among the dead, special mention should be made of Mr. Nathaniel Swan, for many facts respecting the Indians; Captain Norman Clark, Capt. Peter Twitchell, and Mr. Charles Stearns. --In private conversation with these, many facts of great value have been unexpectedly brought to light, which will be interwoven into the History from time to time.

In the entire absence of any Plantation Records, it is not to be expected that a complete history of the town can be given, or of its first settlement. This is now impossible.

One great object we have in view is to embody such facts as may come into our possession for the entertainment of the present generation, and which may serve to aid the future historian of the town and state.

N. T. TRUE

Bethel, Me. Jan. 1, 1859.

The Bethel Courier.

A Weekly Family Newspaper, Neutral in Politics, devoted to Literature, Agriculture, Education, the Mechanic Arts, and the News of the Day.

VOL. 1. BETHEL, ME., FEBRUARY 4, 1859. NO. 8.

The Bethel Courier.

SMITH & NUTTING, Proprietors.

Published every FRIDAY MORNING—Office in FOSTER'S Block, BETHEL HILL

TERMS:

One Copy one year, (if paid in advance) - $1.00
" " " " " six months, .50

If payment is delayed till the close of the year, $1.50 will be charged.

All communications of a business character should be directed to the "BETHEL COURIER."

TERMS OF ADVERTISING.

Square of 16 lines or less, 3 insertions, $1.00
" " " " 1 month, 1.25
" " " " 3 " 2.00
" " " " 6 " 3.50
" " " " 1 year, 5.00

Transient Advertisements payable in advance.

☞ S. R. NILES, (successor to V. B. Palmer,) Advertising Agent, No. 1, Scollay's Building, Court street, Boston, is authorized to receive advertisements for this paper, at the same rates as required by us.

☞ DAVID C. LITTLE, Jun., Exchange street, Portland, is our authorized Agent, to receive Advertisements and Subscriptions for the Courier.

☞ Paper discontinued, unless at our option, till arrearages are paid.

No deductions will in any case be made from the advertised rates of the Courier.

Job Printing of all kinds executed with neatness and despatch at this office.

Business Cards.

History of Bethel.

BY N. T. TRUE.

CHAPTER V.

Among the first who came to Bethel was Lieut. Nathaniel Segar. Having recently succeeded in recovering a sketch of his life written by himself it will be well to transcribe in this chapter a brief account of the "BETHEL CAPTIVES." It is to be regretted that in a business character of the narrator tell his own unvarnished story.

"I, NATHANIEL SEGAR, was born at Newton, in the County of Middlesex, and Commonwealth of Massachusetts. I resided here until the year 1774. In the spring of this year, I went to a place called Sudbury Canada, now Bethel, on the great Androscoggin river, Maine. I worked here several months, and then returned back to Newton, the same fall, and remained there during the winter.

On the 19th of April, 1775, the British troops made an excursion a fort at Montgomery. We worked ed into New Jersey. We arrived upon this fort about three weeks, and here some time in the month of December. I was not able to do duty, got the fort in a good way before we sailed, the fort is a good way before we left it.

After this, our regiment was ordered town, in the Jerseys, until the 3rd of up the North river for Canada. We Jan. 1777. On this day, I received sailed to Albany, and then marched my discharge; and also a passport to Lake George. We then went in that I might pass all guards till I bateaux, and rowed in them 45 miles came to Boston. After most fatiguing to another landing. We landed here, ing journey, under my feeble circumstances, and hauled our boats and baggage by stances, I arrived to my father's house land about a mile and as half, to the in Newton, and into the bosom of my waters of Lake Champlain, and there friends, very much to my own and we rowed to Ticonderoga. Some days their great joy and satisfaction. after we arrived here, we marched to I received no pay nor provisions to Crownpoint. Soon after we marched bear my expenses on my long and tedious journey home. I sold what to St. Johns, in Canada. We had not clothing I could possibly spare to help it was said, marched 120 miles. me on the road. I was under the Here we hired a Frenchman to pilot necessity to beg, and to make use of us to Chamblee, about 12 miles. all lawful means to help me along on In a few days we set out again with my journey to my friends, but through our baggage in bateaux, down the the mercy and goodness of God, and river St. Lawrence for Quebec. We the charity of many friends, I accomplished my journey in the latter part plished my journey in the latter part rowed 40 or 50 miles, to a place, cal- of January. After some time, I regained my health and strength, and I led Sorel. Here the enemy met with us, and we were obliged to retreat was able to do some business. back to Chamblee with some loss.— My journey reminds me of the We made our stand here for some

---

Original Tale.

A HEART'S HISTORY.

"Go opened the whole wide universe
Before your spirit as a chart;
You'll find no greater mystery
Than that dark novel—the human heart."

How the gay world, in which I move, will scoff at the mention of a heart by me, Helen Clarendon,—whose cheek they ne'er saw blanched; whose lip, in their presence, never trembled; whose eyes, they think guileless of tears, and whose proud step, and firm tones were never known to falter.—How often as I have moved in their midst, have I heard them saying in low tones, "She is beautiful, but all so cold—so heartless." Ay—even when I stood over the form of my dead child, with my own hands arranged its little shroud, and with undimmed eyes, pressed my last kiss upon its marble brow, they whispered—

"Cold, proud woman! even the loss of her only child fails to move her. She could not have loved it!"

Love thee! my Allme, my beautiful sinless one; did I not love thee; his affections undemonstrated, and now as I look back to the days of childhood, I cannot remember ever to have received our kisses from the lips of either parent. How often have I watched my little playmate, Bell Enfield, when in her father's arms I she laughingly resisted his fervent kisses; or listened to her mother's soft voice, as it called her by a dozen endearing names, till my childish heart overflowed in tears that such love was not for me.

I remember well how? one day, I stole up to my father's side, and gently possessing myself of his hand, timidly imprinted a kiss thereon. Not being repulsed, I grew bolder and with the ardent impulse of a loving nature, I twined my arms close about his neck and kissed his cheek. He seemed surprised at this unwonted display of affection, and when, with a full heart, I looked in his face and asked if he did not love his child, he replied, though not unkindly, "Pooh foolish child! but run away now, I am tired!" and as I turned to leave the room, the loud derisive laugh

Chapter 1
Sudbury Canada Grant

In the year 1770 what now constitutes Oxford County was nearly an unexplored wilderness. The western portion of the County, on the Saco River, had long been known to the earliest settlers of the country as the residence of a powerful tribe of Indians, the Pequakets, whose headquarters were about two miles west of Fryeburg village.

On the eastern boundary of the County were located the Rockomekoes at Canton Point, on the "Amariscoggin River," which is defined by some "the banks of a river abounding in dried meat," while the interior of the County was almost wholly unknown, save to the hunter, to whom this was long a favorite region, who followed up the tributaries of the Great and Little Androscoggin Rivers in quest of game.

The few remaining Indians had been reduced by war and disease to an insignificant number, and previous to this time had nearly all removed to Canada and united with the St. Francois Tribe, located on the St. Francois River, where quite a large tribe still resides.

A few permanent localities were then known by their Indian names, as Ogiochee, the White Mountains; Umbagog Lake, signifying shallow water; Pennacook, now Rumford Falls; Songo, "the place where they set traps and caught nothing," a pond near the south corner of the Town; Pequaket, which Molly Ockett defined, "*Dust from leaves*," alluding to the rising of the dust from the leaves when walking over them after a freshet in the Saco; Connecticut, Coos, *crooked* or *Long Rivers*. Others have obtained different definitions of these words. Different tribes and individuals gave various interpretations to the names of these localities. It is sufficient to state that at this time these were the most important and best known names occurring in this vicinity previous to its settlement. (Of the Indian history of the Town, I shall write more fully in another chapter.)

The towns around the White Hountains in New Hampshire appear to have been generally opened for settlement earlier than those of Oxford County. The Town of Shelburne, 12 miles west of Bethel, received a charter as early as 1768, though it was not surveyed for a settlement till 1771. Most of the towns in that vicinity were chartered and settlements commenced previous to the Revolutionary War.

In 1762 Gen. Joseph Frye received a grant from the king of the present town of Fryeburg, in consideration of his services as an officer in the king's army. The first settlement was made in 1763, and was consequently the earliest in the County. A few families had made an opening in Bridgton previous to 1776, but to reach Fryeburg, the nearest important settlement from Bethel, was a distance of 35 miles through an unbroken forest.

A person starting from Bethel in 1776, in a south easterly direction, would have traveled as far as New Gloucester, a distance of more than 40 miles, without meeting a settlement.

About this time families had moved into Jay, 40 miles below on the Androscoggin River, and still farther down, at Lewiston Falls.

The first step towards the settlement of Bethel took place in June 1768, when a grant of land, by the name of Sudbury Canada, six miles and three-quarters square, situated on the Androscoggin River, in the supposed County of Cumberland, was granted by the General Court of Massachusetts Bay in New England, to Josiah Richardson and his associates residing in Sudbury, Mass., and vicinity, for services rendered in the French and Indian wars. Some of these claims extended as far back as 1690 for services rendered in an expedition to Canada that year, as it appears from two quitclaim deeds now in the possession of Mr. John A. Twitchell of Bethel.

An extract from the early history of New England may serve to show the connection between that and the history of our town:

"About this period, the French in Canada and Nova Scotia instigated the northern and eastern Indians to commence hostilities against the English settlements. Dover and Salmon Falls, in New Hampshire, Casco, in Maine, and Schenectady, in New York, were attacked by different parties of French and Indians, and shocking barbarities committed. Regarding Canada as the principal source of their troubles, New England and New York formed the bold project of reducing it by force of arms. For this purpose, they raised an army under General Winthrop, which was sent against Montreal, and equipped a fleet, which, commanded by Sir Wm. Phipps, was destined to attack Quebec. The season was so far advanced when the fleet arrived at Quebec, Oct. 5th, 1690, the French so superior in numbers, the weather so tempestuous, and the sickness so great among the soldiers, that the expedition was abandoned. Success had been so confidently expected, that no adequate provision was made for the payment of the troops. There was danger of a mutiny. In this extremity, the government issued *bills of credit* as a substitute for money; and these were the first ever issued in America."

It was for services in this expedition that the grant of land, known as Sudbury Canada, was made, after more than three-fourths of a century, to the descendants of those engaged in that expedition.

Such are some of the connecting links, small to be sure, which unite the history of Bethel with that of our common country.

A meeting of the proprietors was held, and Joseph Twitchell, Esq., of Sherborn, Mass., and Isaac Fuller were chosen to survey the township and divide it into lots that year. Assessments were made, from time to time, by the proprietors to meet the expenses attendant on its affairs.

As the proprietors, by their grant, appear not to have been very much restricted in their location farther than to locate on the Androscoggin River, six and three-fourths miles square, they extended their survey along the best intervales of the river for a distance of nearly 17 miles. From a plan of the river and lots drawn by them, now before me, it appears that they did not at first extend their survey to the upland until the intervale lands were entirely secured. -- These lots were long and narrow, each containing 40 acres.

On the uplands the lots were divided into squares of 100 acres. The town is now about ten miles in length and an average of four in width.

After the return of the surveyors to Massachusetts, Twitchell saw and appreciated the future value of these lands, and as many of the proprietors refused to pay the assessments, he commenced buying up their claims until he eventually had in his possession no less than 40 shares.

The earliest record that has come into my possession is the following quitclaim deed, dated Sept. 7th, 1768. It is here given *verbatim et literatim*:

Know all Men by these Presents that I Ebenezer Twichell of Sherbourn in the County of Middlesex and Province of the Massachusetts Bay In New England -- Husbandman

In Consideration of Six Shillings -- Lawfull money paid me by Joseph Twitchel of Sherbourn a fore said gentleman

Have Remissed Released and for ever quit claimed and by these presents for my self my Heirs do Remiss Release and for Ever quit Claim unto the said Joseph Twitchell and his Heirs for Ever all my Ritte and title to a Township of Land granted to Josiah Richardson and others June 1768 whose ancisters ware for the Expedition to Canada in 1690 to gether with all the Rite title Intrest use and property Clame & demand what so Ever

to Have and to Hold all the be fore granted and Bargained Premises with the Apurtenances to Him the said Joseph Twitchel and to His Heirs and asigns for Ever and to Covinant with the said Joseph Twitchel His Heirs and asigns that I am Lawfully seazed in fee of the Premises and Have good Rite to Convey the same to the said Joseph Twitchel and to His Heirs and asigns for ever

In witness where of I Have Hereunto Set my Hand and Seal this seventh day of September 1768 in ye Eighth year of His Majestys Reign George ye 3d King &c

Signed Sealed
and Delivered In Presents of
    EBENEZER TWITCHEL
    ABIJAH TWITCHEL
    EBENEZER TWITCHEL
Middlesex ss March 10th 1770.

then the above Named Ebenezer Twitchel Personally appeared and acknowlledged the above wrighten Instrument to be his Free act & deed
    Before me --

Jos. Perry Justice Peace.

Chapter 2
Joseph Twitchell

Before proceeding farther in our history, it is necessary to give a sketch of the life of Capt. Joseph Twitchell, who had the most direct interest of any one in the earliest history of the town, although he never became a resident. Additional interest will be given from the fact that he was the ancestor of all the numerous persons of that name in this vicinity.

Joseph Twitchell, Esq. was born in Sherborn, Mass., Feb. 13th 1718-19. His forefather, Joseph Twitchell, *alias* Tuchill, of Dorchester, was admitted to the freeman's oath May 14th 1634. "He was a man of irreproachable character; and tradition represents him to have been a Cyclops in stature, and a Hercules in strength," traits not altogether eradicated from his descendants. Benj. Twitchell of Dorchester, probably his brother, is supposed to have removed to Medfield as early as 1663 where he and his family took the name of Twitchell. Joseph had a son Joseph, who enlisted with others to extinguish the Indian title to lands in Sherborn, in 1682. A son of his, Joseph, was born in 1688, and married Elizabeth Holbrook. His son Joseph Twitchell Esq., was the subject of our present sketch, who married Deborah Fairbanks, June 20th 1739, daughter of Joseph Fairbanks of Sherborn, and with her was received into the church, July 27th 1740.

He settled in Sherborn, on the east side of a place known as Dirty Meadow, on the south side of a steep rocky hill, and became the leading citizen of that town for many years. He served as Captain of the Militia, and was a Commisary for the Army in 1776. He was chosen Representative to the General Court, a Justice of the Peace, and for fourteen years acted as Town Clerk and Treasurer. He was appointed guardian to settle the estate of deceased Indians at Natic. Long after the estates were settled, and after his death, the Indians came to Sherborn, to his son Peter's house, to see if they did not still have an unsettled claim.

An anecdote is related of him as follows: He had been to Halifax on some business, and on his return home the vessel encountered a violent storm, during which the rudder head was split to pieces, and the vessel rendered unmanageable. The captain gave up in despair, and said that they must go to the bottom. Capt. Twitchell examined the nature of the accident, and being of an inventive turn of mind, suspended a man headforemost over the stern of the vessel, a man holding on to each of his ankles, who with an axe cut a hole through the vessel into the cabin. Through this he fastened a temporary tiller with which they managed the vessel, so that she arrived safely at Boston. He drew a plan of the course of the vessel from Halifax to Boston which is now in my possession.

He married for a second wife, widow Deborah (Sanger) Fasset, June 5th, 1786, and died with the apoplexy March 12, 1792. He sustained a high reputation among his contemporaries, and his memory is still cherished by his grandchildren. He had fourteen children. As we may frequently refer to some of them we will insert them here: 1st Samuel; 2nd Joseph; 3d Elizabeth, married Joel Wight; 4th Eleazer, resided in Bethel; 5th Ezra, resided in Bethel; 6th Martha, married Nathan Bixby; 7th Deborah; 8th Abel; 9th Deborah, married Joseph Maynard of Framingham; 10th Molly (Mary), married Moses Rider; 11th Amos, died unmarried in the army; 12th Eli, resided in Bethel; 13th Peter, resided in Bethel; 14th Julia, born March 18th, 1766, married Wm. Tucker, of Framingham. Captain Twitchell never resided in Bethel, but having a good opportunity to become acquainted with the natural resources of the town, he immediately commenced buying up the various claims of others.

At a meeting of the proprietors April 6th, 1774, they voted to sell the Mill Lot, so called, being the 24th lot Range 3rd, and the 23rd lot Range 4th, to Capt. Joseph Twitchell, for the sum of fifteen pounds silver money. This was a higher sum than Peter Minuits paid 125 years previous, for the whole of Manhattan Island on which New York city now stands. The price paid by him was twenty-four dollars. It may not be uninteresting to many, to know the boundaries of lot 24, in Range 3rd.

Commencing at the Mill-dam near Caleb Rowe's dwelling house, it runs easterly, between the house and stable of Dr. N. T. True, to a stake in the swamp on the Frye estate, thence northerly, back of John Hasting's and Dr. Moses Mason's buildings, running through the Parsonage, now occupied by Rev. E. A. Buck, and extending into the lot owned by Stiles and Chapman, thence westerly through a house lot recently fenced out by Valentine Stiles, and extending to the road north of Josiah Brown's dwelling house, and thence southwardly to the first mentioned bound.

This lot it will be perceived embraced a large portion of the village at Bethel Hill, including also the mill privileges. Capt. Twitchell built a saw mill that year, 1774, on the fall near Eber Clough's Starch Factory. The remains of the dam are still to be seen. This appears to have been the first building erected in the town. He did not, however, secure a title

Site of Eleazer Twitchell's saw mill on Mill Brook

to the lots till 1783. That same year he built a grist mill at the lower fall on the spot where the present grist mill now stands at Bethel Hill. On the opposite side of the street on land owned by Mr. David Brown was erected the first dwelling house at Bethel Hill, which was built for the accomodation of the miller. This was in 1779.

Capt. T's primary object was to induce settlers to move into the town, but for several years after settlers came, there was no miller. Each patron carried his grist to the mill, ground it, and left it for the next customer. The same was the case with the saw mill. The natural consequence was, that the grist mill soon became out of repair, and as it had a large undershot wheel it required more water than the stream was able to supply. This rendered the situation of the early settlers very trying.

Chapter 3

Proprietors and Surveys

Among the *original* proprietors who received the grant of the Township, I find only the names of Richard Burtt, Isaac Baldwin, Joseph Morse, Nathaniel Morse, Lodwick Dows, who, by the records went in the expedition to Canada in 1690; Edward Twitchell, who probably went in the same expedition, Moses Noyes, Joseph Twitchell, who was probably the father of Capt. Joseph Twitchell, Esq., John Green, Daniel Walker, Joseph Trumbull, Abner Newton, Joseph Merion, John Fay, James Paterson, Edward Clap, Richard Ward, Nathaniel Dike. The rights of the last nine individuals were drawn by Elijah Livermore of Waltham, Mass., Gentleman, and sold to Aaron Richardson and Jonathan Clark of Newton, in Dec. 1774, for the sum of one hundred and eighty pounds, lawful money.

Among the second class of proprietors, or those who petitioned the General Court for the grant, as the lawful heirs of the former proprietors, I find the names of Joseph Twitchell, Esq., of Sherborn, Josiah Richardson, of Sudbury, Jeduthan Baldwin, Esq., Thaddeus Richardson, Capt. Josiah Stone, Framingham, Thomas Parker, Aaron Richards, Newton, Nathaniel Eames, of Framingham, Cornelius Wood, Sudbury, Elijah Bent, Sudbury, Nath'l Morse, probably son of the same name, Joshua Kibby, Ebenezer Twitchell, Sudbury, who drew the right of Edward Twitchell, Nath'l Belknap, Brookfield, John Noyes, Esq., Nath'l Sparrok, from whom Sparrowhawk Mountain in Bethel received its name, and Capt. Jonathan Fay. None of this class ever settled in Bethel. It is possible, though I have no evidence, that some of the original proprietors may have performed public service at a later period than 1690. Each grant was composed of three lots. From the original plan of the Town now in my possession, it appears that the surveyors at first only laid out into lots the intervales and islands along the Androscoggin River, as being of primary importance.

The first meeting of the proprietors of which I have any record was held Dec. 5th, 1769, when the following transactions occurred: --

"Whereas the Proprietors of A Township of Land granted by the General Court to Josiah Richardson and his Associates of the Contents of six miles and three quarters square and is now Layed out on Androscoggin River In the County of Cumberland, and at a meeting of the said Proprietors of said Township on the Fifth day of December a.d. 1769 they did order their comm'tt to Post and Sell Every of the said Proprietors Rights that Had not Payed Their Tax of Fourty Shillings taxed on their Rights and we Josiah Richardson, Esqr, Cornelius Wood, gentleman, Both of Sudbury and Josiah Stone of Framingham, gentleman, and all of the County of Middlesex. the said Proprietors committe By them chosen Impowered to Sell the delinkquent Proprietors Rights who had not payed -- Said Tax. and we having observed the directions of the Law in that case made and Provided. Now Send greeting. Now know ye that we the said Josiah Richardson, Esqr Corneliues Wood gentleman Both of Sudbury and Josiah Stone of Framingham gentleman & all of the County of middlesex & Province of the Massachusetts Bay in New England In our Said Capacity, for the Consideration of the sum of four Pound, one Shilling to us in hand well and Truly Payed before the Ensealing and delivery hereof By Joseph Twitchel of Sherbourn in said County of Middlesex gentlemen. The Receipt where of we do hereby acknoledge and for that Consideration Do Sell and Confirm to Him the said Joseph Twichel and to His Heirs & assigns for Ever two whole Rights in the said Township the first Lott of one of P. Knights is No. 9 on the South side the River and was drawn on the Right of Joshua Kibby, the first Lott of the other Right is No. 13 or the forth Lott on the East End, and was drawn on the Right of Nath'l Morse. To gether with all the Right and after Draughts to Each of the said Rights Respectively Belonging, or in any wise appertaining to the same. To them the said Joshua Kibby & Nath'l Morse To Have and to Hold to Him the said Joseph Twitchel and to His Heirs and assigns for Ever to His and Their only use Benefit and Behoof for ever all the afore granted and Bargained Premises with all the appurtenances and we the said Josiah Richardson Corneliues Wood & Josiah Stone In our said capacity do Covenant to and with the said Joseph Twitchel -- and His Heirs and assigns that before the Ensealing and delivery here of we have full Power and Lawful athority to sell convey and the before granted and Bargained Premises with all the appurtenances in manner afore said and that he the said Joseph Twitchel and His Heirs and assigns shall and may from time to time and at all times For Ever here after have Hold use occupy and Injoy all the afore granted Land, Premises with all the appurtenances free and clear freely & clearly In witness whereof we the said Josiah Richardson Cornealiues Wood and Josiah Stone have Hereunto Set our Hands and Seals this 21st day of March Anno que Domini 1770 and In tenth year of His majestys Reign

JOSIAH RICHARDSON

CORNELIUS WOOD

JOSIAH STONE

Signed Sealed and Delivered in Presents of us

PETER BETH

CYPRIAN HOW

Middlesex ss., on the 26th day of March A D 1770 the within Named Josiah Richardson Corneliues Wood Josiah Stone the Ensealed hereof Personaly appearing Acknowledged the within Written Instrument to be their free and vollantary act and deed
Before me
JOHN NOYES Justis of Peace"

Similar meetings were held in 1773, 1774, 1777, and 1783. These were held chiefly for the purpose of selling the rights of those who had failed to pay taxes assessed by the proprietors. It does not appear that any of second class of proprietors ever settled in town, but generally sold their claims for a small consideration, as must naturally have been the case during the Revolutionary War. Capt. Joseph Twitchell appeared always ready to purchase the rights of those who failed to fulfill the requirements of the proprietors.

Other names of the original and second class of proprietors may, at some future time, be obtained from the Colonial Records of Massachusetts, and from the Records of the proprietors, should they be in existence.

The original survey extended on the borders of what are now the towns of Albany and Greenwood, a distance of nine miles, on the east and west sides, about four and a half miles. -- The town, including Hanover, resembled the gable end of a house; the S. E. side being the base, and the ridgepole being a few rods from Bear River Bridge in the extreme north part of the town. From this point the town is about six miles in width. Probably there were not far from thirty-three thousand acres of land in the survey. The Androscoggin River runs about eighteen miles through the town, embracing sixteen islands, nearly all of which are most valuable for cultivation. The number of intervale lots were some over one hundred.

The original base line ran E. twenty degrees N. There is now a variation of the needle from one and a half to two and a half degrees W. of N.

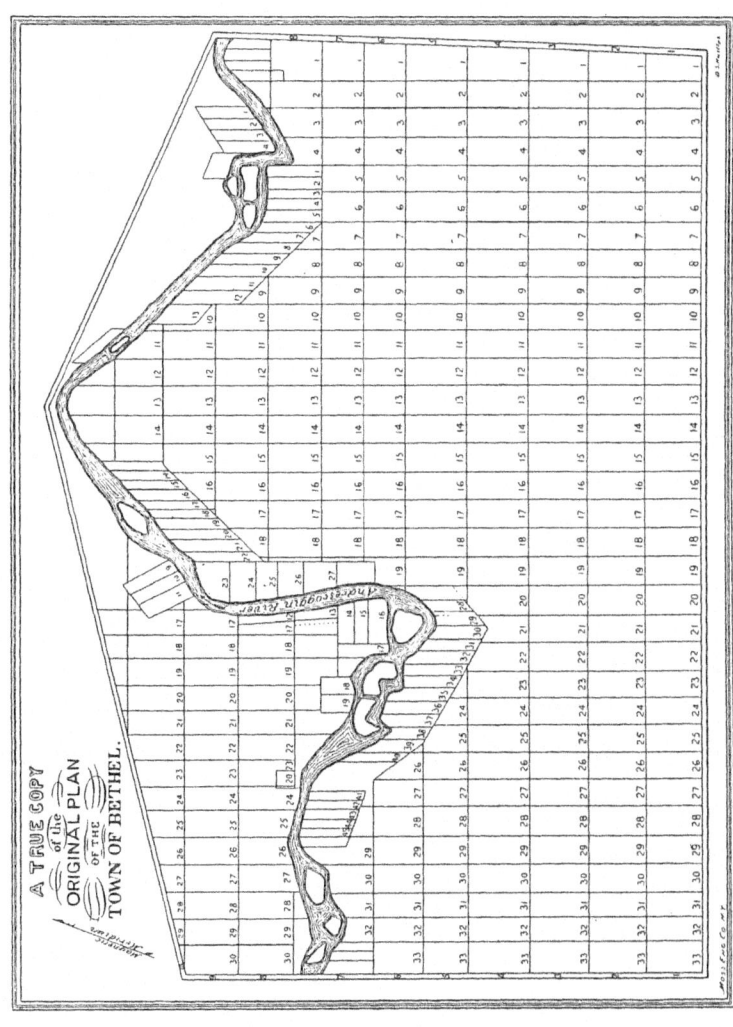

Chapter 4
Early Settlers

In the entire absence of any records, I am compelled to rely on the memory of our oldest citizens for the facts and dates in this and the next chapter. It would be strange if, in every instance, they should be correct. Subsequent investigations will, no doubt, rectify any errors that may occur, and which will be noticed before I complete what I have to say respecting the history of the town.

Immediately after the survey of the town, attention was directed to the fertile lands in the *Androscoggin country*, as this portion of the State was then called.

In the year 1773, ten men came through the forests to Sudbury Canada -- brought their provisions with them -- built camps and felled five acres each on ten different lots, but the Revolutionary War breaking out, they became frightened and left. In May 1776, three of them returned, viz.: Jesse Dustan, who settled on the farm now occupied by Adam Willis of Hanover, John York, who came from Standish and cleared up the farm now occupied by Amos Young in the lower part of the town. One man by the name of Kimball settled on the farm now owned by Foster Farwell, but afterwards left the town. There also came with them Benjamin Russell, Esq., and his brother Abraham. From his grandson, Abbott Russell, I learn the following facts:

Benjamin Russell was born in Andover, Mass., Jan. 27th, 1737, on the spot, according to tradition, which the first of that name occupied in America. His wife, Mary Proctor, was born in Salem, Mass., Mar. 1st, 1739. He came to Fryeburg among the first settlers, where he resided thirteen years -- was chosen Justice of the Peace while there -- and used to say that he was the first in that office that ever resided in Oxford County. He came to SCOGGIN, as it was then called, with the four others mentioned above, in May, 1776, cleared up three acres of that which had been felled two years previous, planted two acres with corn, and sowed one bushel of rye from which he harvested forty bushels. This was on the farm now owned by his grandson, Abbott Russell. He built a log house below the present buildings that year, as did the others, and returned to their homes for the winter. Abraham Russell built a house, a few rods west of Alder River Bridge, on the land now occupied by Gilman Chapman, Esq. This was carried off by the great freshet in 1785, after which he built the house now occupied by John Russell, near the Narrows.

In the fall of 1776, Mr. Samuel Ingalls and wife came to town from Andover, Mass., and spent the winter on the farm now occupied by Asa Kimball. She rode a part of the way on horseback and the rest of the way traveled on foot. She was the first white woman that came to the town. In consequence of this fact, the proprietors gave her one hundred acres of land. He subsequently removed to Bridgton, and then returned to Bethel, where he died on the farm now occupied by Amos Young. The farm on which he first commenced operations was first occupied by Jonathan Keyes, who afterwards went to Rumford, and was the first settler in that town.

To return to Benj. Russell, Esq. -- The next March 1777, he brought his family to Bethel. Himself and Gen. Hastings, then living in Fryeburg, being mounted on snow-shoes, hauled on handsleds his wife and daughter, then fifteen years old, who afterwards married Nath'l Segar, a distance of fifty miles in two days. They camped the first night near Pettee's Mills in N. Waterford. His wife was consequently the second white woman that came to town.

Mr. Russell performed the business of the plantation, and celebrated the marriages, which were quite as frequent as at the present day. He wrote an elegant hand. He died Nov. 1802. His wife died in 1808.

Jesse Dustan moved to Bethel in 1778. His wife was the third woman that came to town. She had the first child born in Town. His name was Peregrine Dustan. He was born in 1782, a few months before Joseph Twitchell, now residing in the village. In consequence of this, the proprietors gave him 100 acres of land, on the farm now occupied by Vincint Chapman. He became a minister of the Methodist denomination, and died quite young.

James Swan came from Methuen, Mass., and settled in Fryeburg, and in 1779 moved to Bethel on the farm now occupied by Ayers Mason and Algernon S. Chapman. He built a house on the east side of the road about half way from Alder River Bridge to Ayers Mason's. He had four sons who were young men when he came: Joseph Greely, who lived with his father; Elijah, who did not make a permanent settlement in the town; James, who settled on Swan's Hill, in the eastern part of the town; and Nathaniel, who settled on Sunday River in Bethel, where he died.

Joseph Greely occupied the log house built by his father, till the great freshet, Oct. 25th, 1785, when it was swept off. As the water rose so high that the inmates could not all be taken off from the door, he took his mother from the chamber window in a boat and carried her to a place of safety. His wife had a web of cloth in her loom, but so sudden and unexpected was the rise of the water that she could not find an opportunity to cut it out, so it was swept away with the house. Fearing that the spot would be subject to inundation, he built on a more elevated position, where the dwelling house of Ayers Mason now stands. His father was known as the person with whom Sabattis, a well known Indian in this vicinity, lived for many years.

Among the first who came to Bethel was Lieut. Nathaniel Segar. Having recently succeeded in recovering a sketch of his life written by himself it will do very much towards settling some points in the most difficult points of our history, especially in our last chapter. I think it better to let the narrator tell his own unvarnished story.

"I, Nathaniel Segar, was born at Newton, in the County of Middlesex, and Commonwealth of Massachusetts. I resided here until the year 1774. In the spring of this year, I went to a place called Sudbury Canada, now Bethel, on the great Androscoggin River, Maine. I worked here several months, and then returned back to Newton the same fall, and remained there during the winter.

On the 19th of April, 1775, the British troops made an excursion from Boston to Concord to destroy some military stores which had been lodged there by the Americans; and a battle ensued between the British troops and the Americans. After this battle, a regiment from the militia was called for to guard Boston, and to prevent the British troops from making another excursion into the country. I enlisted into this regiment and marched with it to Cambridge.

Soon after, I enlisted as a soldier into the eight month's service, under the command of Capt. Nathan Fuller of Newton. We marched to Cambridge, and joined Col. Gardner's regiment in the continental service, and in the Massachusetts line. We remained at Cambridge for some time. On the 17th of June, Col. Gardner's regiment was ordered to march to Bunker Hill after that bloody battle was commenced; but not having correct information, we were too late to reinforce those on the hill seasonably to afford them much assistance, as our men were retreating when we had gotten to the hill. However, one of our company, named James Walls, who was near me, was wounded, though not mortally; and Colonel Gardner was mortally wounded. In a few days afterwards, he died of his wounds. We retreated with the rest from the hill, and were met by a party, who were bringing refreshments for those who had been in the battle, which were very acceptable to us; as the day was very warm, and we were very much fatigued.

After the battle, our regiment was stationed on Prospect Hill, under the command of Lieut. Col. Bond. We remained here during the eight months' service.

Before my eight months' service was completed, I entered in the same company and regiment as before. Lt. Col. Bond now received a Colonel's commission. In the spring of the year 1776, when the British had evacuated Bunker Hill, I, with a number of other soldiers, went unto the Hill, and found bottles on their tables with the appearance of spirits in them, as though they had run away in great haste. Soon after the British troops had left Boston, our regiment, with the rest of the continental troops, received orders to march to New York. We went to Norwich, in Connecticut, by land. Here we were ordered on board of sloops, and we soon arrived at New York in safety.

In two days after this, 50 men were called from our regiment, and two from our company. I was one of them, to march up the North river, to erect a fort at Montgomery. We worked upon the fort about three weeks, and got the fort in a good way before we left it.

After this, our regiment was ordered up the North river for Canada. We sailed to Albany, and then marched to Lake George. We then went in batteaux, and rowed in them 45 miles to another landing. We landed here, and hauled our boats and baggage by land about a mile and a half to the waters of Lake Champlain, and there we rowed to Ticonderoga. Some days after we arrived here, we marched to Crownpoint. Soon after we marched to St. Johns, at the outlet of Lake Champlain, in safety. We had not, as it was said, marched 120 miles.

Here we hired a Frenchman to pilot us to Chamblee, about 12 miles.

In a few days we set out again with our baggage in batteaux, down the river St. Lawrence for Quebec. We rowed 40 or 50 miles, to a place called Sorel. Here the enemy met with us, and we were obliged to retreat back to Chamblee with some less. -- We made our stand here for some time. Here, too, many of the soldiers caught the small pox. We were all of us in danger of taking this dreadful disease. After proper arrangements had been made, general orders were given, that every man might innoculate. We, however, held our stand, till the army had recovered of this terrible disstemper. After we recovered of the small pox, the army retreated to St. Johns, and from thence over Lake Champlain.

Our army was very feeble at this time, and much debilitated for want of proper medicines, to carry off the relics of the small pox. Many had died, and but a few were fit for duty. However, as we were, we were ordered on board the boats, and to retreat back to Crownpoint. On our passage we rowed day and night, as the Indians were watching our motion. Some of our men, however, landed and were killed by them. We were therefore in danger of being attacked by them.

The waters of the Lake were, at this season of the year, extremely unwholesome. But after great exertions, we arrived at Crownpoint, nearly worn down by hard labor and sickness.

Soon after we arrived at this place, a number of us were ordered to Mount Independence to build barracks and many other employments. We were not here long before very many of us were taken sick with the camp disorder, and the fever and ague. These disorders greatly increased, till it was impossible to carry any more to the hospital. At Fort George, it became so sickly, that our regiment was exempted from duty, as there were scarcely well men enough to take care of the sick. But through the mercy of God, I recovered, while hundreds died with the disease. Col. Bond, the commander of our regiment, died here. But after some time, through the goodness of God, the sickness abated so that in the month of August, all our regiment who were fit for duty were ordered to march under the command of the Lieut. Colonel and Major to Albany. At this time, however, only two companies were fit for duty. I went with them in hopes to be discharged when we came to Albany. When we were ready to march, we were taken over Lake George, and were marched to Albany, but not discharged, as we hoped. Here we remained some days. After this, we were put under the command of Capt. Hatch and being taken on board some vessels, we sailed down the North River, and then marched into New Jersey. We arrived here some time in the month of December. I was not able to do duty. We, however, continued in Morristown, in the Jerseys, until the 3rd of Jan. 1777. On this day, I received my discharge; and also a passport that I might pass all guards till I came to Boston. After a most fatiguing journey, under my feeble circumstances, I arrived to my father's house in Newton, and into the bosom of my friends, very much to my own and their great joy and satisfaction.

I received no pay nor provisions to bear my expenses on my long and tedious journey home. I sold what clothing I could possibly spare to help me on the road. I was under the necessity to beg, and to make use of all lawful means to help me along on my journey to my friends; but through the mercy and goodness of God, and the charity of many friends, I accomplished my journey in the latter part of January. After some time, I regained my health and strength, and I was able to do some business.

My journey reminds me of the prodigal son, when he returned to his father's house in poverty and distress; though I had not spent my time and property in riotous living and with harlots, but in the service of my country. I returned home in poverty and want, yet I found my friends as ready to receive me, and to administer to my necessities, as his were. I had none to reproach me; but we all rejoiced together in that I returned alive, after this fatiguing and distressing campaign.

When the army came to Bennington, in Vermont, there were orders to raise men from the Militia to go there. I enlisted for this service, in a company commanded by Capt. Joseph Fuller, of Newton. We marched to Bennington. When we arrived, we were ordered to Skeensbury, where we continued for some time, as a guard. -- Col. Brown with a party of men, and Capt. Allen, with his rangers, were ordered to march to Lake George landing. We went and destroyed the enemy's Batteaux, took about 200 Hessian prisoners, and a considerable of plunder, which we brought in with us to our camp.

After this, we were ordered to Stillwater, where we arrived not long before the battle at that place. I was not in the battle. I had turned out in a volunteer company of 50 men. We were ordered to guard a swamp, where it was thought the Indians would come, and harass our army. But none came to trouble us. We were continued at this place till the battle was over, and then the company was called in. Our company was left here, as we were not wanted to pursue General Burgoyne and his army.

Some time after this, our company was ordered to White Plains. We tarried here till our time was out, in June, 1778. We had our discharge, and I again set out for Newton, where I safely arrived and rejoiced with my friends and fellow citizens upon the capture of General Burgoyne with his whole army. This memorable event took place Oct. 17, 1777. It so occupied the attention of myself and friends, that we almost forgot the labors and toils I had undergone the present season to accomplish this memorable dispensation of Providence in favor of the American cause. -- Blessed by God for all his favors and mercies.

Lieut. Segar thus continues his narrative: After I returned home to my native town, and had recruited myself, I went to work until August, 1778, when men were called for to march to Rhode Island. I enlisted again in the militia for this service and soon after, we marched to Rhode Island, and the next day after our arrival, we marched toward the enemy, where we remained some time.

While we were stationed here, we had the most severe storm of wind and rain, that ever I had experienced in my life at this season of the year. Many men died through fatigue and drinking cold water, and severity of this cold storm. Many horses likewise died in the storm. There were not half barracks enough to receive the troops and shelter them from the storm. We were unable to secure our cartridges from the wet, and they spoiled. However, we soon drew more, and were prepared for action, should we be called to it.

Soon after, we marched nearer to Newport. The British troops were at this time in possession of it. Our army made a stand here for several months, and made great preparations for battle and for winter quarters, but, on a sudden, we were ordered to retreat from the Island. The enemy being informed of our design, closely pursued us, but we did not experience much injury in the retreat from the Island. After some days, we left the Island, and retreated about six or seven miles to a place called Fall River. Here we kept guard till the first of January, 1779. At this time I was again discharged from the public service of my beloved country; and returned once more to Newton, and into the bosom of my friends with great joy, after a fatiguing campaign. Here I tarried till the spring of this year.

I was one year and eight months, that is, in the years 1775 and 1776, in the continental service; six months in the militia in the year 1777, when Gen. Burgoyne and his army were made prisoners by General Gates; and I was five months in the militia, at Rhode Island, in the year 1778. I was also in the militia two months, at Boston, but do not recollect the time when. The whole time I was in the public service of my country was two years and nine months.

In the spring of the year 1779, I concluded to set out again for Sudbury Canada (Bethel) where I had been the year before the American Revolutionary War commenced. I went in company with my friend, Mr. Jonathan Bartlet. We carried kettles with us to make sugar. The remainder of the season, after we had made several hundred weight of sugar, we spent in clearing land, with a view to make us farms, and to make a permanent settlement in this place. In the fall of this year, we returned to our friends at Newton, where we tarried through the winter.

In the spring of the year 1780, I set out again with my friend Bartlet, and also Mr. Thaddeus Bartlet and a boy by the name of Aaron Barton, for Bethel. When we had arrived here, we employed ourselves in making sugar, and then in clearing and working upon our land. We had very good crops of corn, and other things. In the fall, we concluded to spend the winter in this place, which we did. The Indians here appeared very friendly towards us. They employed themselves in hunting; and we could barter with them for corn and sugar, and for which we received wild meat, tallow, and fur; and hence we lived quietly and comfortably with them. We labored to live in good friendship. However, we had many difficulties to encounter, as is always the case in settling new countries. We had no roads; we went by marked tress, and hauled in our necessaries on hand-sleighs. We had no neighbors settled near us; and there being but few families in this place, it was for our interest and safety to cultivate peace and a good understanding with the savages of the wilderness.

There had been a Mill built in the upper part of the town, by Capt. Joseph Twitchell, one of the original proprietors of the town, which was about ten miles from where we had pitched; it was now out of order, and could not be repaired till another season. But to remedy this evil, we went to work and made us a little Hand-mill to grind our corn. We succeeded very well with our mill; and ground our corn in it till the next spring when the former mill was repaired. We all enjoyed good health during the winter.

There were only five families, at this time, that were settled in this part of the town, and not very near together viz. Mr. Samuel Ingalls, Mr. Jesse Dustin, Mr. John York, Mr. Amos Powers, and our family. In the upper part of the town, five familes had settled, viz. Capt. Eleazer Twitchell, Benjamin Russell, Esq., Abraham Russell, Lieut. Jonathan Clark, and Mr. James Swan. The nearest of them was six miles, and some of them were ten or eleven miles distance from us; therefore, we could afford but little assistance to each other, should the Indians molest us in any part of the town.

In the spring of the year 1781, the Mill was repaired, and we concluded to reside here, and to call it our home. We, therefore, went to work in sugaring, and in clearing and tilling our land for farms and a crop, in high spirits, as the land was good, being much intervale on the river.

The Indians were often in among us, and appeared very friendly. We sold them corn, and other things, for meat, fur, &c. In the first of this season, they appeared very friendly towards us, which we labored to cultivate; and they were pleased in trading with us. Afterwards they grew morose and surly; but still we were not apprehensive of any mischief from them, as we had heretofore lived quietly with them. But at length they came in very much emboldened, and painted, and more in a hostile manner than heretofore. We inquired of them the reason of their painting themselves, and of their being so merry; they told us, that it was a high day with them. They pleased themselves in talking with each other in their own language, which we did not understand. We did not know or even surmise any harm from them. Their conduct at this time, and the manner in which they appeared, were very different from what they were before; but still we kept about our work, not being much afraid of them, as we knew of no reason why we should be afraid of them, or why they should, in the least, injure us, as we had always lived in harmony with them. There were none of these Indians in the party when I was taken prisoner."

Lieut. Segar's account of his capture by the Indians is reserved for a future chapter.

Capt. Eleazer Twitchell, third son of Joseph Twitchell, Esq., was born in Sherburne, Mass., Jan. 22nd, 1744-5. He married, April 4th, 1768, Martha Mason, born May 20th, 1751, daughter of Moses Mason, of Dublin, N. H. He first settled on the "Yeardly Place," in Packersfield, now Dublin, and then removed to Nelson in what was then known as the "Scripture Place." Mrs. Twitchell was a companion every way qualified to counsel, aid and encourage him in all the trying scenes through which he passed. Her generosity, kindness and affability secured the esteem and friendship of her Indian neighbors, and contributed much to the good understanding between the infant settlement and those with whom they mingled.

I find some doubt in regard to the year when Capt. Twitchell moved to Bethel. His daughter, Mrs. Martha Rowe, now living (1859) at the age of 85, informs me that she was five years old and that her then youngest brother Moses was nine months old when they came to Fryeburg in the winter previous to coming to Bethel in March. This would make it in 1780. As confirmation of this, her brother Simeon used to say that he brought through the woods a yearling boy, which must have been Moses, her younger brother. It is singular that there are so few positive records of the town at this date.

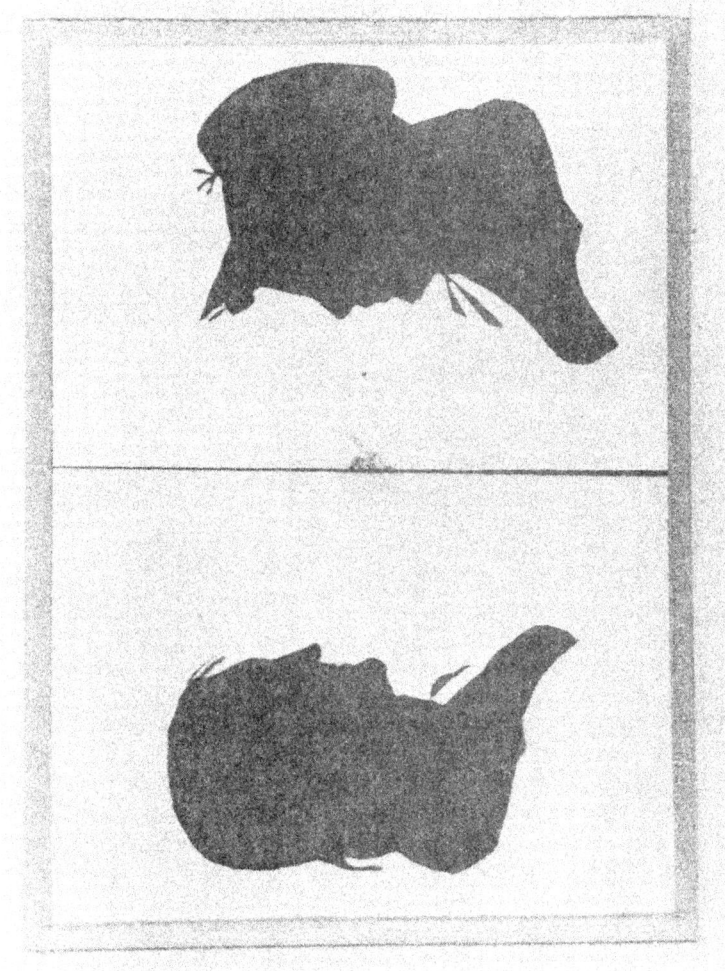

"Captain" Eleazer Twitchell and wife, Martha Mason

Capt. Twitchell's father having so large interests at stake in Sudbury Canada, and having no one to take charge of the mill, pursuaded his son to sell his property, and remove with his family to a new home on the Androscoggin.

Capt. Twitchell, his wife, and wife's sister (Betsey Mason), five children, and six hired men, viz. John Grover, Jeremiah Andrews, Gideon, Paul and Silas Powers, and a Mr. Fisk, left Nelson, N. H., in the winter of 1780 and came as far as Fryeburg, where in consequence of a severe injury which Capt. Twitchell received, they remained till March. Capt. Twitchell sent his men through to Bethel on snow-shoes to make a path, when they returned to Fryeburg, packed their baggage on hand-sleds and started for Bethel, the women following in the rear. Mrs. Martha Rowe, now living with her son residing in Gilead, was one of the children from whom I have received many interesting facts which will be made use of from time to time. They camped the first night by a large rock, near Kezar Ponds, in the extreme west part of Waterford. A camp had been fitted up with conveniences for a stopping place. When they arrived at Bethel, they moved into the house on the island near the grist-mill. This was a small framed house, consisting of two rooms, the first of its kind in town, which had been previously built to accomodate the workmen connected with the mill. The Grist Mill got very much out of repair, and it was very difficult to obtain provisions for his family. The children obtained subsistence frequently by picking berries, while occasionally a moose served them for meat in the winter. Capt. T. caught seven one winter. These were obtained on the hills in the vicinity.

In 1781 Capt. Twitchell repaired the Grist Mill. The inhabitants had to grind their grain much of the time in hand-mills, as the wheel of the Grist Mill was a large undershot, and was liable to be frozen up in the winter. Capt. T. was very active in promoting the interests of the town. -- There is an old ballad, one line of which runs --

"And if a Twitchell, strong."

Capt. Twitchell seemed to fulfil the requirements of his ancestors in this respect.

He frequently sent his men and team to meet and aid persons coming in to settle. He ran out the town line soon after he came, and surveyed the lots of many of the first settlers. His field notes are now in my possession.

The men who came with him through his assistance secured lots for a settlement, and he kept men almost constantly in his employ. He subsequently commenced clearing the farm now occupied by Moses A. Mason, cutting the pine timber which grew on it of the best quality. This was hauled to the river and floated to Brunswick.

Of his capture by the Indians in 1781, we shall speak in another place.

He lived in the house on the island in the fall of 1785 when the great freshet rose nearly to the beams of the house. He made a raft, took off his family and made a camp of boards where his family spent the night. -- The upper dam near Caleb Rowe's gave way bringing down with it immense quantities of wood which fortunately passing to the west of the house left it uninjured.

Soon after this, he built a house on the hill which was the first built near the Common. This was situated in the rear of the Hotel and was the first clapboarded house in this part of the town. The clapboards shone most beautifully in the sun when new, and attracted much attention. But this was soon too straight for him, and in the year 1797-8 he built a large house which was known as the *Castle*, and which he used as a public house. In this was a large hall where the young people of that day congregated to enjoy themselves much to the annoyance of their more staid fathers and mothers. In this house was the first regular cellar with an arch and brick chimney. It was torn down in 1834. A good story, current here 60 years ago, is told by our townsman, Dea. George W. Chapman: -- Rev. Caleb Bradley, now of Westbrook, was a teacher here in 1798. He preached a Thanksgiving sermon that year, the first of the kind ever delivered in town. This was subsequently printed. In the evening, Mr. Bradley and Dr. Brickett, both young men, and full of Thanksgiving glee, spent the evening at Capt. Twitchell's. These were invited to go down to the cellar for the purpose of seeing the arch where Mrs. T. had some nice mince pies. Mr. Bradley suceeded in roguishly purloining one of these and secreting it in his overcoat pocket. When supper came there was a general laudation of Mrs. T.'s pies, when Mr. Bradley declared that he could furnish a better one than any on the table. The challenge was accepted, but on going for his pie, what was his surprise to find the dinner turkey bones in its place. The sharp sighted Mrs. Twitchell had completely outwitted him.

Capt. Twitchell built a road from the mill up the hill as far as the Common. This was the first road in town.

In 1788 Capt. Twitchell thoroughly rebuilt the mill. Mr. Samuel Redington, father of Judge Redington, of Augusta, was the mill-wright. It commenced running Sept. 2, when he ground "one bushel of rie," and the second day "three bushels of rie, and one of whet." In 1789 his father gave him a deed to the mill and the land adjacent. About 1804, tub-wheels were introduced into the mill by one Hitchcock, and was a great improvment.

One of the best of his deeds was the gift of the beautiful Common to the town. The wide street above the Common was also given by him. -- His original design was to make this a parade ground for a regiment. -- Broad Street was designed for the parade of companies, and the Common for Regimental parade. He was elected to fill the various offices in town ever after it was incorporated. Every settler was entitled to fifty acres of land in addition to his lot after he had occupied it, and the duty of surveying for the proprietors fell on him.

Capt. T. had twelve children: Simeon, Deborah, Martha, Amos, Moses, Joseph, Lydia, Eleazer, Sylvanus, Asa, Cynthia and Adeline. He died June 1819 aged 74.

Among the earliest settlers was John Grover, father of Dr. John Grover. Respecting the genealogy of the family, an interesting communication from his grandson, Hon. Lafayette Grover, Member of Congress from the State of Oregon, will be read with interest.

"In late researches into the early history of New England, I have quite satisfied myself as to what time our family ancestors came to this country. I find that John Grover, the first of our name in this country, was living in Charlestown, Mass., in 1634. He was probably among the first who arrived after the landing of the Mayflower in 1620. John Grover had a son John, born in 1640, (as the old records of Charlestown still show), whose oldest son John settled near Andover, Mass., where our great grandfather James was born, who with his five sons and three daughters (James, John, Jedidiah, Eli, Elijah, Sarah, Olive, and Naoma) soon after the close of the Revolution, purchased extensive tracts of land in Bethel, Me., from whom all of our names descended, who live in this town.

Our great grandfather was a man of great piety and some learning, and was a Deacon in the church. He died in Bethel, and was the first man interred in the old cemetery on our old farm. John Grover, our grand father, was the second son of the family, served in the Revolution, was at the battle at Princeton and Trenton, N.J., returned home when the year's service expired, married Jerusha Wiley in Fryeburg (who was a sister of Gen. Hastings, father of John Hastings) and settled as a farmer at West Bethel. His farm included all the land upon which is built the village at West Bethel. Father was the oldest son and called John, which seems to have been a family name for many generations.

Our ancestors came from England. The name is purely English; and in my antiquarian researches into the genealogical history of the middle ages, I have found the "coat of arms" belonging to our family. The escutcheon is surmounted by a crest, and an arm, embowed, from the clouds holding a wreath. There is but one "coat of arms" representing the name of Grover in all Heraldry, and that established beyond all history of dates, consequently there never was but one original head, so the descent is not questionable."

Mr. Grover came to Bethel in company with Capt. Eleazer Twitchell in 1780. He had a camp in company with Mr. Peter Austin on the farm now owned by Capt. Samuel Barker. He was engaged the next spring in making sugar and in clearing land. When the Indians came to Bethel in 1781, they visited his camp and destroyed the sugar he had made. He happened to be from his camp and escaped to the house of Capt.

Twitchell where he with the others spent the night expecting an attack at every moment. The next morning he started without ceremony for Fryeburg, and arrived there a distance of 30 miles by noon; Capt. Twitchell soon after sent off a man on horseback, but Mr. Grover arrived there first. Grover Hill took its name from him.

An incident or two of him is worthy of record. He was stationed for a time at Dorchester Heights when the British occupied Boston; a detachment was ordered to throw up an intrenchment during the night for the purpose of annoying the British in the city. A fire was incautiously built which served as a capital mark for the British Artillery. They immediately commenced a brisk cannonade; the balls flew thickly. One arrested Mr. Grover's attention by cutting its way through an oak tree near by him. Another struck a man in the chest standing close by cutting him nearly in two. The detachment sought refuge in the rear of the hill where they were safe. The next morning a large number of balls were collected by the soldiers. Powder carts loaded with sand arrived quite frequently, giving the enemy to understand that they were well supplied with ammunition. Mr. Grover was one of the hardy pioneers well fitted to begin the world in a new country. A few years before his death he removed to Mercer, Me. His son Moses was in the war 1812 and being taken sick his father went to see him. This was in the direction of Montreal, but the father died on the way. This was in 1814-1815. He had ten children. His wife died in Bethel, June, 1839.

Lieut. Jonathan Clark was born in Newton, Mass., March, 28, 1747. When yet a young man, he bought in 1774 a lot where Lewis Sanborn now lives. He made but little progress towards a settlement, and returned to Massachusetts. He was a Commissary in the army for a few months, but returned to Bethel in 1778-9, during which time he cut the first hay in town, up the brook opposite the Steam Mill. The scythe which he used is still in the possession of Jed. Burbank, Esq. He afterwards exchanged and obtained two intervale lots, on one of which is the farm now occupied by A. L. Burbank, Esq. During the years 1778-9 he built a plank house a few rods east of Mr. Burbank's barn. On May 27, 1780, he married Miss Esther Parker, of Newton, Mass., born Aug. 26, 1753, and with her moved to Bethel the following June. They came on horseback from Newton to the head of Long Pond in Bridgton and the rest of the way on foot. They had several children, all of whom died of consumption. Esther, their daughter, was married to Jedediah Burbank Esq., Nov. 13, 1803, and died July 20, 1827.

During the freshet in 1785, he made a raft of the great doors of the barn, and carried his family to a place of safety. He made a shelter for the night opposite Mills Brown's house. The water came up to the summer shelf, suspended from the beams, and spoiled his books and papers. He afterwards built the house which is still standing on the hill, and is known as the "Frost House."

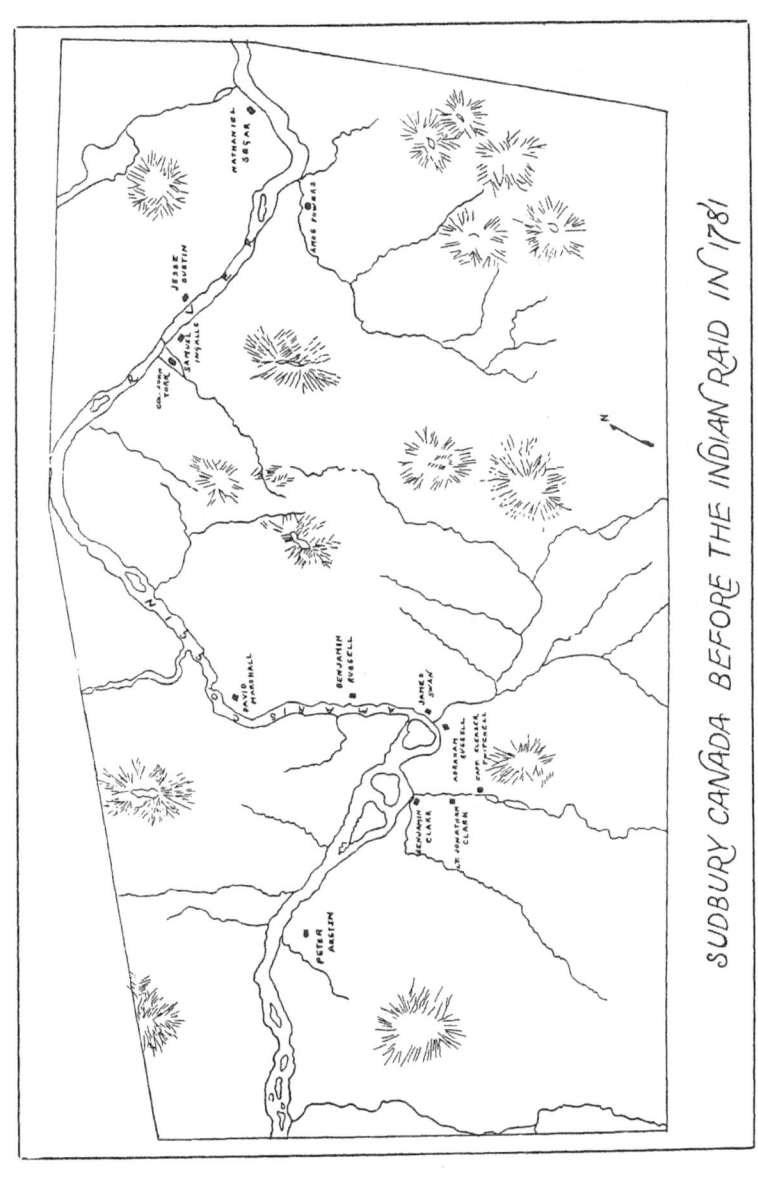

Lieut. Clark appears to have been an active man, and enjoyed the confidence of the citizens by being elected to fill the various offices in town.

Mrs. Clark appears to have been a woman of uncommon resolution. When the Indians came to the house in 1781, and took her husband captive, she manifested such courage as but few men could exhibit. After seeing the Indians carrying her husband away handcuffed, she fled to the woods and there remained during the night all alone. The next morning she passed through the woods and went to the house of Capt. Eleazer Twitchell, where was the greatest consternation.

Lieut. Clark died, Aug. 23, 1821. His wife died, Feb. 13, 1815. They have but one descendant residing in Bethel, Mrs. Sarah J., wife of Nathan Twitchell.

In the spring of 1781, the Grist mill was repaired and an effort made to induce settlers to move into Sudbury Canada. Five families were now settled in what is now the west Parish, viz: Capt. Eleazer Twitchell, who lived on the island where the present Grist Mill stands, Benjamin Russell Esq., who lived on the farm now occupied by Mr. Abbott Russell, Abraham Russell, on the land now owned by Gilman Chapman, Esq., near Alder River Bridge, Lieut. Jonathan Clark, who lived on the farm now occupied by A. L. Burbank, Esq., and Mr. James Swan, who lived on the farm now occupied by Mr. Algernon Chapman, near Alder River Bridge.

Other young men had commenced an opening. Among these was Peter Austin, who had a camp and commenced operation the year before on the farm now occupied by Captain Samuel Barker. Mr. Austin was fortunately away from home when the Indians arrived at his camp with their captives. He settled there and remained till about the time the town was incorporated in 1796, when he removed to Canton Point, where he became a wealthy and enterprising farmer and raised up a large family. He has but one descendant in this town, Mrs. Betsey, wife of Mr. Pinckney Burnham, his grand-daughter.

In the lower part of the town were settled Mr. Samuel Ingalls, on the farm now occupied by Mr. Peter Kimball, Mr. Jesse Dustin, on the farm now occupied by Mr. Adam Willis in Hanover, Mr. John York, on the farm now owned by Mr. Amos Young, Mr. Amos Powers, on the farm known as the Arnold Powers farm, and Lieut. Nathaniel Segar, on the farm now owned by Capt. Wm. Barker in Hanover.

The only connecting links between the earliest settlers and the present now living are two individuals, Mr. Peter York, who came with his father, John York, to Bethel in 1779, and Mrs. Martha Rowe, who came with her father, Capt. Eleazer Twitchell, in 1780. Consequently Mr. York has lived in the town a period of 80 years, being a longer time than that of any other person. They lived to see greater changes in the conditions of mankind than ever fell to the lot of any other generation that has lived since the flood.

Their fathers enjoyed the blessing of a country comparatively old, and moved to a wilderness that had been known only as the hunting grounds of savages.

Their route from Massachusetts to Bethel was either by way of Fryeburg or to Standish and then across Sebago and Long Ponds, on the ice in winter or in boats in summer, and the rest of the way through a dense forest. Their most frequent visitors were the Indians who still occupied the region as their hunting ground and who still claimed a legal right to the country. The settlers bartered with these, giving them corn and sugar, and received from them wild meat, tallow and fur.

They had no roads. Spotted trees were their guide-boards, and the general course of the Androscoggin was the line of direction. They seemed to be in a measure exiled from the world. The country was engaged with Great Britain in the contest for freedom. Luxuries were unknown; but they had stout hearts and the earth, as soon as the trees were felled and burned, yielded most bountiful crops. Marvellous stories were related of their crops of wheat, potatoes, and corn on the intervale.

Yet they had their luxuries. They employed the spring in making that inimitable production, maple sugar. Hulled corn boiled in maple sap is no mean luxury anywhere. Fresh moose steak was as nice then as now. They could raise the finest wheat so that in the quality of their food they might even then set a table good enough for an epicure.

Their sleep was just as sweet in a log house as in a palace. The rousing hardwood fire, blazing away in one corner of their rude home, sent rays of comfort to its healthy inmates that can be but poorly enjoyed in these latter days of close rooms and air-tight stoves.

Never is necessity more sensibly made the mother of invention than when it is exhibited in a newly settled country. A sap trough could easily be converted into a cradle. The manufacture of wooden bowls, plates and spoons made good employment for their long winter evenings and were a very good substitute for something better. For the want of bricks to make a chimney, they could make a hole through the roof and top one out with mud and sticks. A moose sled of peculiar and ingenious construction answered a great variety of purposes during the long winter, while the long poles could be lashed to the sides of a horse and made to draw their supplies through the woods. There was but little need of breaking roads, for every body could use snow-shoes. A hole dug in the ground was a place of deposit for potatoes while some poles set up made a crib for their corn.

Seven years had now passed since the first trees were cut for a settlement, yet but ten families had now in 1781 concluded to make this their home. Not a child had been born, nor a person died up to this date. No carriage or cart of any kind had as yet been made in town. Their salt and other supplies had till this time to be drawn through the woods from the head of Long Pond in Bridgton.

But after all it was not so difficult to make a home. There is more romance and more reality united in making a home in the wilderness than perhaps under any other circumstances; such individuals have high hopes and these give energy of character that is often lost in their more favored descendants. No higher aspiration can really well fill a man's breast as when he builds his framed house after having lived for years in his humble log tenement. Improvement marks his every step. This compensates a thousand inconveniences incident to a new country.

Even now we almost envy the man who with a loving wife starts for the Aroostook. Let a man be assured of a healthy climate, a good soil, a good constitution, and a good wife and he can shake his fist at kings in defiance of all dependence on regal favors.

Chapter 5

Indians and the 1781 Raid

Before proceeding further with the history of the town, I propose to give an extended account of the Indian tribes in this portion of the state. It is peculiarly fitting to do so, because the last of those outrages committed on the early settlers from the time of King Philip's war, terminated by the descent of the Indians upon Bethel, and carrying away several of the inhabitants into captivity.

Of the eight distinct families that occupied N. America the largest was known as the Algonquins. If the reader will take the trouble of looking on a map at the source of the Mississippi River, follow that down as far as Tennessee and thence across to the Atlantic, thence following the coast eastward to the mouth of the St. Lawrence River and across the Canadas to the first mentioned bound, he will enclose the territory of the Algonquins, except that the Huron Iroquois occupied what is now the state of N. York and the peninsular adjacent in Canada, formed by the Lakes Huron, Erie and Ontario.

Thus about one half the territory of the U. States east of the Mississippi was occupied by the Algonquins. Consequently all the N. England tribes belonged to this great family, all speaking one language, though broken up into various dialects.

The Algonquins, so called by LaHontan and others, called themselves *Leni Lenapes* (original men), and they were also called Wapanachki, Abenakis (men of the east). A more poetical definition is given Abnaki: "the place where the sky is white, or, where our ancients arose." The Abenakis were called Tarratines by the English. This name seems to have been afterwards restricted to certain tribes inhabiting Maine. A peculiarity of the Abnaki tribes is said to be in their custom of making mounds over their dead.

The tribes of New England were settled on the principal rivers. On the Connecticut were the Mohegans, subdivided into several tribes inhabiting Massachusetts, R. Island and Connecticut. Those on the sources of the Connecticut were called Nipmucs, or Fresh Water Indians. On the Merrimac were the Pennacooks, on the Saco, the Sokokis, of which the Ossipee and Pigwackets in and near Fryeburg were branches.

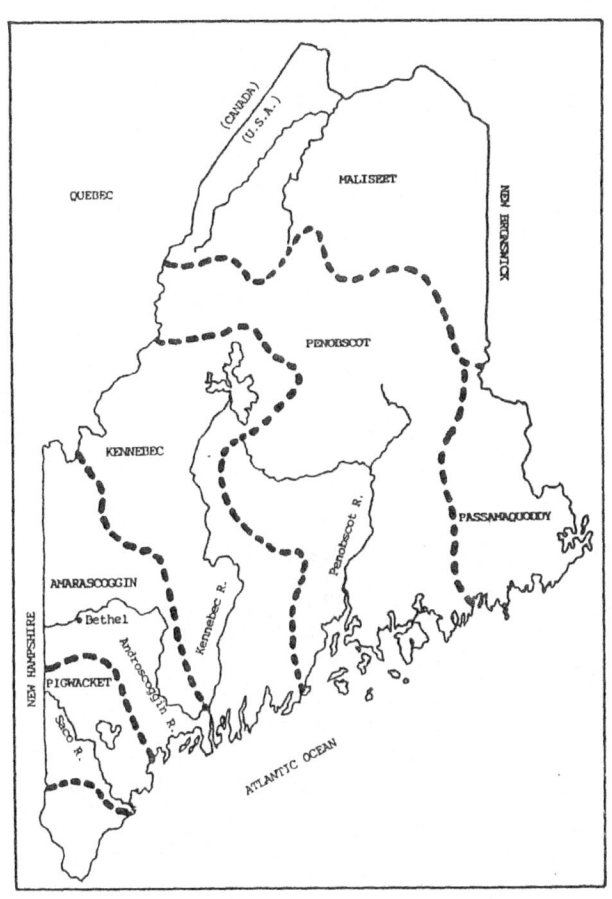

Map of Maine Indian tribal lands with Bethel shown on the upper Androscoggin River

The Anasagunticooks, of which the Rokomeko tribe formed a part, claimed possession of the Androscoggin from its source to Merrymeeting Bay where it empties into the Kennebec. The Norridgewocks lived on the Kennebec, the Penobscots, or Tarratines, on the Penobscot, the Wawenocks on the St. Georges River, the Passamaquoddies on the St. Croix, the Marchites on the St. Johns, and the Micmacs in N. Scotia.

Each of these tribes was made up of smaller divisions. The present situation of the Penobscot and Passamaquoddy Indians will illustrate their condition for centuries past. Although the Passamaquoddy tribe has its principal location towards the mouth of the St. Croix, a respectable portion of them reside farther up the river on the Schoodic Lakes, each division having a chief, but considering themselves members of the same tribe.

Different tribes at different times had those around them as tributaries. Thus a Mohawk from N. York was for a time no less a terror to an Eastern Indian than to a white man. The principal chief was called the *Basheba* and held control over all the subdivisions of his tribe. Their councils were held at his residence.

Sassacus, the chief sachem of the Pequots in Connecticut, had twenty-six sachems under him when the English settled that state. Having thus given a mere outline of the different tribes in New England, I shall, in my next give some account of the language of the Algonquins.

The language of the Indian tribes of North America has been, perhaps, the most interesting feature connected with their history. Frequent attempts have been made to trace its connection with the languages of the eastern continent, but thus far without success. The Algonquin language was the most extensively spoken on the continent. Different tribes had their respective dialects, but could converse readily with each other. The language evidently became changeable in its character. Thus, a modern Indian being asked to give a definition of *Androscoggin* might not be able to do it. He would reply, "that is old Indian," plainly evincing that the name was ancient, or that such changes had taken place as to cause him to lose sight of the original definition. As a specimen of the similar and dissimilar aspects of the same word in different portions even of the same tribe, I present the word *wigwam* in the Ojibway language. At St. Mary's, it is *Wegewom*, in another, *wegewaum*, while in another, its connection is hardly recognized, *makakeokamic*. Other still more striking examples might be given. The Canada Indians, from their great intimacy with the French, frequently adopted the French numerals instead of those of their own language. Other French and English words gradually crept into their language after the settlement of the country such as *canoe*, from the French, *canot*. On the other hand quite a number of significant words have been added to the English language which owe their derivation from the Indians. Thus *wigwam* is derived from *wikwam*, a house, moccasons, from *maxen*, shoes, tomahawk, from *tamahican*, a hatchet. A squaw, probably from *ochqueu*, a woman. Occobee (orthography doubtful) from *okkepee*, rum; hommony, boiled corn; *samp*, corn pounded and boiled. *Sanhop*, a husband; *Pappoos*, or *Pappoose*, a child; *Tabaco*, a province of South America, gives us tobacco, because according to Webster it was first discovered there by the Spainards. Then we have *wampum, quahaug, tumpline, caoutchouc, powow*.

The termination *cook*, so common in many Indian names of places, has become quite Americanized. It is derived from *c*, euphonic, and *auke* signifying a *place*. Thus *Pennacook*, from *Pemaquis* crooked *c*, euphonic, *auke*, a place. Pequaket seems to have had the same derivation, though Mollocket, an Indian woman who resided in Bethel and vicinity many years after its settlement, gave the definition, *the place where the dust arises from the leaves*, alluding to the dust that rose from the leaves while walking over them after a freshet in Saco River. The termination *auke* is spelled so differently by early French and English writers that it is not always easy to recognize the derivation. Thus we have *Potomac*, the place of the porpoise; *Chesapeake*, the place of the great river; *Penobscot*, rocky place; *Kennebec*, place of residence at the long water; *Cushnoc*, overtaking place; *Aroostook*, good river; *Abnaki*, place where the sky is white; *Winnipisseogee*, beautiful lake of the highhlands; *Umbagog*, lake with shallow water. All these words terminated in *auke*. *Androscoggin*, probably first noticed by Capt. John Smith, and spelled by him *Aumoughcougen*, and by others *Amarescoggin, Amoscoggin, Ammonoscongan*, was by the early settlers frequently abridged to *Scoggin*. Vetromile, a recent investigator of the Indian languages, defines it the Fish Spearing River. Another writer analyzes it thus, *Amarescoggin*, from *Namaos*, fish, *kees*, high, and *auk*, a place, which may be defined, the high place where fish are caught. The present name of Androscoggin is supposed to have been given out of compliment, and perhaps from some similarity of sound, to governor Andros, as it assumed that form of spelling about the time that he was in this country, although the name Amarescoggin was often retained in records a century later. The Indians limited the name to the river above Lewiston Falls. Between the latter place and Merrymeeting Bay, they called it *Pejepscot*, or the river like a diving snake, a definition exceedingly applicable, as any one acquainted with the river would recognize. From the latter place to the mouth of the Kennebec, it was called *Sagadehoc*, or the mouth of the river. Then there are other terminations in auk, as *Saco, Norridgewock*. Sometimes they applied the same name to different places, as *Pennecook*, on the *Merrimac*, and *Pennecook* at Rumford Falls on the Androscoggin; *Chatauque* in New York, and *Chatauque* on Sandy River in Phillips, Me.

Sometimes they would coin a word from the English, as *Peol*, from the English *Peter*, which they could not so readily pronounce.

A few Indian words are still remembered by our oldest inhabitants. Mrs. Martha Rowe, now residing in Gilead, who was familiar with the Indians in her youth, defines *Kussa*, go away; *Alum*, come here; *Quallimosit*, the name of an Indian who formerly visited Bethel, was defined, Roll up cloth.

The names of many places were very significant. *Songo*, a pond in the town of Albany at the source of the Presumpscot, was the place where they set traps and caught nothing; *Connecticut*, the long deer river; *Susquehanah*, the winding river; *Allegany*, cold river; *Norembegua*, still water before the falls; *Damariscotta*, Alewive river; *Cobosseconte*, sturgeon river.

They had their favorite names of persons. Thus there was a *Sabatis* who lived at the head waters of the Kennebec, who also accompanied Arnold in his expedition to Quebec. Another lived near, or in the town of Lisbon, from whom a pond and a mountain take their names, while another was familiar to the early settlers in Bethel, who came from Canada.

A curious analogy may be traced between the words Amoscoggin and Anasagunticook. The latter word was the name of the Indian tribe that lived in Bethel and other places on the Androscoggin river. Let the reader compare the definition with that of Androscoggin given above.

Anasagunticook, rather, *Amas-a-conte-cook*, from *namacs*, fish, *a*, euphonic, *konte*, stream, *cook c,* euphonic and *auke*, place, or locality, i.e. the region of the Fish River, or simply, Fish River.

For the analysis of this word and for other favors, I am indebted to the Rev. E. Ballard of Brunswick, who has entered upon this new field of classical study with much zeal.

Like the nomenclature in chemistry, where the name signifies the composition of a body, so these Indian names all have a descriptive meaning, often very expressive and elegant.

The following anecdote is from a correspondent of the *Boston Journal*, which illustrates the manner in which words are sometimes transferred from one language to that of another. "Apropos to aboriginal names, there is a story afloat which I have never seen in print, but which is too amusing to be lost. I will not vouch for its truthfulness, but all who are familiar with Indian phraseology will recognize in it what Mr. Choate calls "a fine touch of nature." Many years ago, in Michigan or Wisconsin (my memory is at fault, and my conscientiousness shall have full benefit of the doubt), there was an Indian brave whose better half had presented him with an almost incredible number of children; but unhappily they were all girls, and, therefore, in the estimation of his race, of very little consequence -- in fact, worse that useless. It was a source of great annoyance to the Chief; but, with the obstinacy of her sex, the squaw continued to make an annual addition of a female "responsibility" to the little army of them which had already taken possession of his wigwam. At last, on one of these occasions, the old brave visited a grocery (for white settlers where beginning to encroach upon the domain), and with great gloom and solemnity refused to join in any of the conversation or conviality. Several of the whites finally gathered around him and congratulated him warmly on the new arrow which had just been added to his domestic quiver. With a look of indescribable and unutterable disgust he ejaculated in reply, "She-boy-gin -- She-boy-gin'" (a she boy again!) strode from the house and was never heard of afterwards. As the last grain of sand broke the camel's back, so this congratulation of his misfortune was too much for Indian nature to bear. But (so runs the tale) the phrase became identified with the locality, and when in due time a flourishing town sprang up around the little frontier grocery, it received, by unanimous consent, the name of Sheboygan."

The Indian languages early attracted the attention of the first settlers in this country. Wm. Penn, in a letter written in 1683 thus speaks:

"I must say, that I know not a language spoken in Europe, that has words of more sweetness, or greatness, in accent and emphasis, than theirs; for instance, *Oricton, Shak, Marian*, all which are names of places and have a grandeur in them. Of words of sweetness, *Anna*, is mother; *Iffimus*, is brother; *Matta*, no; *hatta*, to have; *matta ne hatta*, I have not; *Sepaffen*, the name of a place; *Menanfe*, the name of a person."

Any person who has heard the Penobscot Indians speak in their own language could but be struck with the peculiarly smooth articulation of words, reminding one of the Italian.

The liquids l, n and r are substituted for each other. The Penobscots pronounce Carritunk, *Calnitunk*. I believe the Indians of this continent generally find it difficult to pronounce the letter r. An amusing circumstance occurred to some explorers in Oregon. They were engaged in boiling some rice for their meal when some Indians came near and wished to know what that was. On being told it was *rice*, they imediately pronounced it *lice*, and this was the best they could do, after all the efforts of their white neighbors to set them right. The Massachusetts' Indians invariably pronounced Winslow, *Winsnow*.

One of the most remarkable peculiarities of the Algonquin language was the facility with which they compounded words. Their names of localities were formed in this way, and have left us a rich legacy in the names of places all over our continent. If the definitions of these places were more generally known, they would be much better appreciated.

There are several places in Maine terminating in *keag* denoting *locality*. The Penobscots pronounce it short as *kik*. It means the earth, as in *Spom-kik*, above the earth, i.e. heaven. *Kenduskeag*, is *Kandoskik*, and means Eel Place, or Eel River. *Che* at the beginning or end of a word means *great*; as in *Chesapeake*, *che*, great, *sepe*, river, *ahke*, or *auke*, place; the place of the great river; *Mattawamkeag*, from *matta*, much, *wampi*, white or clear, *keak*, or *kih*, earth; it means the gravelly bottom can be seen through the clear water. *Magalloway* is unsettled. It has had three definitions: 1. Large Tail, 2. Crooked, 3. Birch Bark River, *Norridgewock*, smooth water falls. Duponceau in speaking of the Delewares who spoke the Algonquin language, illustrates their facility of combination in the word *Kuligatschis*, which is composed of parts of six different words, but which must be translated into English thus -- *Give me your pretty little paw.*

There is sometimes a peculiar delicacy of expression worthy of the most refined language. Thus, *Pilape*, a youth, is formed from *pilsit*, chaste, innocent, and *lenape*, a man. In consequence of these peculiarities they have but few adjectives, while the verb undergoes a great variety of inflections and combinations in which to express their ideas. In common with most savage nations, they uttered the subject first in a sentence. An Indian presenting his gun to the smith would say, "Gun, me want mended."

There certainly must have been a peculiar force in the use of some words; thus in the Shawnee which belongs to the western branch of the Algonquins, a woman was *s'squawowah*, the accent on the last syllable. Nursery maids might find a good word for a child, or an infant, *mieminlet*, sounding the *i* in the first syllable like *ee* and the *e* like a in hate, while the Delawares in the west give us for the word *day*, the very suggestive and expressive one of *kisqui'k*, and, today, *uquekisqui'k*. Then what is more rythmical than their word for the numeral eleven, *telenohcote*, sounding the *e* like a in hate, also hundred, *telentumtelen*. Virgil would have been glad of the last word to express the tramping of horses, while Homer could have made use of the Shawnee for night, *tebethki*, and for moon, *tebethtikishthoi*, on which volumes might have been written by his admirers.

The Indians were unacquainted with writing, and their skill in drawing never surpassed that of an ordinary school boy. The best specimen I have ever seen was a map of the Magalloway River drawn on white birch bark by Natalluck, the last of the Anasagunticooks on the Androscoggin river, which is now in the posession of Hon. Moses Mason, of this town.

Probably not less than a thousand Indian names may be found in the State of Maine. Could their definitions all be unravelled, they would furnish materials to reconstruct a language.

The Indian tribes occupied the fertile intervales on all the principal rivers of Maine from a remote period. The lands gave indications of having been cleared for centuries.

As early as 1504 claims were made in this part of the world by the English and French governments, and in 1535 Cartier explored the St. Lawrence as far as to the principal Indian settlement at Hochelaga, now Montreal, which, says Roger in his recent *History of Canada*, was ever a first class city and their chief emporium in Canada. From this date may be reckoned that influence which the French exerted, and which is felt to this day, over the Indian tribes of Maine and Canada.

But little is known of their history till about the year 1617, when a plague broke out and swept off a large portion of the Indians in N. England. Of the nature of that disease historians are not agreed. Powerful tribes were nearly depopulated.

It was in consequences of this fact that an important reason was presented to the English Monarch by the Plymouth Company, that the country was nearly depopulated by a pestilence and offered no hindrance to a settlement. Amid all the changes of government I am not aware that the Indians ever surrendered their right to the sources of the Androscoggin.

The first tribe which we shall particularly notice is that of the Pennacooks, who occupied the Merrimac River in N. Hampshire, and who exerted a powerful influence among the surrounding tribes. This tribe seems to have migrated from southern N. England as they spoke the same language with those of that region.

They were under the control of the Sagamore Passaconnaway who was first known to the English in 1629 and with their power seemed to rise and fall for a hundred years, for he was supposed to be 120 years old when he died.

The word Pennacook is derived from *Pennaqui*, crooked, and *auke*, a place, in consequence of the crooked manner in which the Merrimac winds through the town of Concord, one of their chief settlements.

During the life of Passaconnaway all the tribes east of the Merrimac as far as to the Ameriscoggin were tributary to the Pennacooks.

Among these were the Coosucks, from *Cooash*, pines, settled in Coos Country at the sources of the Connecticut.

Those tribes in the interior were called by those on the sea-shore, *Nipmucks*, or fresh water Indians, from *Nip*, still water, and *auke*, place, but retained the general name of Pennacooks.

The Coos Country extending from Haverhill to the sources of the Connecticut River was occupied by a band of Pennacooks, attracted there by its hunting and fishing grounds, and who kept a kind of armed possession of that country for the protection and relief of the frequent parties which were passing and repassing from the various points upon the Merrimac to the Aresaguntacook Indians upon the river St. Lawrence, a tribe with whom they lived on the most friendly terms.

A branch of Pennacooks removed to the Androscoggin River near Rumford Falls, who gave the name of Pennacook to this place. The Pennacooks were known as distinct from the other Indians on the river, though they appear to have lived on the most friendly terms with them. They seem to have remained longer on the river than the other Indians, as they were known to the earliest settlers of Bethel after the Revolutionary War. As the intimacy between the Coosucks and the Anasagunticooks was very great, they passed through Bethel on their journeys to each other. One of their camping grounds was in Bethel and is now known as Powow Point, situated down the river about a mile from the Depot at Bethel Hill. Here a spot of land was cleared where many a council was held. What a history this spot might reveal! No mortal knows what nights of anguish may have been spent there by captives on their way to Canada.

The Pennacooks were a semi-agricultural tribe, and it is a noticeable fact that where they engaged in agriculture, there they became more civilized.

Passaconnaway was alive in 1663 and at the head of his tribe, but died prior to 1669. He had one son, Nanamacomuck, who was inimical to the English and removed to Amariscoggin in Maine sometime after 1648. Probably no more powerful tribe of Indians lived at that time east of the Mohawks.

The Pennacooks gradually diminished in number until the remnant removed to Canada sometime during the last century.

The Pennacooks in common with neighboring tribes had the greatest veneration for *Agiocochook*, the Indian name of the White Mountains. There is a curious tradition, preserved in Josselyn's N. England, of the veneration of the Indians for the summits of these mountains.

They considered them the dwelling places of invisible beings, and never ventured to ascend them. They had also a tradition, that the whole country was once drowned with all its inhabitants, except one Indian with his wife, who, foreseeing the flood, fled to these mountains, were preserved, and afterwards *repeopled* the country.

The next tribe in order was that of the Sokokis, on the Saco River. These Indians were located chiefly in two divisions, the one on the Ossipee River in N. Hampshire, and the other on the Saco, in Fryeburg. The location of the latter was about two miles from Fryeburg village. Their Chief Sachem resided on Indian Island, situated in the Saco River a little above the Falls in Saco village.

The Sokokis were a fierce, cruel and warlike people. Whether their proximity to the mountain region gave them greater developement or not, they certainly were remarkable for their physical prowess. In the pestilence of 1617 they appear to have suffered in common with the other tribes in Maine. They were also engaged about this time in a war with the Eastern Indians and lost their chief.

Among the early Indian Chiefs, Squando figures prominently. His wife and child had been upset by some sailors to see if the latter could swim, as it had been asserted that they could do so naturally. Squando was exasperated and expended his savage cruelty in every possible way against the whites. This was in 1675-6. There was another chief by the name of Assacumbuit, and another called Polan who was killed in Windham in a skirmish in 1756. Another was called Chocorua from whom one of the White Mountain peaks was named. But no Indian has left his name in the memory of the whites like Paugus, chief of the Pequakets. Subtle and brave, he commanded a band of as brave warriors as ever were found among savages. There are but few incidents of him except what may be found in the account of the Lovewell fight, which we shall give in another chapter. There was also his successor, Wawah, who was engaged in several excursions against the whites.

After the Lovewell Fight in 1725, the Pequakets removed to the Coos country on the Connecticut river, while a few lingered around their old home, among whom was their Chief Philip and Swarson, who fought with the Americans in the Revolutionary War. The latter received an elegant sword from Congress. These frequently came to Bethel after the settlement of the town. Philip is still remembered as being a very old man at that time. Another Indian was Sabattis. He was taken captive by Maj. Rogers when a boy in his expedition against the St. Francis Indians in 1759. He came to Fryeburg, and made that his home much of the time in the house of Mr. James Swan, who afterwards removed to Bethel. Sabattis had a reputed, though it has been said, not a lawful wife in Mollyocket. They often came to Bethel together. Sabattis was fond of rum, and on a certain occasion, it is said, that he attempted to wring Mr. Swan's neck, but he being the stronger man gave him such a whipping as ever after made him a friend. He would go out a hunting in search of fowl and choice bits of moose, and bring these in to gratify his master.

Although the Lovewell Fight in Fryeburg has but little direct connection with the History of Bethel, it may be of interest to a portion of the readers of the *Courier* to describe one of the fiercest encounters recorded in the annals of N. England.

Let us imagine ourselves in the town of Dunstable, in Mass., in the year 1724. Eleven of its citizens have been killed by the Indians this year. The town is in mourning, while a spirit of revenge is aroused to punish the enemy for their bold and savage deeds.

The General Court offers a bounty of one hundred pounds for every Indian's scalp. This is a great temptation to bold spirits. Among those who are determined on some daring adventure was Capt. John Lovewell. He collects forty men, plunges into the forest as far as what is now Wakefield, N. Hampshire, and kills ten Indians while asleep, scalps them and procecds to Boston where he and his companions received more than 3000 dollars. One can imagine the effect of such a success on the little town of Dunstable. Volunteers from this and the neighboring towns surround the bold Lovewell, and another expedition is well fitted out against the Pequakets. Captain, Lieutenant, Ensign, Sergeant, Corporal, Chaplain and Doctor are provided for the expedition. The whole company numbers forty-six men.

This expedition started from Dunstable April 16th, 1725, just 134 years ago to the day on which we are writing out this sketch, on a journey of a hundred or more miles through the wilderness to attack a dangerous enemy. After a perilous march they arrived on the shores of Ossipee Pond, where they erected a fort in which the Doctor and seven men were left to take care of several who were unable to advance.

The whole number who were in the engagement was only thirty-three. They were still forty miles from the Pequaket settlement, and it was not till they had been from home twenty-one days, that they arrived at the western shore of Saco Pond, May 6th, 1725. Here they remained concealed during the next day.

But who can imagine the excitement of these men who had spent the weary hours of nearly a month in relating stories of Indian warfare. The Lieutenant, Josiah Farewell, had escaped, the only survivor on a previous excursion, while the scenes of the past year were fresh in their minds. But when they were within hearing of the din of an Indian village, that day must have been one of awful suspense. During the night as they lay concealed, they imagined that Indians, having got scent of them, were lurking around ready to raise the yell of the war-whoop. On Saturday morning, they breakfasted, held their devotions, and started around the northern shore of the Pond. Here they crossed the Indian Path to the Pond; as they approached the North Eastern shore, they deposited their packs. Here, Ensign Wyman discovered an Indian having in his hands some fowls and two guns. They immediately sunk to the ground and allowed him to approach, when several guns were fired at him, but so excited were the men that they failed to hit him. The Indian resolved to make the most of his situation, raised his gun and mortally wounded Capt. Lovewell, and slightly wounded a soldier. Ensign Wyman then took deliberate aim and killed the Indian. The interesting work of scalping the Indian devolved on Mr. Frye, the chaplain, and a soldier. This was their first trophy after so long a march. They then returned to where they had left their packs.

During all this time Paugus had been down the river with eighty men on a scouting party, and was on his return. Landing at the shores of the Pond they found the packs of the men, and traced their footsteps. In a moment they counted their packs and sprang into the adjoining swamp. As Lovewell and his men returned to their packs the Indians sprung forth, uttered their horrid yell and fired their guns over the heads of their white foes, at the same time bringing with them ropes to tie their prisoners, but they counted not rightly, their host. Lovewell would accept no quarter, but sprang forward with his men and killed a number at the first fire. The Indians after retreating a few rods rallied and returned the fire, killing nine, and wounding three more. Among the killed was Capt. Lovewell.

Slowly the English retreated, but still firing upon their enemy at every opportunity, until they reached the shore of the Pond where were a few pine trees which served as a protection, while a stream of water on one side, and a ledge of rocks on the other, served as a most favorable position. Taking their station here, they continued the fight during the day, the Indians repeatedly shouting and yelling like demons, while the English echoed back the shout as they gave them volley after volley during the day.

At this time but nine of their whole number were uninjured, while the enemy could scarcely retreat with twenty men. Paugus, the hero of the day, had bravely led on his men, but descending to the stream to wash out his heated gun, he was met on the other side by John Chamberlain, who had gone there for the same purpose. While washing their guns Chamberlain told Paugus he should kill him. Paugus dared him to the trial. They dry their guns and load them at the same time, but Chamberlain not stopping to prime his gun, struck the breech on the ground, by which it primed itself, and raising it, fired, and shot Paugus dead, while the ball from his own gun grazed through Chamberlain's hair.

The successor of Paugus was Wahwa, who not long after withdrew from the contest -- a contest never forgotten by the Indians in this part of New England.

The Indians having withdrawn, the remaining men held a consultation at midnight. Nearby lay nine of their company dead, and fourteen more were wounded, three of whom were unable to move. What a trying scene for nine uninjured men in the heart of the enemy's country, and without food or shelter! One of their wounded died during their deliberations. Two others pressed their companions to return and leave them to the mercies of the savages.

They commence their retreat, but had proceeded only a mile and a-half when four of their number are unable to proceed.

One of the wounded rolled himself into a canoe and was drifted by the wind towards the fort, at Ossipee, and arrived there as soon as the others. They found the fort deserted by those who were left behind in consequence of the report of a deserter who fled at the beginning of the fight.

Frye, the Chaplain, who was wounded and was left behind, was never heard of again. The others after incredible suffering all reached their homes.

A company of men afterwards returned to the spot and buried the dead. They dug up three Indians, among whom was Paugus.

The spot where the battle was fought is a delightful one. The tourist should leave the pleasant village of Fryeburg, and pass over the pine plains which gradually descend to the shores of what is now known as Lovewell's Pond. Let him first ascent Jockey Cap, a bluff half a mile from the shore of the pond, and survey the whole route. Descending, he will proceed to the shore where all the points of interest are shown. It is a lovely, quiet spot. The pond was formerly the resort of waterfowl which rendered it pleasant and profitable sport for the Indians.

But the Indians are not there. The terrible loss of one half of their warriors caused them to leave their homes and flee to the Coos Country, on the Connecticut River.

It is probable that the Indians residing in Bethel were frightened at this invasion into the forests of Maine and fled to the same section of the country.

The name of Paugus will always be remembered as a brave warrior. We cannot clothe him in long flowing dress covered with various ornaments, as a recent writer has done, but rather like the ballad writer, describe him in a huge bear-skin; yet he must have been no ordinary Indian.

Aged people can still remember the bitter hatred that continued to exist long after the contest with them. The name of *Indian* was the watchword by which to rouse up every evil passion in men's natures.

The wrongs of that period were mutual. Bad men lived then as now who would not scruple to defraud the simple native, and excite in him a spirit of revenge.

The Indians living on the Androscoggin River played no inconsiderable part in the early Indian wars.

From Merrymeeting Bay at the mouth of the Androscoggin, to its source, and probably on the St. Francis river in Canada, dwelt the Anasagunticooks. They had a place of rendezvous at a fort which they built near Brunswick Falls. The Anasagunticooks were divided into several tribes. There was a settlement on a branch of the Androscoggin in the vicinity of the town of Lisbon. From rather slender information I infer that all the Indians residing below Lewiston Falls were called Pejepscots, or Pejemscots, while those above the Falls were called Androscoggins or Rokomekos. Whether those as far up as Bethel had a distinct name I have never learned. All those tribes met the other Indian tribes in council at Merrymeeting Bay on what is called Abagudasset Point, on the north side of the bay. In their palmiest days they are said to have numbered 1500 warriors, but they suffered in common with other tribes in the plague of 1617 and in their wars in 1747 they could not number more than 160 men fit for service.

About 25 miles above Lewiston Falls, they had a settlement called Rouameuo, now Canton Point. Here they had five hundred acres of land under cultivation. This was the head quarters of the tribe. Here they had a fort, a chapel and a priest. The fort was destroyed by Capt. Church in 1690.

At Rumford was the Great Androscoggin Falls where a branch of the Pennacooks resided, and who afterwards gave it the name of Pennacook Falls. It appears that the Indians sometimes gave the name of Anasagunticook to the villiage on the St. Francis River. It does not appear that the Indians ever deeded away the territory of the Androscoggin River above Rumford Falls. Hence in the early History of Bethel the Indians claimed a right to the country. It has been said that the Indians were instigated by this fact as much as any other to make their attack on Bethel in 1781. Mollocket always claimed the right of a proprietor as long as she lived.

In our next chapter we shall give some account of Worombo's Deed.

The Anasagunticooks were exceedingly hostile to the English. The names Tarrumkin, Warumbee, and Hogkins, their Sagamores, figure largely from 1675 till 1700. They were brave men.

We shall take the liberty to insert a letter written by Judge Potter, President of the N. Hampshire Historical Society, which will throw some light and start some important questions.

HILLSBOROUGH, N. H.
Feb. 9, 1859.

DEAR SIR: -- Yours of Jan. 24th is at hand. It is true that the Pennacooks settled at Rumford or near there on the Androscoggin. It is probable that the first settlers of Rumford (Pennacook or Rumford men) learned of the lands and fisheries there from the Indians at Pennacook (afterwards Rumford, now Concord, N.H.).

Nanamocomuck, the oldest son of Passaconnaasoay the Sagamore of the Pennacooks, was the chief of the Wachusets, in Massachusetts, near the Wachusett Mountain. He was cast into prison in 1659 -- being the indorser for another Indian to one John Tinker for the sum of forty pounds. His friends sold an island in the Merrimack, called Wickasauke, to pay the debt. After leaving the prison he became the enemy of the English, and with his family and friends moved to the Androscoggin country, the Androscoggin Indians being subjects of his father Passaconnaway. Nanamocomuck became distinguished, if not sagamore of the Androscoggins -- as his son upon his death became a noted Sagamore among them. This son was Kancamagus -- known among the English as *John Hogkins*. Nanamocomuck died probably before his father Passaconnaway, as the latter was succeeded on his death about 1665 by his second son, Wonnalancet, and had his eldest son been alive he would have succeeded to the Sagamoreship of Pennacook.

In 1677, Wonnalancet returned to Canada -- abducting the Sagamoreship of Pennacook. Upon this, Kancamagus, the chief to the Androscoggins, succeeded to the vacant Sagamoreship. In 1685, Hogkins or Kancamagus, fearing the Mohawks, and not receiving assistance from the English, which they had asked, fled with his people to the Androscoggin, where he built a Fort. The Mohawks not appearing, at the solicitation of the English, the Indians returned to their homes and entered into a treaty with the English, which was executed at Portsmouth, Sept. 8, 1685.

Kancamagus was not present on this day, but came into Portsmouth and signed, the 19th of September. Bagerson, or Joseph Traske, signed it at the same time and probably came with him from the Androscoggin. In 1676 many of the friends and an uncle of Kancamagus had been taken at Cocheco by Major Waldron and Capt. Syll and Hathorne, from Massachusetts, and sold into slavery. This insult was to be avenged, and accordingly in 1689, Kancamagus having formed a confederacy of the Pennacooks, Pequauquets, Sacos, Androscoggins and other eastern Indians fell upon Cocheco, killed Major Waldron, and killed or captured fifty-one men, women and children, and almost entirely destroyed the settlement. This attack proves Kancamagus to have been a skillful warrior. The English immediately went in pursuit, and in September took Worombo's Fort in which was the sister and two children of Kancamagus. The sister was killed, and the children were taken prisoners. On the 21st of the same month Kancamagus with Worombo attacked Capt. Church at Casco, killed seven, and wounded twenty-four of his men before they were repulsed.

In 1691, Kancamagus signed the truce at "Sackatahock." After this truce we hear no more of him. Where was the Fort of Nonannocomuck? and where was the Fort of Worombo?

Yours respectfully,
C. E. POTTER.

Among the prominent Indians of the Anasagunticooks was a Sagamore named Worombo, who with his family appear to have lived in a fort at Canton Point as early as 1684. He seemed to figure largely in the Indian treaties of that period. He gave a deed of the country as described in the following instrument. It has been a matter of doubt what was meant by the "upper falls." Could they be the Rumford Falls? We may well suppose that Worombo was well acquainted with the country at Bethel and probably the Indians there were tributary to him. When Capt. Church destroyed his fort in 1691, the Indians were gone up the river some fifty or sixty miles after corn, which must have been at Bethel, and as Worombo was absent, he was probably in that company. Worombo's two children were taken captive by Capt. Church.

It will be perceived that if Rumford Falls were those intended, that the Indians never gave away the lands on the upper Androscoggin.

WOROMBO'S DEED.

To all People to whom these Presents shall come Know yee that whereas near three Score years since Mr. Thomas Purchase, diseased came into this Country as wee have been well informed, and did as well by Power or Pattent derived from the King of England as by Consent Contract & Agreement with Sagamores & Proprietors of all the lands lying on the Easterly sides of Androscogan River & Kennebecke River; enter upon & take possession *of all the Lands, lying four Miles Westward from the uppermost falls, In sayd Androscogan River to Maqqait* in Casco Bay & *on the lands on the other side* Androscogan River *from above said falls down to Pejepscott & Merrymeeting Bay* to bee bounded *by a South west & North west lyne, to rune from the Upper part of said falls to Kennebecke River, & all the Land from Maqquait to Pejepscot & to hould the same breadth where your land will beare it, down to a place* called Atkins his Bay near to Saggadahock on the Westerly side of Kennebecke River all the Islands in this Kennebecke River & the lands between the sd Atkins his Bay & Small paynt Harbour, the lands & Rivers & Ponds interiacent *Containing yr. in breath about three english Miles more or less* and whereas wee are well assured that Major Nichols Shapleigh in his life tyme, was both by purchase from the Indians Sagamores our Ancestors & Consent of Wm. Gorge Commissioner possessed, & dyed seized of the Remaynder of all the lands lying and Adjoining upon the Mayne, and all the Islands between the sd Small Point Harbor & Maqquait aforesaid, & particularly of a neck of Land called Meraconeg & an Island called Sabascon Diggin, & whereas the relects & Heyrs of sd. Mr. Purchase & Major Nicholas Shepleigh have reserved accommodations for their several Familys sould all the remainder of the aforesaid Lands, & Islands to Richard Wharton of Boston Merchant & for as much as the sd mr. Purchase did personally possess, improve, & Inhabit, at Pejepscot aforesaid near the Centor of middle of all the lands afores'd for near fifty years before the late unhappy war and whereas the sd Richard Wharton hath desired an enlarqement uppon & between the sd Androscoggan & Kennebecke River & to Incorage the sd Richard Wharton to settle an English town and promote the Salmon & Sturgeon fishing by which wee promise ourselves great Supplies & Relief Therefore & for other good Causes & Considerations & especially for & in consideration of a valuable sume received from the sd Wharton in Merchandize Wee Warumbee, Darumkine, Wehickermett, Weedon, Damhegan, Neanongasett & Numbenewett, Chief Sagamores of all the afores'd & other Rivers & Lands adjacent, have in confirmation of the sd Richard Whartons title & Propriety fully freely & absolutely given granted ratified & confirmed to him the sd Richard Wharton all the aforesaid Lands from the upper most part of Androscoggan falls foure miles, Westward & so down to Maqquait & by sd River of Pejepscot & from the other side of Androscoggan falls, all the Land from the Falls to Pejepscott & Merrymeeting Bay to Kennebecke, & towards the wilderness to be bounded by a Southwest & Northwesterly to extend from the upper part of the sd Androscogan uppermost falls to the said River of Kennebecke and all the Lands from Maqquait to Pejepscot & rune & hould the same breath where the Land will beare it, unto Atkins his Bay & Kennebecke River & Small Paynt Harbour. In Casco Bay, & all the Islands In Kennebecke and Pejepsoct River and Merrymeeting Bay and within aforesaid bounds especially the afores'd Necke of land called Merriconeage and island called Sabascon Diggin together with all the Rivers, Rivulets, brooks, ponds, pools, Waters, Water Courses, all the Wood Trees of timber or other frees and all mines minerals quaries, & especialy the soole Use and benefit of Salmon and Spurgeon fishing in all the Rivers Rivulets or Bays of aforesaid and in all Rivers, brooks, Creeks or ponds within any of the bounds afores'd & also Wee the said Sagamores have upon the Consideration aforesaid, given granted, bargained, & souled enfeoffed & confirmed, And do by these presents give, grant, bargain, & sell, allience Inteoff & confirm to him the sd Richard Wharton all the Land lying mites above the uppermost of the said Androscoggan Falls, in length & breadth houlding the same breadth from Androscoggan Falls to Kennenebecke River, and to be bounded by the aforesaid Southwest & North East tyne & a parcell of Lands at five miles Distance to run from Androscoggan to Kennebecke River as afores'd to gether with all the profit privileges Commodities Benefits & advantages and particularly the soole property benefitts & advantages of the Salmon & Sturgeon fishing within bounds & lymits afore's To have and hold to him the seid Richard Wharton, his Heirs & Assigns forever, all the aforenamed Land Priviledges & Premisses with all benefitts, rights appertenances or advantages y'r now do or hereafter shall or may belong unto any part or parcell of the premises fully, freely & absolutely acquited & Discharged from from all former and other gyfts, grants bargains & Sales Mortgage & incumbrances whatsoever; and Wee the sd Warrumbee, Darumkine, Whihhermete, Wedon, Dumhegan, Neonongassett, & Nimbatsett, do covenant & gyant to & with the s'd Richard Wharton, that Wee have in ourselves good Right & full power thus to confirm & convey the premises and that Wee our Heirs successors shall & will warrant and defend the s'd Richard Wharton his heirs and assigns forever in the Peaceable enjoyment of the Premises and every part thereof against all and every person or persons, that may legally claim any Right, Title, Interest or propriety in the Premises by from or under us the above named Sagamores, or and of our Ancestors or predecessors. Provided nevertheless that nothing in this Deede be construed to Deprive us the sd Saggamores successors or people from improving our Ancient Planting grounds, nor from hunting in and of the said lands being not Inclosed, nor from fishing for our own Provision, so long as no damage shall be to the English Fishery; provided so that nothing herein contained shall prejudice any of the English Inhabitants or planters being at present actually possessed of any part of the Premises and legally deriving Right from sd Mr. Purchase, and or Ancestors. In Witness whereof -- We the aforenamed Sagamores well understanding the purport hereof do set to our hands and seals at Pejepscott the sevententh day of July in the thirty fifth year of the Reign Sovering Lord -- King Charles the second *one thousand six hundred eighty four*.

The Androscoggin Indians appear to have played no inconsiderable part in King Phillip's War. They made excursions to the sea coast, and attacked the settlers in Yarmouth, Falmouth, Scarborough and Wells, and retreated with their captives. It is singular that so little record is made of their locations. In Drake's Book of Indian History is the following passage:

"In 1690 Tobias Oakman was taken by the Indians at Black Point. At which time he says he personally knew Edgar Emet, who was then Chief Sachem of Kenebeck, and Squando who was then Chief Sachem of Saco, and Moxus who was then Chief Sachem of Noridgework, and Shepscot John, who was Chief Sachem of Shepscot, and with Oorumby who was then Chief Sachem of Pejemscot, Madokawando was Chief of the Penobscots at that time." Now, where was Pejemscot, and where was Pejepscot?

A prominent Chief of the Androscoggins was *Mugg*, who made an attack on Scarborough in 1676 with 100 warriors. In immediate relationship there was a tribe known as early as 1630 by the name of Aucocisco who lived between the Saco and Androscoggin Rivers. They probably occupied the Presumpscot and Royall's Rivers. They had a camping and burial ground on Cousen's Island at the mouth of Royall's river. An immense pile of shells still remain there, and their skeletons frequently cave out of the bank. They appear to have retired at a very early period.

Expedition of Col. Church.

The following relation of Col. Church is copied from the Hinkley papers, vol. 3d, in the Massachusetts Historical Library. It is a transcript of what he wrote or indited. Time has made it almost illegible -- it was copied & brought to light by the Rev. Mr. Greely of Turner. It is much more correct in its geographical statements than the account given of the same expedition in the life of Col. Church by his son. It seems to confirm the position taken by the Pejepscot Proprietors in their contest with the Commonwealth of Massachusetts -- in relation to the extent of the claim of the Proprietors -- that "the uppermost falls on Androscoggin river" mentioned in the Indian Deed of Worumbee and others, was not the upper falls at Brunswick, nor the falls at Lewiston. The Proprietors produced many depositions to make it appear, that the river from Merrymeeting Bay, to Lewiston Falls went formerly under the name of Pejepscot -- and the continuance of the river beyond was called Amascoggin or Androscoggin.

Portsmouth Sept. 30, 1690.

MAY IT PLEASE YOUR HONOUR: -- After the tender of all humble service -- these are to give your honour a brief account of our proceedings since we set sail from Piscataqua upon the 10th inst, at 2 in the afternoon. At first I must beg your honour's pardon for my backwardness herein; but indeed I intended to have had more to write before I did send; also I heard that Maj. Pike had given your honour account of the substance, but to prevent mistakes I will here be a little more particular.

We sailed, as aforesaid, I came the 11th at night, in the night amongst the islands in Casco Bay: -- laid the vessel close, out of sight: -- went on shore at break of day upon an Island, that had been inhabited by the English (called "Capeag") we ranged about, -- found where the enemy had lately been, but were drawn off. This was the 12th day. In the evening we weighed, & came to "Macquait." & the 13th day, about two of the clock in the morning -- we landed our men silently upon the main and leaving soldiers on board to keep the vessel -- we marched in the night up to 'Pechipscutt' fort -- divided the army into three companies, surrounded the fort, and when daylight appeared, we found that the enemy were removed, not long before we came there. Also, the soldiers found some little plunder and a barn of corn. The same day we advanced up the River towards "Amascoggin" on the S. W. side of the river, although the way was extremely difficult; yet it was a more obscure way, the enemy using to march on the N. E. side. We marched that day above the middle Falls about 20 miles. There it began to rain hard, where we encamped and built fifty tents and lay there that night & at break of day, put out our fires and marched as soon as it was light. It being the 14th inst., and the Sabbath day, the soldiers marched briskly and came within sight of the fort about 2 o'clock P. M. Then we turned into the woods and fetched a circumference and waded over a little River not much above the knees -- and in a short time came to the westerly branch of the great River -- and there left our baggage and those men that were tired and made up 40 more to guard the Doctor, and looking over the brow of a hill by the river, espied two English and an Indian moving towards the Fort -- ran after them and soon took the English, but the Indian got clear. Then I feared he would inform the Fort; gave order, that all with one consent should run through the River and not mind any other form; but be that could get first to the Fort; -- if they had opportunity, to offer them peace; -- if they would not accept it, to fall on, and by that time they were well entered, the rest would come up. Also I gave order to two companies to spread between the woods and the Fort, to prevent the escape of the enemy that way. All which was attended. We were very wet, running through the River; but got up undiscovered to the Fort till within gun shot. Few Indians we found there; but two men and a lad of about 18 with some women and children. Five ran into the river, 3 or 4 of whom were killed. The lad of 18 made his escape up the river to another place where there was corn, about 40 or 50 miles up, as afterwards we were well informed. We killed 6 or 7 and took 11; Lodged in the fort that night. Only one of our men was wounded in that little skirmish. We made use of no other firewood but the fort all the time we were there. Monday, being the 15th inst., we having examined the Indian and the English captives, made search for corn and other plunder. We found a pretty deal of corn in barns under ground and destroyed it. Also, we found guns and ammunition a pretty deal with beaver and we took five English captives, viz: Lieut. Robert Haskin's widow of Oyster River, Benj. Barnard's wife of Salmon Falls, Ann Heard of "Cochecha," one Willis' daughter of Oyster River and a boy of Exeter. Both Indians and English inform us that the enemy had lately had a consultation; many of them were for peace and many of them were against it; and had hired and procured about 300, and advance to Wells with a flag of truce and offer them peace: -- if they could not agree, then to fall on. If they could not take Wells, then they resolved to attack Piscataqua. The which when we were well informed, we left two old squaws that were not able to march; gave them victuals enough for one week of their own corn boiled and a little of our provisions and buried their dead and left them clothes enough to keep them warm and left the wigwams for them to lie in; gave them orders to tell their friends how kind we were to them; bidding them do the like to ours: Also, if they were for peace to come to good man Small's at Berwick within 14 days -- who would attend to discourse them. Then we came away with our own 5 captives and 9 of theirs and waded through the River and returned in that day and one more to our vessel at "Macquait." We made all haste imaginable, for fear some of our Towns should be attacked before we came home and through the goodness of God, we were most of us well and found all the vessels well and went all on board and set sail; only, (as God would have it) one of our vessels ran aground, which we did not understand, being in the night, and having left her --and soon missed her, Capt. Alden concluding she had run aground, and before she came clear, there escaped one Anthony Bracket of Casco, who was informed by the lad that escaped from "Amascoggin" aforesaid of our army. He made his escape -- got into our track and came to "Macquait," hallooed to the vessel, that heard him and gladly took him on board. The rest of our fleet bore up and came to Winter harbor, where I sent out a scout of 60 men to 'Salco' Falls to make discovery -- the rest in arms ready on shore, intending at their return to march by land to Wells. The Scout met with a small party upon the River, making fish and other provisions, viz: -- old 'Dong' and his crew about 40 in all. The enemy being on the other side of the river, ours could not come at them. They made shot at them, killed one 'Dicks, a baso man' (a Chebacco man) and got him on shore, 2 more men sank in the river. Some of ours swam over the River, took their canoes and plunder. At this skirmish, Lt. 'Hunniwell,' was shot through his thigh. There we took a pretty deal of powder, shot and lead and other plunder and 8 or 9 canoes. Also we destroyed 4 or 5 canoes at 'Amascoggent.' The man we took from them at 'Salco' told us the enemy from Cape Sables and all quarters were looked for by that time to rendezvous at 'Pechepscutt;' also that he knew that the enemy had brought Beaver and goods to 'Pechepscutt' plain and bid them. We supposed it was a gratuity for the Eastward Indians; -- also, that he himself knew within half a mile where it was hid. This made us alter our former intention and took ship and sailed to a place more Eastward than 'Macquait' (called Mare point) landed our men by day light, about 250 -- marched around in the woods -- came upon the Eastward of Pechepscutt plain. In our march we espied a canoe with 3 or 4 Indians in 'Macquait' bay. We made after them, but they got out of our reach. When we came upon the plain, we parted into 3 companies, found none of the enemy, but we found plunder -- of which a pretty deal of powder and shot. Then we returned and embarked and made the best of our way to Casco; came in there in the evening, being the 20th inst. There I concluded to land and send the ablest part by land towards Wells; but I landed the most part of the men and went on shore and ordered them where they should lodge; -- but the Indians, in particluar I ordered to such a house or else to go on board again; -- but, they, contrary to my order took up their lodge on the River by "Papooducke" side were the enemy had lately rendezvoused, all the rest of the Commanders and companies were where I ordered them to be. The enemy discovered the Indians' fires, came in the night and discovered where the companies lay and ambushed them at day light -- made shot upon our Indians. It being the 21st inst., and the Sabbath day. Our English arose to the succour of the Indian friends, being all ready at break of day per my order and drawing up towards them many were wounded and slain, the enemy having great advantage of ours, -- for the light of the day and stars reflecting upon the waters gave them advantage to see us, when as we could not see them at all against the dark woods, especially we could not see to distinguish between our Indians and theirs. Whereupon I ordered to lie still under the sea bank till day light. I coming on shore the second boat and saw the difficulty. But the enemy fired hard upon the vessels and boats coming on shore and when the day was light enough, I ordered the men to rise from the banks and run all upon them at once. The which we did and soon put them to the flight -- followed them hard through a swamp -- firing briskly. They knowing where their canoes were, got their wounded men into them before we came up and most of them put off. Our men affirmed but two they saw killed. We took 2 guns and many blankets and gun cases and 4 canoes. The rest of the enemy run into the woods. We went on board, sent away two vessels with the captives and sick and wounded men and buried our dead -- which were 3 English and 4 Indians. The wounded were 17 English and 8 Indians. Those that were slain were chiefly Plymouth. The wounded of Captain 'Connyeres' 6; Capt. 'Floid' 3; Capt. Southworth 4; Capt. Walton 3; of Capt. Andrews 1. -- Since that one Englishman of Plymouth is dead of his wounds and an Indian; and as Englishman, both of Plymouth, dead of the small Pox.

We embarked and came to Cape 'Neddicke' the 25d day and marched with about 200 men, all we had fir for service to Wells. Sent a scout the next day to "Salco" and Winter harbour, about 24 miles, made no discovery of the enemy later than we were there before. Then we returned and came to Portsmouth the 26th instant, because our doctor was gone home with the wounded men and our men were several of them sick and lame and wanted "shoose" (shoes) and other recruits; -- or else we would have gone farther before we had come home. The Indians we brought home were John Hawkins' wife and four children. We took his brother in law, who ran away from us in our return home. This John Hawkins is the Sagamore that headed the Indians that took 'Cocheche'. Two children also of "Welumbee," and one girl more, whose father and mother were slain in the skirmish. John Hawkins' sister was also slain at the same time and we returned to Portsmouth 26th Instant -- intending with all haste to go to "Socconock," but many cross things falling out to frustrate the design too long here to relate. But from Major Pike your Honour will here more at large. -- Thus with my service to your honour, I rest and remain your honours most humble servant -- ready to serve

your honour
BENJA. CHURCH.

In 1703 Gen. Dudley, of Mass., had a conference with the Indians at Casco, which was represented by a large delegation from the Pennacooks, the Sokokis (Sacos), the Anasagunticooks, the Canibas, and the Tarratines. All the Indians appeared to great advantage. They were well armed, handsomely clad, some of them, fancifully decorated, and most of their faces so painted, as to give them looks truly terrific. Probably no one tribe was so fully represented as the Anasagunticooks, for about 250 of them arrived in a flotilla of 65 acres. A tent was spread, large enough to enclose and accommodate the Governor and his attendants, with the principal Sagamores and Sachems. Among these, when seated, the English promiscuously disposed themselves, being not wholly without apprehensions for their own safety. Among the Sagamores present, Wattanummon, of Pegwacket, Mesambomwtt and Wexar from Androscoggin (Anasagunticooks), Adewando and Hegan, from the Pennacooks.

The missionaries and friars from Canada had just been among them to withdraw their allegiance from the English.

In 1703 Calliaos and M. de Vaudreuil, his successor, persuaded the Indians of western Maine to settle at Becancourt and St. Francois, two small rivers in Canada. The Sokokis, and the Anasagunticooks from Maine, were among the number, and these were called the St. Francis tribe. This was the head quarters of the Indians in this section, in the subsequent Indian wars. The Indians did not entirely leave the Androscoggin as a tribe till a half century later. So great was the diminution of this tribe by the war of Queen Annie, that in 1713 they did not with the eastern Indians number more than 300.

In 1751 the Sokokis Indians, whose families had been with the English, while they themselves were at Louisberg, had of choice returned to their former places of abode and hunting grounds at Pegwacket, satisfied with the treatment received, and much attached to their English friends.

In 1754 hostilities breaking out, a bounty of 100 Pounds was offered by the General Court for the scalp of any St. Francis Indian, and ten Pounds more additional for any one taken alive -- such was public indignation against that tribe.

In 1755 the General Court declared war against the Anasagunticook Indians, and all the other tribes eastward of Piscataqua, excepting those upon Penobcot River.

In 1756 a small force of men was sent up the Androscoggin in whale boats, a distance of 65 miles probably as far as Rumford Falls. They found no Indians, but measured distance and noted the features of the country.

In 1757 the Anasagunticooks, who originally inhabited the banks of the Androscoggin, still viewed the country as their own, and often visited it. They made an attack on a party of eight men near the fort at Topsham, and wounded two at the first onset. A severe skirmish ensued, in which the Indians, on seeing two of their number fall dead by their side, seized their bodies and fled. Two Englishmen were killed farther up the river.

In 1775 Sabbattis and Natanis accompanied Gen. Arnold to Quebec.

Bethel was the 108th town incorporated in Me.; John Grover says it was settled in 1773, and had 14 families in 1781.

Among the most noted Indians whose name is remembered by the whites was that of Sabattis, or Sabatiste, who was Sagamore of the Anasagunticooks, and who requested government to keep some supplies; for, said he, in "Cold winters and deep snows, my Indians, unable to go to Fort Richmond, sometimes suffer." The government always in such instances cheerfully administered relief; and the tribe remained quiet though constantly viewed with distrust.

In 1744 several Sokokis families at Pegwacket, knowing their own weakness, renounced their allegiance to the French and united with the English.

The Indians on the St. Francis (probably) excited by the French, committed the most cruel depredations on the lower English settlements, killing some and carrying others into captivity. But when peace was declared between France and England in 1748, it was hoped that no more of Indian warfare would be heard of in Maine. The Indians seemed to be desirous of peace, and sent a delegation to Falmouth when a treaty was made in 1749.

Among the Anasagunticooks I find the names of the following Chiefs, who signed it: -- Sawwaramet, Ausado, Waaununga, Sauquish, Warcedeen, Wawawnunka, names as musical as those of the most cultivated nations.

In consequence of the unsettled state of the country particularly in New Brunswick and Nova Scotia, the French continued to excite the Indians, when in 1750 the St. Francis tribe to the number of 80 descended to the sea coast and committed several murders and carried away captives to Canada.

In 1750 the St. Francis Indians made an attack on the lower settlements in Maine.

"Boldly resisted, or foiled in their assaults," says Williamson, "they withdrew, carrying away with them between 20 and 30 prisoners. In passing through New Gloucester, they met Joseph Taylor and Mr. Farewell, near Seabody Pond, whom they seized, and proceeded with them through the woods towards the sources of the Little Androscoggin in the northerly part of the present town of Paris. Discovering a new track, they pursued it to the height of land, where they found the camps of two hunters, Snow and Butterfield. At the moment of discovery, the Indian file leader, hooded with a large hawk-skin retaining its feathers and hanging down upon his shoulders, raised a hideous yell, and quickened his pace. Snow, having been a captive in a former war, and conceiving a great antipathy to the Indians and their manner of living, determined to sacrifice his life, rather than be again their prisoner. When he heard the shout, he was in a sitting posture, pecking the flint of his gun, which was at the time loaded with only a partridge-charge. Deliberately rising on his feet, and taking good aim, he brought the foremost Indian to the ground only a few feet distant. He was their Chief. This so infuriated his companions, that they instantly fired upon him a volley, which pierced his body through with several bullets. To satiate their rage, they then cut and mangled it till tired, leaving it above ground and forbidding Butterfield and the other prisoners to bury or touch it. The body of their chief they carried into a bog where Moose Pond empties into Little Androscoggin; and after breaking the turf and forming an aperture, they crushed it deep into the mire, and departed, uttering expressions of intermingled grief and respect. At Umbagog Lake, they fell in company with another party of Indian plunderers, where all of them joined in something like funeral solemnities, commemoration of their Sagamore's death; then wiping the tearful eye, they rehearsed to each other their adventures and feats, with the same God cheer, as if nothing melancholy had happened. Taylor was with them five years, became acquainted with both the French and Indian languages, and was afterwards instructor of Indian youth at Dartmouth College. Mr. Taylor lived in Claremont, N.H. His oldest daughter was the wife of Col. E. Rawson of Paris, Me."

In 1759 the French had drawn the Indians into their interests so completely that they became exasperated by the French themselves and came to be among their most cruel enemies.

General Amherst having reduced "Ticonderoga despatched thence, Sept. 13. Maj. Robert Rogers, with about 200 rangers, to destroy the Indian villages at St. Francois and Becancourt. After a fatiguing march of 21 days he came within sight of the places, which he discerned from the top of a tree. Halting his men at the distance of three miles, he rested till twilight. In the evening he entered the former village in disguise, with two of his officers. The Indians being, unfortunately for them, engaged in a great dance, he passed through them undiscovered. Having formed his men into parties, and posted them to advantage, he made a general assault Oct. 4th, just before day, while the Indians fatigued by exercise, were in a sound sleep. So completely surprised were they that little resistance could be made. Some were killed in their cottages, and others, attempting to flee were shot or thrust through by those placed in the avenues. Several of them actually fell upon the spot; about 20 were taken prisoners, and five English captives rescued from suffering. Daylight disclosed to the assailants a horrid spectacle. It was the sight of several hundred scalps torn from the heads of their countrymen, elevated on poles and waving in the air.

St. Francois was a village which had, through a period of many years, been enriched with the plunder of the English frontiers and the sale of captives. The church was adorned with plate, and the houses were decently furnished. The apprehension of alarm and of pursuit did not allow much time for pillage. The rangers only took such things as they could conveniently bring away, among which were 200 guineas in money, a silver image weighing ten lbs., a large quantity of wampum, and some articles of clothing. Having set fire to the village, Rogers made his retreat up the River St. Francis, intending that his men should meet in rendezvous at the upper Coos on Con. River. Rogers, having one man killed and 6 or 7 wounded, was under the necessity of diminishing his prisoners on their parole; and after this, he was pursued and lost 7 of his company. The whole party kept in a body about ten days, and then scattered, some died in the woods, and all the rest suffered the extremes of hunger and fatigue before they arrived at any habitation of the settlers." Williamson Vol. II., P. 341.

After the attack of Col. Rogers on the St. Francis tribe in 1759, we hear but little of the Indians in the western part of Maine. They ceased to exist as tribes. Scattered families lived in Fryeburg, and at Canton Point, and other places, but their political power was forever gone.

They, however, still felt a secret desire to be avenged upon the whites for seizing their right to the soil. It is said that this was one motive which excited the Indians to make their attack on Bethel.

The following narrative is the finale of Indian warfare in Maine, and in fact in New England, extending from King Phillip's War, with but little interruption to the close of the Revolution. The narrative of Lieut. Segar, it is understood, was written out by Rev. Daniel Gould, the first settled minister in Bethel, who received it from Mr. Segar. The truthfulness of the narrative is evident on every page.

THE CAPTIVITY OF
LT. NATHANIEL SEGAR,
DURING THE REVOLUTIONARY WAR.

"On the 3d day of August, 1781, there came six Indians from Canada; I knew one of them, named Tomhegan, for he had been often at my house. They were all painted and armed with guns, tomahawks and scalping knives. I, and Lieut. Jonathan Clark, and Capt. Eleazer Twitchell, were at a little distance from a piece of woods, when five Indians came running out of the woods, and told us that we were their prisoners, and must go with them to Canada. Lieut. Clark's house was near by. They took us to the house, and bound us.

After they had bound us, they went to plundering the house, and told us to sit down, and sit still, or they would kill us. While they were plundering the house, they found several gallons of rum in the cellar, a part of which they put into their bottles and carried away with them. They found sixteen dollars in money, some clothing, provision and many other things, which they found in the house, and converted them to their own use. While they were plundering the house, Mrs. Clark had embraced her opportunity, and hid her husband's silver watch in the ashes, so that she saved it from the Indians. They attempted to take her gold necklace from her neck, but the string broke and the beads were scattered about the floor. When they were gone, she found nearly all of them. They also attempted to take her silver buckles from her shoes; she asked them what business they had with her feet, and they finally left them. My fears were that they would kill her she -- was very bold towards them, and shewed no fear.

While these things were doing, an Indian came out of the woods with Mr. Benjamin Clark, another prisoner, whom he had taken. In the meantime Capt. Twitchell, by watching his oppertunity, had absconded,

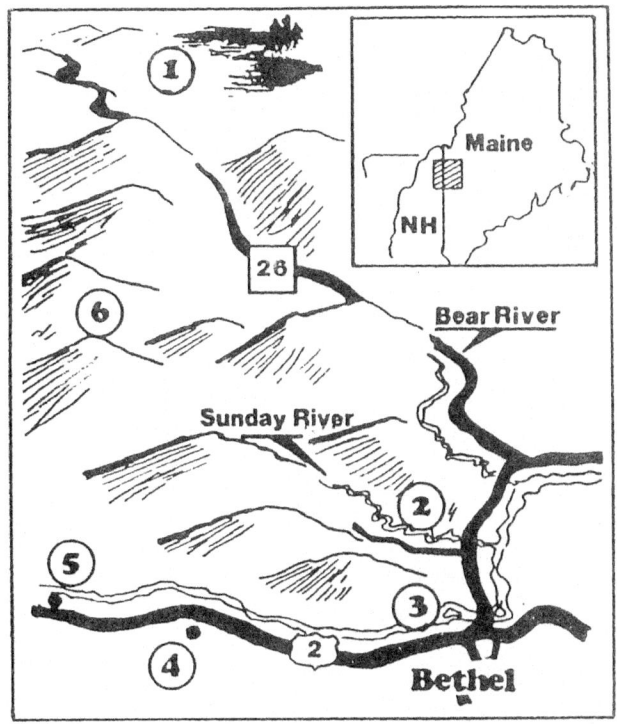

Map of Sudbury Canada Raid

LEGEND
1. Raiding party beaches canoes at Lake Umbagog.
2. First attack at Barker homestead on Sunday River.
3. Captives taken at Clark house in Bethel.
4. Gilead settler killed and scalped.
5. Shelburne, N.H. settler killed and a black man captured.
6. Raiders with captives flee over Mahoosuc Mountains to Canada.

and had so effectually secreted himself in the woods among the logs, that they could not find him; and night coming on, he remained here during the night. In the morning, he returned home in safety to his family, and rejoiced with them for his deliverance from the power of the savages of the wilderness. Mrs. Clark had secreted herself within a few rods of the Captain, where she lay all night, wholly unknown to each other, until the morning, when both returned home.

When the Indians had taken what they pleased, they packed up their plunder, and told Mrs. Clark to tarry in the house, and she would not be hurt, but if she went abroad, she would be killed, for there were hundreds of Indians in the woods.

When their matters were adjusted, the Indians loaded the prisoners and themselves with heavy packs, filled with plunder, and, our hands being bound, we were ordered to march. With heavy hearts, as well as packs, we obeyed their commands. It was now dark, so that we could not travel more than one or two miles before we were under the necessity of encamping for the night; and a dismal night it was to us. I had often heard of people being taken by the Indians, and I now found myself in this dreadful situation, not knowing what evils would befall us, and whether we should ever see our friends again, whom we were now leaving in anxiety, uncertainty and distress.

However, we traveled and found a deserted camp, or hut, where Mr. Peter Austin had lived, while he was felling trees, and making a farm; but happily for him, he was now gone. Here we tarried during this distressing night. The Indians entered the hut, and made search for plunder. They found some sugar, and two guns -- one they broke, and the other they took away with them. It was now so dark that we could go no farther. The Indians ordered the prisoners to lie down, and they laid down around them. Here we spent a gloomy night, which none can realize except those who have been in a like condition. After a sleepless, distressing night, not knowing what a day might bring forth, and being in the hands of cruel and barbarous savages, we arose early in the morning, even before it was light; and lest we should escape from them, or rise upon them, they tied the bridle with which I was bound very straight, as well as the others' bandages, so that our hands were much benumbed. We now needed all the fortitude of Philosophers, and resignation of Christians, to support us in our melancholy situation.

Before it was light, the Indians could not easily find the baggage. One of them missed his tomahawk, and accused me of having taken it, and would have given me a heavy -- perhaps a deadly -- blow, had not another Indian stepped between us and prevented it. When the light was more clear, he found it.

Early in the morning, we were ordered to travel up the river. We came to a place called Peabody's Patent, now Gilead. We went to a house owned by Mr. James Pettengill. He was at a little distance from his house, when we came to it. He was making towards the house; but seeing the Indians at the house, he stopped. The Indians discovered him, and called to him to come to them; and he did. They then searched the house, and they found some sugar, and in a tub some cream. They put the sugar into the tub of cream, and they fell to eating like hogs, but they gave us none to eat. Mrs. Pettengill and a number of children were in the house, but they received no abuse from them.

After a short stay here, the Indians told Mr. Pettengill that he must go with them to Canada. He told them he had no shoes. They searched the house, but they found none. They told him that he might tarry at home, but charged him not to leave the house.

We then went on, I should suppose, a mile or more, and were ordered to stop. Two of the Indians went back, and soon returned, and Mr. Pettengill with them; we traveled some distance together. On a sudden, Mr. Pettengill was missing. I thought they had sent him back; but they killed him about half a mile from his house. Some days after, his wife discovered his dead body in the bushes, where they had left it. Mr. Joseph Greely Swan, with several others from Bethel, went and buried him. His body was in a high state of putrefaction when buried.

After this melancholy event, though we did not know it at the time when it was done, we went on to a brook in Shelburn, N.H. Here we found a number of children at play. When they saw the Indians, they were much terrified. One of the Indians asked them, if there were men at the next house; they said there were ten. They asked them, if they had guns. They said they had. There were not ten men in the place; but the children, being so much terrified at the sight of the Indians, did not know what they said to them.

The Indians were so much terrified at the answers, which the children had given them, two of them threw off their packs in great haste, and put them on us, one on me and the other on Mr. Benjamin Clark. We were now loaded with two packs apiece for us to carry on our journey, with our arms tied fast.

In this situation, the Indians ordered us into the Androscoggin river, and to march through it, and to get over as well as we could, with four of us. We obeyed their orders, and with great exertions, we arrived through the goodness of God safe to the other shore; but I know not how, for people tell me, "that it was never forded before or since that time, at that place." As the prisoners could not swim, and the water being deep, it is the more difficult for me to account how we did so safely cross this river. Those two Indians, who loaded us with their packs after we were over, crossed the river themselves in great haste, and came to us. Then we all travelled on, till we came to a small house, owned by Mr. Hope Austin. His wife and children were in the house, but Mr. Austin was not at home at this time. The Indians searched the house for plunder. They found a little money and some other things in the house, which they took. They told Mrs. Austin to tarry in the house, and promised that she should not be hurt.

After this, we were ordered to resume our march. We travelled some miles, and were ordered to stop in some woods. Tomhegan took his gun and went from us. We soon heard the report of a gun. Tomhegan soon came back to us with a colored man with him, named Plato. He began to inquire of Plato, how many men there were in a house near by; he said there were two, besides the one whom Tomhegan had shot. Little did I think, when I heard the report of the gun, that a man was killed. It was Mr. Peter Poor who was killed. Mr. Poor and Plato were going out to work after dinner. Tomhegan had secreted himself among fell trees, where they were passing to their work. As soon as they came near him, he raised himself, and called them to him. "Poor," as Plato said, "turned to run, and Tomhegan instantly shot him, and he died immediately." The Indians told me, now they had Plato, they would let one of the prisoners go back; accordingly, one of the Indians said to Lieut. Clark, "you may go back, provided you will keep the road." With a joyful heart he embraced the opportunity to gain his desired liberty, and to return into the bosom of his family and friends. But he did not keep the road as he was ordered, but crossed the river, and turned into the woods and went through them to his family, and thus undoubtedly saved his life. For an Indian or two, who were left behind to bring up the rear, would have killed him on his retreat home, as a deserter.

After this, we went with the Indians to the house where Capt. Rindge, the owner of the house, with his wife and children were. Capt. Ridge was amazingly alarmed at the approach of the Indians. He told the Indians that he was "on the king's side." Notwithstanding, they plundered his house, and got a great deal of value. He was so terrified, that he brought many things to them, which belonged to his wife. We all fared well there, and had victuals enough. The Indians went out and scalped Mr. Poor. Hope Austin was there; he had deserted the house, and fled into the woods before the Indians entered the house, and so escaped any personal injury from them. The Indians told Cap't. Rindge, that he might tarry at home. They made a prisoner of Elijah Ingalls. He was a boy; but Capt. Rindge so far prevailed with the Indians, in his behalf, that they dismissed him.

The Indians were now preparing to proceed on their journey for Canada. We all set out, as we were ordered, though with aching hearts and trembling limbs, and with heavy packs on our shoulders, leaving our friends behind us, fearing we should never see their faces again on this side of a boundless eternity, not knowing what would befall us on the way, as we were liable to perish by hunger, or by savage cruelty. But God has seen fit to order it otherwise for us.

Under the most gloomy apprehensions, we entered the wild, howling wilderness, with cruel and blood thirsty savages, for Canada. When we had travelled some miles in the wilderness, we came to a large mountain. Here we tarried for the night. The next morning, as soon as it was light, we set out again; and by great exertions, we ascended the mountain to its summit, where we had a fine prospect around us, of this wilderness, and mountainous country. But making no tarry here, we were hurried on till we came to the height of land between Androscoggin river and the Umbagog lake, from whose source this famous river takes its rise. Here we had a short respite, being allowed to rest and refresh ourselves.

Here an Indian pulled off some spruce bark, untied my hands, and told me to write, that if ever we were overtaken by Americans, they, the Indians, would kill the prisoners. This bark he stuck on a tree, and then bound my hands again.

After we had travelled on several miles in the wilderness towards Umbagog Lake, the Indians ordered the prisoners to sit down. Upon this, they took three scalps from their packs; but we did not know whose they were, nor where they had obtained them. We knew that Mr. Poor's was one, but whose the others were, we could not conjecture at this time; we feared that they were obtained from our friends, whom we had left behind. However, the Indians informed us, that they overtook a man in the woods, when they were on the way to Bethel. They supposed him to be a deserter from Canada, and had killed and scalped him; and afterwards we were informed that they had scalped Mr. Pettengill, which make the three scalps.

A bounty had been promised the Indians by the British officers, of eight dollars for a scalp, or for a prisoner. This is the most savage and abominable act, even for a savage, but much more so for a civilized people, as the savages would be as likely to scalp on one side as the other, whether friend or foe and, therefore, must be the most savage act ever practised by man.

The Indians gave me a journal, which they said they had taken from the man whom they overtook in the woods; but I could not read it. I believe it was written in the French or Dutch language.

At St. Francois, I was asked where the Indians had obtained so much money, as they had. I told them I did not know of more than twenty dollars, which they had plundered while we were with them. I was told the Indians had a large sum in gold. I believe they got it of the man whom they overtook and killed in the woods.

During our tarry at this place, we were permitted to sit down and rest ourselves, but they would not permit us to sit together. This was a very rocky place. Here they took the hair of their scalps in their teeth, and began to shake their heads, to cohoop, to jump from rock to rock, and conducted and acted in such a hideous and awful manner, as almost to make our hair stand upright upon our heads, and to fill us with fear and trembling. I had heard of an Indian powow; but what tongue can tell, or imagination can describe the looks and actions of these savages on such occasions? Such scenes are beyond description. Their actions are inconceivable. *It would seem that bedlam had broken loose, and that hell was in an uproar.*

After the horrors of this scene were over, we were ordered to pursue our journey. We travelled on till we arrived at Umbagog lake, which lies partly in New Hampshire, and partly in Maine. We arrived here the fifth day after we were taken prisoners. The Indians here had three canoes, which were made of spruce bark. They made them, as they said, when they came to make prisoners of us. In these canoes we all passed safely over the lake. They now considered themselves safe. They had a little flour, and some moose scraps, with half the hair on; this they gave us to eat. We could eat but little, as hungry as we were. It was not fit for the dogs to eat. This was the last food we had to eat for several days, excepting some sugar, which the Indians had taken by plundering the inhabitants. Here they divided their plunder among themselves, and they had a very merry time of it indeed. Here, likewise, they took off their lousy shirts, and employed themselves in killing their lice with their teeth, as dogs kill their fleas.

After we had rested here some hours, we set out on our journey for Canada in their canoes. They having got rid of their fears, unbound us by day and bound us by night, till we had got to our journey's end.

They conveyed us from Umbagog lake in a small river, which, I believe to be the Magalloway. They went some way on this river. Here they shot a moose; and boiled and roasted some of the meat, and fell to eating like dogs; but we poor prisoners could eat but little, having neither bread nor salt; yet we were hungry. We tarried here some time. They cut some meat from the body of the moose, and partly dried it in the smoke, and put it into our packs. Our packs being heavy already, and we much worn down with hunger and fatigue, could not carry much of the moose meat with us. The Indians expected to kill more on the way, but they did not. Three of the Indians made themselves moccasins of the hide of the moose.

We set out on our journey for Canada, by land. We had high and rough mountains to travel over, and dismal swamps to pass through, day after day. We were weary and faint. The Indians could get nothing for themselves, or for us to eat. We had now very serious thoughts, lest we should perish in the wilderness. Our strength and spirits failing and sinking so fast in our deplorable situation, that we feared the Indians would kill us, if we gave out; but we mustered all the courage and strength possible, lest we should be destroyed by them.

One night, where we stopped, the Indians took their moccasins, which they made of the hide of the moose, which they had killed before, from their feet. They were much worn at the bottom and tainted, by reason of the hot weather. They threw them away, and we prisoners picked them up, roasted and ate them. This poor repast strengthened us a little. The Indians had a calf moose skin with them. They burnt off the hair from it, they boiled it, and gave us a part thereof to eat. Through the goodness and mercy of God, we had strength to go on our journey, in hopes we should soon get to the end of it.

We, after some time, struck upon the waters of the river St. Francois. It was at first but a small brook. On the second day, we found it grew much larger. This night we came to the main branch of this river, and encamped for the night. The next morning an Indian told me, that, after travelling a little way, we should come to three canoes, which they took up the river in the spring, when the water was high; and that they had some corn, and spears to catch fish. We were very glad to hear this welcome news. We took courage and travelled on till night. When we came to the canoes, we were weary and tired, and almost worn out with hunger and toil. They boiled the corn, and gave us some of it to eat. We were now somewhat refreshed and encouraged, hoping we should soon get through the wilderness, and our toils and anxiety would come to an end; besides, we had water and canoes to help us along our tedious journey.

In the morning, we set out with our canoes down the St. Francois river. The Indians went on shore and pealed some birch bark from the trees to make torches to catch fish with in the night. They caught a large fish, called Sturgeon, with their spears. This rejoiced us very much. They cooked it, and gave us some to eat. Then we pursued our course down the river. We had many carrying places, over which we carried our canoes. At length, we arrived at a man's house. He had a number of cows. The Indians milked them, and *we had good bread and milk to eat,* which was a very luscious dish and highly pleasing to us; and we eat as much as we wanted. This house was a mile and-a-half from the village.

After stopping an hour or two at this place, the Indians ordered us on board our canoes, and we sailed down the river, with all possible speed, in hopes that our fears, danger and toil would soon come to an end, though not our captivity. As we approached the village, the Indians cohooped six times, three times for the three prisoners they had taken, and three times for the three scalps which they had obtained in the excursions which they had made. They were soon answered from the village. They cohooped very often, during this mile and-a-half.

We soon came to the village. It was dark, but the Indians made it as light as day with their torches. There were seventy Indian warriors at this place. When we came near the shore, an Indian clinched me by the arm, and violently pulled me to him, swaggering over me, as though he would have killed me. I was surrounded by the Indians on every side, with terrible countenances, and of a strange language, which I did not understand. At this time there were great rejoicings among them over the prisoners, scalps and plunder which they had taken in this nefarious enterprise. I was afraid they would abuse the prisoners. But while serious thoughts filled my mind, and awful apprehensions troubled me respecting my situation, a man crowded in among the Indians, took me by the arm, and bid me go with him. When we had gotten from them, he told me the Indians did not abuse the prisoners, provided they were taken from them as soon as they brought them in.

This man took me to the guardhouse, and delivered me to the guard. He inquired of me, how many prisoners there were of us. I told him there were three, viz: a white and a colored man, besides myself. He then went in search of the other two. He found Plato surrounded by the Indians, who were throwing firebrands at him. Plato was crying like a child through fear. He was taken from the Indians and conveyed to the guardhouse, where I was. Then they went in search of Mr. Benjamin Clark. They found him safe among the Indians. He was taken from them, and was brought to us in the guard house. The guard seemed really to pity us.

The next morning ten or twelve Indians came to the guard-house, and requested Mr. Clark; the guard told him he might go with them. The Indians took Mr. Clark, cut off his hair, painted him, and dressed him in an Indian dress, like an Indian chief. It seems they intended to make him a chief among them. He was now at liberty among them.

It was fourteen days after we were taken prisoners before we arrived in Canada. And we then felt and said within ourselves: these have been very gloomy and dangerous days to us, and still remain so; for we know not how soon our captivity will come to an end, nor what troubles and dangers still await us, during our confinement from our friends and among our enemies. But we must patiently wait till our deliverance comes, trusting in the mercy of that God, who has hitherto preserved and carried us through so many dangers and hardships as we have experienced already in our afflictions, and prepare us for deliverance from savage cruelty, and the hands of our enemies, and restore us in his good time, in safety, into the bosom of our friends, to rejoice in his mercy.

We were here under guard two days. After this, we were given up by the British guard to the Indians, with an interpreter, to carry us in their canoes to Montreal. About ten Indians took the charge of us. On account of contrary head winds, we were many days in going up the river St. Lawrence. The prisoners were sometimes ordered to march by land, with a number of Indians to guard them. When we were in the canoes, we were not permitted to wear our shoes. The canoes, as soon as we were on the land, left the shore, even before I could pick up my shoes. When the Indians came up again, I immediately went for my shoes, but I could not find them. I asked for them, but an Indian told me, they had sold them for pipes. I found some fault with them for their conduct; but they told me, the King would find me shoes. These were the last things they could take from me. They had ordered me to give them my shirt before, and they gave me an old frock for it, without giving me any boot. I could not help myself, for I was a prisoner and in their power.

We at length arrived at Montreal, and were conducted to the commander. There were three of us. They examined us and asked us many questions; where we were taken prisoners; how long we had been in the American service, and many other like questions.

The Indians requested the commander, that they might keep Mr. Clark, but he would not grant their request. The Indians then took off all the ornaments from him, and every rag of clothes, except a very short shirt. They now received their bounty money for the prisoners and scalps. They took Plato away with them, and sold him to a Frenchman in Canada. Afterwards he was sent back to his old master, Capt. Rindge. The rest of us were given up to the British. We were ordered to go with a man who conducted us to the jail and delivered us to the guard, where were ten prisoners; and some of them confined in irons. Our situation was now truly distressing. We had been so worn down with hunger and a fatiguing journey through the wilderness, and distressing fears in our minds, that we were almost ready to despond. Our allowance was not half sufficient for us. In this place were multitudes of rats, which would devour the whole allowance that was granted us, and was of itself too small for us; but we took every measure to secure it from the rats. The lice, which we caught of the Indians, were a great annoyance to our bodies. We were, therefore, afflicted on every side.

We were kept in this miserable situation forty days. After this, we were taken away and sent up the river St. Lawrence, with forty or fifty other prisoners, collected from various other places, forty-five miles, to an island, where were a guard-house, a block-house and barracks, and also a guard of thirty men. In this tour, we were escorted by guards, till we arrived at the Island. This movement was made in October, the same year we were taken.

There were other prisoners brought here, to the amount of one hundred and eighty. We were guarded by men who deserted from the States. They were cruel, and abused many of the prisoners, and cheated them of part of their allowance. We continued here till the next spring, 1782.

During the time of our imprisonment here, our sufferings were great and very distressing. We had to endure a hard winter, which was tedious to us under our other sufferings. We were cooped up in a dismal place. However, we made the best of our circumstances that we were able as bad as they were, and under tyrannical oppressors; we were breathing for our deliverance, and longing to return home to our beloved country and friends, and to our wonted occupations again. None can know our distresses but those who have felt the same. Hunger, fatigue, confinement, and anxiety, we experienced during our captivity, together with cruel savages, and unfeeling soldiers to guard us. Those who have experienced the same, know how to pity and can sympathize with us, and we with them.

However, in the summer of the year 1782, we heard that Lord Cornwallis and the whole army were taken by Gen. Washington, and there would be a general exchange of prisoners; which information greatly rejoiced our hearts, and gave us a lively hope that our deliverance from bondage would speedily come, which we had so ardently longed for.

Not long after these glorious tidings were announced, and proper arrangements were made, we were taken from this Island, and were conveyed down the river St. Lawrence to Quebec, and ordered on board a ship; but we were detained here twenty days in anxious suspense. Here was another ship provided to take in other prisoners. The vessel we were put on board of was to sail for Boston, and the other was to sail for Philadelphia. We sailed about the tenth of November, 1782. We were in high spirits, and had a pleasant passage, and landed at Castle William, three miles below Boston. The same night we landed at Dorchester point. Mr. Benjamin Clark, my fellow prisoner and sufferer, and myself, set out immediately for Newton, and arrived before we slept, to the great astonishment and satisfaction of our friends.

Our friends had not heard from us after we were taken, till the night we returned home. They could hardly believe their eyes, when they saw us. We approached to them, as though we had risen from the dead. Surely this was a joyful season to us and them. We all now rejoiced in the gladness of our heart, for God's wonderful kindness towards us in our long and distressing captivity, and in delivering us therefrom under circumstances of comfort, and in safety.

And what still added to our joy, we soon heard that preliminaries of peace had been signed at Paris by plenipotentiaries for the purpose. Soon after, this treaty was ratified by the belligerent powers, in which they acknowledged the United States free and independent.

I tarried at Newton some time, to refresh myself, after I returned from captivity; and soon after the peace, I returned to Bethel, and have made me a small farm where I have resided ever since, and have reared up a large family. I have undergone all the hardships, and self denials, which are incident to those who are engaged in settling new countries; but have lived to see the town rise from a howling wilderness into fruitful fields, and in flourishing circumstances, and peace and order promoted therin, and blessings laid up therin, for the rising generation yet unborn.

But age, and the infirmities thereof, are crawling upon me, and my labor is almost finished, and I soon must go whence I shall not return, which is only the common lot of all mankind. I hope, when I am called for, to go where sorrow is unknown, and where all tears shall be wiped away from mine eyes, where the wicked shall cease from troubling, and where all the weary are at rest.

I spent two years and nine months in the public service of my country, and about sixteen months in a most disagreeable captivity by the Indians. This was done in the prime of life, when it was my duty, as well as all young men, to make provisions for future life, and for a family, should they live to enjoy them. My aim was, when I first went to Bethel, in 1774, to make me a farm there; but my attention was arrested by the revolutionary war, and my long captivity in Canada. I was thus defeated for several years in my designs of making provision for future life; and lost the prime of my youthful strength and activity. The hardships I underwent while young greatly debilitated my constitution, and I have been obliged to labor under these disadvantages, which have, in a great measure, brought on premature old age, and the infirmities thereof. However, I have this consolation, that I labored for the benefit of my beloved country and posterity. I hope the results of my toils and sufferings will be acknowledged by my country, and prove a lasting blessing to it, and be handed down unsullied to the latest posterity.

I have yet to labor hard to support myself and family, under the infirmities of age and a debilitated constitution; had it not been that I was interrupted in my designs in the early part of my life, by the cause of my country and the hardships I underwent at that period, I might have been exonerated, at this period of my life, from being necessitated to labor in making provision for myself and family; and the evening of my life might have been spent with much more ease and happiness than it is possible for it now to be. The comforts of the world and religion are as much as I may expect in this life, and all I ask for, and are what I earnestly desire, and hope to obtain; and then I shall be satisfied.

It may not be amiss to mention here that when the Indians were on their way from Canada to Bethel, in their nefarious design upon the inhabitants, and when I and Mr. Benjamin Clark were made prisoners, they passed through Newry, and entered the house of Capt. Benjamin Barker. Miss Mary Russell and Miss Betsey Mason were at Capt. Barker's on a visit. The Indians entered the house and plundering the house, they must also plunder these young ladies, and took several articles from them, which they carried away with them. This was a most cruel and barbarous act in them; but the tender mercies of the wicked are cruelty!

After Mr. Clark and I were released from our captivity, we both returned to Bethel. We found the young ladies here, and we married them. I married Miss Mary Russell, and Mr. Clark married Miss Betsey Mason. Both of us have had, and reared up, large families by them. Mr. Clark died several years ago. The rest of us are yet living, and through the mercy of God, are in comfortable health; and for which we have abundant reason to rejoice in his mercy towards us.

I would further remark, that for the services which I performed in the revolutionary war, I received the then currency, which afforded but little compensation for these toils in the defence of my country, owing to the rapid depreciation of the money in which I was paid; that my time was almost lost to myself. Indeed, the country was not able at that time to properly satisfy the soldiers for their labors in that service. And furthermore, I have had no compensation for the time I was in captivity. The loss of time, and the hardships I then underwent, were felt as in the service of my country; and were so considered, as I was *exchanged* as a soldier, taken in actual service, or in time of battle; and therefore, I always thought, and still think, that I, in *justice*, ought to have received some compensation from my country; but as I have received nothing, it still adds to my calamity, and which has been sensibly felt through life."

Thus ends the last of those thrilling adventures which occupy so conspicuous a position in New England Indian history. Lieut. Segar lived to see his country grateful for services rendered in her defense. He died Sept. 1847, at the advanced age of ninety-two years and eight months.

After the Indians had left with their captives, there was the greatest consternation among the inhabitants. Among those was a family by the name of Marshall who had settled on the farm now occupied by David Sanborn, near the Town House. I shall therefore give a sketch of him as published by me several years since in connection with his flight from the town.

Mr. David Marshall and wife moved to Bethel in March 1781. He was born in 1751, and was married in 1776 to Miss Lucy Mason, who was born in Newton, Mass., in 1753. They had eleven children. He was in the battle of Bunker Hill. "I saw (he would say with tears in his eyes) during the heat of the engagement my fellow soldier fall prostrate by my side. Full well I knew from whence came the deadly shot, for I saw the enemy when he stepped out from behind a tree which stood a little way from the main body of the haughty veterans of the British monarch, and observed his well directed fire. This was a striking crisis with me, for I might well expect to be the next mark for the Briton, as I stood next in place. But the same hand of Providence that prospered us in our cause protected me then, and enabled me to reload and be in readiness for my enemy, when he might step out again in order to shoot me. The steady level and waiting aim of my gun came in direct sight of his own. I fired, and saw my poor victim fall. I felt victorious and justified, as he had made aim at me, and an unerring aim at him who lay weltering in his gore by my side."

Mr. Marshall and wife lived in Bethel till August 5th 1781, when they were informed by a Mr. Russell that a party of seven Indians were on the opposite side of the river, and had taken three women prisoners, but who told them that if they would remain where they were, they would not be killed, but if they should attempt to escape, they would most certainly be put to death; for there were four or five hundred Indians in the vicinity killing the inhabitants at their pleasure. "At this moment," said Mrs. Marshall, "what shall I do, as my husband is gone from home on an errand." "Hide in the woods," was the reply of my informer. "While I was hastening to the woods with my children, I saw my husband coming home. I beckoned to him to hasten, and on his coming up, I hastily related what I had heard. He ran to the house and took such provisions as he could readily seize, and throw into a sack, and then started with his little store and family into the woods. We traveled lightly, and looked cautiously around, expecting every moment to see the face of the red man, but after a few hours our fears considerably subsided, and we sat down to rest. On examining my condition, I found myself very much fatigued, and without my ordinary dress, for during the morning I had slipped off my shoes and dress, having nothing on except a thin skirt and a hankerchief over my shoulders. This caused my heart to ache, for we had resolved not to turn back, but to pursue our journey which lay through a waste, howling wilderness. After a short halt, we set out again, and traveled till dark. We did not dare to strike the least light to cheer us in the dark woods for fear of being discovered by the Indians. We sat down impatiently waiting the rising of the morning; the 6th, we renewed our journey, but with a much slower pace than on the day previous.

During the afternoon we were overtaken by a Mr. Dodge, who had set out from Bethel by request of some of the inhabitants to go to New Gloucester for help. I requested him to inform the first inhabitants that he met of my situation, and give them the course as near as he could, and ask them to come to meet us. Mr. Dodge missed his course to Jackson's Camp in No. 4, now Paris, which he expected first to reach, and came out at Lieut. Bearce's, in Hebron. He informed Bearce, who immediately set out for said camp, and on his arrival obtained two men who went with him as far as the river in the North of Paris, and there struck up a fire, and prepared some food, while Bearce went on in search of the family. He first found my son David, whom his father had carried a short distance ahead, and left on a log, telling him to be quiet, while he went back after me, for he was obliged to take this course, as I had become so weak that I could not travel without help. We arrived in a short time at the river, took some refreshment, and then proceeded to Jackson's Camp where we arrived on the 9th after having undergone more than we can possibly describe. We remained here three or four days. Consequently, I was the first white woman who took lodgings in what is now the town of Paris.

Mr. M. and family went from Paris to N. Gloucester, where they remained a few months, and then removed to Minot. From the latter place they removed to Hebron, where they lived many years and died.

David Marshall died Nov. 20th, 1828, aged 77. Lucy, his wife, died August 25th, 1824, aged 71.

For the foregoing sketch, I am indebted to Hon. Moses Mason, nephew of Mrs. Marshall, who obtained it from their son, Moses Marshall, of Hebron.

After the Indians had left with their captives, there was the greatest consternation among the inhabitants. Capt. Twitchell had escaped and hid beneath a log over which the Indians had passed in pursuit. Here he remained concealed all night. Lieut. Clark's wife fled to the woods and lay concealed not far from Capt. Twitchell, but unconscious of each other's proximity.

In the morning Capt. Twitchell cautiously crept out of his hiding place, which was not far from the railroad bridge over the Mill Brook, and passed through the woods within sight of his house by the grist mill. Not knowing what might have been the fate of his family, he stopped at a distance, when he was spied by one of the inmates who were watching for the Indians. His family consisting of his wife and children, and some young men, had passed the night in the greatest anxiety. Mrs. Rowe now living in Gilead was one of the children. They fancied that the Indians were concealed in the mill nearby ready to shoot them should they appear out of the house. But as soon as Capt. Twitchell gave them the true state of affairs, John Grover started off for Fryeburg on his own responsibility, while soon after, Capt. T. sent a messenger on horseback. But Grover arrived first on foot.

Nobly did the gallant little settlement respond to the call. The messenger arrived at Fryeburg a little past noon; immediately two men mounted their horses, and, proceeding up both banks of the Saco, summoned all the men, with their guns, to repair at once to the house of one Nathaniel Walker. Quickly they assembled, and learned from the messenger the terrible fate which seemed pending over their neighbors. When the call was made for volunteers to march at once to their assistance, thirty brave men stepped forward -- thirty brave men, but in no condition to undertake such an expedition. Many of them were barefooted, some bareheaded, and a few nearly as destitute of clothing as the foe they designed to encounter. Before nightfall, however, the thirty men were all armed and equipped, and comfortably prepared for the march. In long Indian file they marched, Sabatis, the guide, leading the way, followed by the commander, Stephen Farrington, on horseback. Nathaniel Walker, junior officer of the expedition, himself on horseback, brought up the rear of the long file. Just after dark they forded the Saco, some two miles above the village, and bidding adieu to their friends, struck out into the wilderness. As the sun rose over Bethel Hill the following morning, they reached the house of Capt. Twitchell. Sabatis had already discovered the Indian trail. Stopping but a few moments at Capt.

Twitchell's for food, they immediately commenced their pursuit of the savages.

The Indians had the start of them more than twelve hours; how they had employed these hours may be learned from Segar's Narrative.

By the aid of Sabatis, who could track them where the whites could see no traces whatever, the party followed the Indians, till coming to a rocky hill, even old Sabatis was at fault. "Me find um quick, " said the Indian, and struck round the hill. Here they met Clark, whom the Indians had permitted to return, on condition that he should stop any party of whites who might pursue them by representing the determination of the Indians to kill the prisoners as soon as they should find any party in pursuit.

But the men would not be persuaded; their blood was up, and, though Clark told them they could not reach the Indians till every prisoner was slain, they would not yield.

The party, old Sabatis having found the track, pushed on. They soon found the piece of *spruce bark* pegged to a hemlock tree, to which Segar has thus referred:

"Here an Indian pulled off some *spruce bark*, untied my hands, and told me to write that, if ever we were overtaken by Americans, they, the Indians, would kill the prisoners. This bark he stuck on a tree, and then bound my hands again."

Still, Captain Farrington was for passing on, but at length yielded to the unanimous voice of the men, who voted to return. "We came back," says one of the company, "buried poor Pettengill, staid over night at Bethel, and the next day returned to Fryeburg."

On the banks of the Androscoggin directly in front of the dwelling house of Timothy Chapman, Esq., and which was first settled by his father, Rev. Eliphaz Chapman, there is an elevation of intervale consisting of three or four acres. On this spot was an Indian village. How long it had been inhabited is of course not known. It is probable that they had not occupied the spot for fifty years prior to the settlement of the town in 1776. It appears that they had cleared about ten acres of the intervale for a cornfield. Pine trees measuring eighteen inches in diameter at the butt had grown up in some places; the rest was covered with bushes.

In all my researches thus far in regard to the Indian settlement in Bethel, I only find two allusions. The writer who describes Church's expedition remarks that the Indians had gone 40 or 50 miles up the river after corn, and this must have been at Bethel. Another was the remark of Mollocket to the early settlers that the Indians lived very happily at Bethel until they were driven away by the whites.

It is pretty evident that the Indians here belonged to the Anasagunticooks as they usually carried their dead to Canton Point for burial. It is said that they hauled one of their number on a handsled to Canada, for the purpose of burial, according to the rites of the Catholic church.

We can hardly believe that the first preaching and instruction of Christianity in this town was by the Roman Catholics. The French priests were assiduous in their efforts to convert them to their faith.

On clearing up the land, about twenty cellars were discovered which seem to have been excavated in a rude manner probably for depositing their corn, and other provisions.

It is pretty evident that the village was suddenly broken up, probably soon after the Lovewell fight in Fryeburg, as a dozen or more gun-barrels were found, besides brass kettles, axes, knives, glass bottles, arrows, and hoes, the latter of which were used by the settlers for several years afterwards. The gun-barrels found there were made up into fireshovel handles by the blacksmith, Fenno, for the use of the settlers. On one occasion he was heating a barrel in a forge when a charge of powder which had been there at least fifty years exploded and drove its contents through his work-bench on the other side of his shop. A single skeleton was discovered wrapped in white birch bark with a piece of ash bark under the head. The bones were those of a young person, who Mollocket said was a young woman that was accidently killed in a drunken frolic. While in the act of drinking from a vessel, she was struck a blow upon the stomach from the effects of which she died.

Mollocket was supposed to be eighty years old when the town was settled. She could remember the Lovewell Fight, and seems to have been acquainted with the Indians resident here. I regret not being able to find the Indian name of this settlement. Judging from the number of houses and the extent of land cultivated, there may have been from one to two hundred individuals. Two miles down the river near the *Narrows* where the river is but a few yards wide, they had a clearing of one or two acres on the east bank of the river known as Powow Point. Here they met in council, and it appears to have been a place of rendezvous for the warriors and hunters of the country around. It was a convenient stopping place for those who had been to the settlements. Tradition says that a camp of Indians was burnt there with its inmates and that their implements, as well as their bones, were afterwards found. It is now the pleasantest spot in town. On a point of land near Mill Brook, on the farm now occupied by A. L. Burbank, Esq., was evidently a burying ground as there was a clearing and a number of graves visible when it was first settled by Lieut. Clark. The Indians in their later visits to Bethel made this their camping ground.

The river is navigable for boats a distance of fifty miles, except in time of very low water, from Berlin to Rumford (Pennacook) Falls. Powow Point was a very convenient position for them, whether they wished to ascend Bear River to L. Umbagog, strike off from the river to the lower settlements, or go up or down the river in their boats. This region was also excellent hunting ground for the most valued furs.

The habits of the Indians in some particulars was worthy of notice even in their descent from Canada after the settlement of the country. They descended the river in their canoes and practised duck-shooting on the wing. When one fell into the water the hunter did not stop his boat to pick it up, but left it for the next boat that came along, when it was safely cared for. If at any time they found a muskrat's nest, they would go to the houses of the settlers, obtain whatever implements they could, without leave, dig out their holes, save the skins, eat the meat and return the utensils to the owner.

It was no uncommon sight for quite a fleet of boats to pass up and down the river in company.

Chapter 6
Molly Ockett

Molly Ockett. The name of this woman is well known to the older inhabitants of this vicinity. The Rokomeko Tribe at Canton Point in 1755 numbered several hundreds, but were visited about that time with the small pox, communicated to them by the French. It swept away nearly the whole tribe. It is probable that Molly Ockett with the few remaining Indians on the Androscoggin River, left for Canada soon after, as she seems to have been called a St. Francis Indian by the early settlers of Bethel. She came, according to Mr. Nathaniel Swan's account, in whose family she lived several years, from Canada to Fryeburg, where she became acquainted with Sabattis, whom we suppose to be the same that Col. Rogers brought from Canada to Fryeburg when a boy in 1759. He lived with her as his assumed, though not his lawful wife and had by her three children. She subsequently refused to live with him on account of his intemperate habits and quarrelsome disposition.

She came to Bethel soon after the settlement of the town, and claimed a right to the land as an original proprietor. The Indians probably never included the upper waters of the Androscoggin in any of their treaties.

She is described by Mrs. Martha Rowe of Gilead, now living, and who knew her well, as a pretty, genteel squaw. She had a daughter, Molly Susup, previous to her acquaintance with Sabattis. She lived with her mother at Bethel, attended school with the whites, and spoke the English language fluently. She possessed a vigorous frame, and engaged in sports with the boys for whom she was frequently more than a match. A circumstance is still remembered when she and her antagonist clenched, and in the contest both rolled down the bank of the river together. She had a child named Molly Peol, by Capt. Swarson, an old Indian, who was very anxious to marry her, but Molly Ockett was opposed to the match. She afterwards married a Penobscot Indian, who quarrelled with her, and left her. Molly Ockett was very much mortified at her daughter's conduct, and felt that her own character, as well as her daughter's, was destroyed.

Molly Ockett was a good huntress and would often go into the woods and over to the lakes, and shoot moose and bears, and return to the settlement for assistance to bring in the most valuable portions of the game. She collected duck feathers sufficient to make a bed, which she presented to Mrs. Swan.

Like most of the Indians, she was fond of rum. She would drink a pint of beer emptyings with the greatest relish. She was well skilled in roots and herbs, and spent the latter portion of her life in going from place to place, and giving advice and medicines to the sick.

She often boasted of her noble descent. Her father and grandfather were prominent chiefs in their tribe, and had passed through all the exciting scenes of warfare between the French and English during the last century.

When the Indians came from Canada and encamped in Bethel, she refused to associate with them. At one time she had a camp of her own on the north side of the river near Curatio Bartlett's, which she had well covered and lined with bark, and where she had her bed and slept, but took her meals in some white family.

She seemed to possess considerable ingenuity. A box made by her of birch bark more than seventy years ago is now in the possession of Mrs. John Kimball of this town.

Molly Ockett sympathized with the Methodists and professed to become a convert. She used to call them "drefful clever folks." She sometimes spoke in their meetings, but could not divest herself of the idea that she ought to make confession to the priest, and occasionally went to Canada for this purpose.

She was easily offended. She had been out one time, and gathered a pailful of blueberries which she carried to her friend, the wife of Rev. Eliphaz Chapman, on Monday morning. Mrs. C. on emptying the pail found them very fresh, and told her that she picked them on Sunday. "Certainly," said Molly. "But you did wrong," was her reproof. Molly took offense and left abruptly, and did not make her appearance for several weeks, when, one day, she came into the house at dinner time. Mrs. C. made arrangements for her at the table, but she refused to eat. "Choke me," said she; "I was right in picking the blueberries on Sunday, it was so pleasant, and I was so happy that the Great Spirit had provided them for me." At this answer Mrs. C. felt more than half condemned for her reproving her as she did. Who would harshly judge this child of nature by the same law that would condemn those more enlightened?

The following paragraph respecting her is from Willey's White Mountain sketches.

A Col. Clark, of Boston, had been in the habit of visiting annually the White Mountains, and trading for furs. He had thus become acquainted with all the settlers and many of the Indians. He was much esteemed for his honesty, and his visits were looked forward to with much interest. Tom Hegan had formed the design of killing him, and, contrary to his usual shrewdness, had disclosed his plans to some of his companions. One of them, in a drunken spree, told the secret to Molly Ockett, a squaw who had been converted to Christianity, and was much loved and respected by the whites. She determined to save Clark's life. To do it, she must traverse a wilderness of many miles to his camp. But nothing daunted the courageous and faithful woman. Setting out early in the evening of the intended massacre, she reached Clark's camp just in season for him to escape. Tom Hegan had already killed two of Clark's companions, encamped a mile or two from him. He made good his escape, with his noble preserver, to the settlements. Col. Clark's gratitude knew no bounds. In every way he sought to reward the kind squaw for the noble act she had performed. For a long time she resisted all his attempts to repay her, until at last, overcome by his earnest entreaties and the difficulty of sustaining herself in her old age, she became an inmate of his family, in Boston. For a year she bore, with a martyr's endurance, the restraints of civilized life; but at length she could do it no longer. She must die, she said, in the great forest, amid the trees, the companions of her youth. Devotedly pious, she sighed for the woods, where, under the clear blue sky, she might pray to God as she had when first converted. Clark saw her distress, and built her a wigwam on the Falls of the Pennacook, and there supported her the remainder of her days. Often did he visit her, bringing the necessary provision for her sustenance.

She afterwards lived in Andover, and was present at the birth of the first child in that town, she and the mother being the only females at that time residing there. She nursed the mother, and continued to reside in the town until her death at the advanced age of more than one hundred years. The Rev. Mr. Strickland, pastor of the church in Andover, conducted the religious services at her funeral, and she was buried in the cemetery of that town. I have not ascertained the date of her death. She could remember the events connected with the Lovewell Fight in Fryeburg, and spoke of the Indians who resided in Bethel as being happy till they were driven away by the whites. She was the last resident Indian in this vicinity.

A short distance south of the outlet of Umbagog Lake is a large smooth rock projecting into the water called Molly Ockett's Rock. Her name is also perpetuated by a mountain named after her in the eastern part of Oxford Co., where she had a camp. She seemed to be a person of more than ordinary ability, possessed a large frame and features, and walked very erect even in old age. She wore a pointed cap, but in other respects dressed in Indian style. She was very loquacious, and entertained the inhabitants with stories and aneodotes.

Her name was spelled and pronounced in several different ways: Mollockett, Molly Ockett, Mollyockett, Mollylockett, Mollyrockett, and

Mollynockett. These changes arose in consequence of the communtability of the liquids l, n and r.

Many apocryphal anecdotes relating to her have been given to the writer; but it is believed the foregoing sketch is the most complete that has ever been made respecting her, and embodies all the leading facts of her history that can now be obtained.

Chapter 7
Matalluck

Matalluck, Natalluc, Metolic. This was the last of the once powerful tribe of Anasagunticooks. It is a mournful termination of the history of a once powerful nation, to record the life of the last of their number who lingered about their old home. Of the early history of this Indian, I have no information, Lieut. Segar was wont to say that Matalluc was the Indian who shook him so violently when he arrived at the St. Francis tribe during his captivity.

The following letter is from Hon. John M. Wilson, who lived on the Magalloway for several years before Matalluc died. It will be read with interest by many.

Wilson's Mills, July 30th 1859.

Dear Sir: Yours inquiring concerning Matalluck, I have received. All that I know of him previous to 1832 I obtained from common reports in this region. It is said he belonged to the St. Francis tribe, from which he was banished for some misdemeanor, some say for abusing his first wife in a fit of jealousy.

He had three children, if no more, I suppose by his first wife, two sons, Parmagimmet and Wilumpi, and a daughter who married a man in Canada by the name of Moulton. He lived several years on the border of Richardson's Lake with his second wife who died there and was buried on a point of land which has since been cleared, and is a part of the lake farms.

He there built his wigwam and lived alone some years at the narrows of Umbagog Lake, on or near what is now the Stone farm. Leaving this, he next took up his residence in Township No. 5. R. 3., where I found him in 1832. Here he subsisted chiefly by hunting, and lived in a camp about 10 feet square made of spruce bark. He was here some ten or twelve years without making any clearing about his camp and would draw potatoes from the settlement in winter 12 miles on a hand sled rather than raise them. At this camp he was several times visited by Gov. Lincoln, who would stay several days at a time. He was very civil and hospitable to strangers, but not very communicative, and the only bad habit he had, probably, was that of taking too much "occoby" when he could get it.

In the winter of 1836 in getting wood at considerable distance from his camp he thrust a splinter into his eye, and was found in that condition by two men who happened that way, in a very cold day, perfectly blind, having lost one eye several years before. He was unable to reach his camp, and would soon have perished without assistance. Without being aware of his condition, his daughter and her son arrived here for the purpose of looking after him about the time he was brought from his camp, and took him with them to Canada.

He was entirely blind and helpless the remainder of his days, and died some six or seven years after he left this place, in Stewartstown, N. H., having been supported for considerable time at the County charge.

It is supposed that Matalluck was at the time of death more than one hundred years old. He was a close built man, of about middling stature, very athletic, and possessed of great powers of endurance.

He came to my house one morning in the winter of 1835-6 about sunrise having laid out about two miles in the woods the night before without fire. A damp snow had fallen the day before, and the weather had become very cold during the night. He had been on the track of a moose all day until dark, "almost see um" he said, and when darkness obliged him to give up the chase, "all wet, no strike um."

Lewis Annance, a St. Francis Indian who was educated at Dartmouth College, could give you more valuable information in regard to Indian history than any other person. He has a family, and when I last heard of him he resided in Lancaster, N. H.

Very respectfully
Your Ob't Serv't
John M. Wilson.

Gov. Lincoln was in the habit of visiting Mataluck and camping with him. Gov. L. left some account of him in his writings, but I do not now have them at command.

One anecdote I believe Lincoln never published. He carried with him on his visit to Nataluc a large penknife fitted up with different blades, awls, saw and the like. Nataluc had his eye on the knife and wished to buy it. Gov. L. told him he could not sell it to him. Nataluc's covetousness was only the more strongly excited, and he at last contrived a plan to secure the penknife. He had a little island in the lake consisting of about an acre on which is a sort of cave in which he kept his furs where they would not be plundered. He invited the Governor to go and see his furs. He took his canoe and landed the governor, showed him his furs, and made him a most liberal offer of them for the knife. The governor told him he could not sell the knife. "Well," said Nataluck, "me no carry you off the island if you no sell me that knife." "But," said the governor, "I told you I would not sell it to you, and I shall keep my word, but I will give it to you as a present." Nataluc was overjoyed in the possession of his knife, and of course reckoned Gov. L. as one of his real friends.

He was visited by Hon. Moses Mason several times while he lived on the Magalloway River. He made a map of that river on birch bark which appears to have been executed with fidelity. He had on one occasion shot an immense moose as he was in the water and dragged him to the shore, and cut off the best parts of meat and dried them. The Doctor bought the horns which now adorn his hall as a hat rack.

We insert the following characteristic letter from that hunter and trapper, J. G. Rich, Esq., which will be read with interest.

Mr. Editor: -- While on a hunting expedition lately, through the forests of Townships Letter C, No. 5, R. 1, No. 5, R. 2, and No. 4, R. 1 and 2 -- about the chain of Lakes known as Umbagog -- one evening after having dug away the snow with one end of my snow shoe, and stuck up a few young firs to keep off the wind and a few pieces of birch bark to keep off the rain overhead, laid a few of the fine boughs of the same for a bed on the ground and cut my night wood and piled it near the camp, I lighted a fire, cooked my cup of Oolong, by boiling in a birch-bark bucket, roasted my partridge by broiling with a few pieces of pork stuck into him, and eat my supper, Robinson Crusoe like, I lit my pipe and set down to look over the *Courier* a few moments in peace. The night was extremely dark, and the rain poured down in torrents -- the wind blew, and a more dismal night we soldom see. My eye ran over the history of Bethel, by Dr. True, and found, by perusal, many Aboriginal names; in fact the chapter I was reading was well lined with them, and my mind after laying down the paper, roamed away to times long ago of similar camp-fires by the red men, and in this vicinity -- many were the joyous nights spent in these wilds by the red hunter, when game was plenty, and it may be tamer than now, and it may even be of kinds now extinct, at least in these parts. Perhaps the American Panther would then be roaming near their camp-fires on such a night as this. Then I thought of old Matalluck in later years, who occupied about the same ground as myself. Camping on Matalluck Point, on the Molechunkemunk, where is now left the remaining rot of the logs of his home camp, and near which is the grave of his lonely squaw, by the side of which the writer buried a lost child some years since, and around which is seen the green grove of pines, and level grounds where the St. Francis tribe used to hold their councils in time of the French & Indian war. Opposite the point of land here alluded to, in the narrow part of the Lake, there used to stand a large pine tree, on which was carved the form of a white man and which was filled with bullets, the effect of the practice of the Indians firing across this narrow pass in the Lake to accustom themselves in target shooting. Matalluck was an Indian warrior and a chief in the tribe spoken of above, and was banished to these Lakes for his love of the white man. Here, on this point, he made his home -- here lived with him his wife Rosalluc many years, until finally she passed away, and then mark the Indians attachment. This old chief took the body of his wife and wound it close in birch bark, and withed it to two limbs of trees, which reached over the smoke hole of his camp, and for three weeks went on the process of preservation. The body was then buried near by and two common rough stones still remain to mark the spot. He then removed to the Magalloway River where he followed his lonely hunting occupation for several years, until finally he became blind and would have starved, having strayed from his camp, had not some men found him feeling around in search of his camp. He was taken to Stewartstown, N. H., where he lived many years in the poor-house, and finally died, ten years ago, at a great age.

Those hard names of the Doctor's still remind me of some others, such as the Indian names of this chain of Lakes, on which the writer has hunted for the last thirteen years. The first Lake commences near Dead and Sandy River waters, which help swell the Kennebec, not many miles away, and is called in Indian "Sawalket." Then comes Kennebago Lake, from which runs the Kennebago River into Cupsuptuc Lake, then Mooselamaguntic, Opquesic, Mollychunkemunk, Weelockennebacook, Allemuntebago, and Umbagog -- also, at the head of the Magalloway River is Parmachenee Lake, and on that river is Azicohos Falls and Mountain. Some of these names are very poetical, and some are hard to pronounce -- like the life of the Indian, many of their acts were very generous, and many very barbarous.

Rough sons of the forest, you have passed away! A few hieroglyphics on the old pine trees, a few mounds and hollows in some secluded part of the woods tell but too truly where thou art; and in a few more moons the white hunter which takes your grounds to follow up your ancient occupation, will follow you, never more to return to these pleasant Scenes -- and Sacred spots and associations, -- peace to their ashes.

HUNTER

Letter B. April 1st 1859.

Chapter 8
Other Indians of Note

Among those who visited Bethel after its settlement was a St. Francis Indian named Lewey. He styled himself a sergeant. On one occasion he came to Capt. Eleazer Twitchell's with a company of his tribe when he was absent. The Indians were very clamorous for some rum. Mrs. Twitchell furnished it, but on the condition that Lewey should see that they did no injury. This he promised, but after they had drunk their first supply, they became clamorous for more and threatened to break down the door. Lewey, who was a stout Indian, stepped into the room among them and threw one on one side and another to the opposite side of the room until he had quelled them. He then told Mrs. Twitchell that he wanted the Captain's drum which the Indians had had before. Lewey took it and commenced drumming; then the Indians staggered out after him in single file, and he marched them round in a circle until they all soon fell to the ground where they lay till they were sufficiently sober, when he roused them up and marched them to their camps down on the Mill brook near where it empties into the Androscoggin.

Another Indian was Capt. Phillip, who occasionaly came to Bethel. He was a Pequaket and lived in Fryeburg. He was in the Revolutionary War, and was quite an old man when the town was first settled.

Another Pequaket Indian who was well known to the settlers was Capt. Swarson. He also fought with the Americans in the Revolutionary War, and was presented with a sword. Capt. Simeon Twitchell went hunting with him to the lakes. He was gone two months, but some other Indians came there and stole provisions which made Swarson cross and Capt. Twitchell returned.

Another was Peol, a corruption I suppose of Pierre, or Peter, Black Susup, Mohawk Susup who came here from the Mohawk tribe, Sawloo, Assabeel, Quallimosit, names whose orthography is doubtful. Mollysusup defined the latter name to signify TO ROLL UP CLOTH. Paseel was the oldest son of Sabattis by his first wife.

Tomhegan, properly Tumtumhegan was the one who led the band that carried Segar and others into Canada in 1781. He was a surly, ugly fellow and among the foremost in instigating the Indians against the whites. He never visited Bethel after this incursion. These Indians were well versed in savage warfare. The French and Indian War was the school of their youth and the Revolutionary War of their riper years.

The Indians found this region one of their best hunting grounds. Moose, deer, bears, beaver, sable, muskrats, and other animals were abundant. The Androscoggin was navigable for their canoes for many miles, while within a short distance a half dozen small streams have their outlet, which abounded in trout as well as game.

Indians of the St. Francis tribe frequently visited Bethel for the purpose of having their guns and jewelry repaired. Simeon Twitchell, Esq., acted as gun smith and jeweller. On one occasion an Indian brought a box of jewelry, probably belonging to different members of the tribe, to Squire T. to be repaired. It was never called for and remained in possession of the family for many years.

This chapter closes our history of the Indians in this vicinity. We have collected all the facts respecting them within our reach. Their history must be necessarily obscure and fragmentary, but we have endeavored to sift out the truth as far as possible. Their memory is fast fading from our oldest citizens, but they will yet form the theme of the poet, the novelist and the historian.

Chapter 9
Block Houses

After all hopes had been given up of rescuing Clark and Segar from the Indians, the inhabitants immediately took measures for their protection. A request was immediately sent to Fryeburg for a company of soldiers to protect the town. Lieut. Jonathan Clark was chosen to meet a committee from Fryeburg and Bridgton, who assembled in the latter town and made choice of Stephen Farrington, of Fryeburg, as commander. He afterwards received his commission, with the rank of Lieutenant. He appears to have been a man well fitted for the situation.

The company came to Bethel and with the aid of the citizens built two Block Houses; the one on the little island near the gristmill, or as Mr. Joseph Twitchell, now living, thinks, it was built near the dwelling house of Mr. Robbins Brown. Mrs. Martha Rowe who was an inmate and is the only survivor of the garrison, describes it as follows:

"Capt. Twitchell's House was built on the island and consisted of two rooms. The garrison was built on the end of this. It was a breastwork made of hewn timbers with port holes, and of such height as to prevent a man from climbing over it. The soldiers had their cabins inside of this against the walls, while the officers occupied one room in Capt. Twitchell's house. Some of the cabins had the boards arranged outside for want of room. The parade ground of the company was on the plank bridge near Burnham's carriage shop, as there was no suitably cleared spot of land for that purpose."

Mrs. Rowe says that she distinctly remembers looking out of the upper window and seeing them on parade. The officers were Bradley, Hutchinson and Lieut. Farrington. These spent much of their time during their stay in relating stories of Indian warfare in which they were well skilled; many a thrilling story was told which would enrich our history could they be recalled. Mrs. Twitchell had places of concealment for her children in case of an alarm from the Indians. They consequently mentally suffered all the fears and trials incident to warfare.

The inhabitants came to the fort during the night, and during the day went out to their avocations. A single gun was the signal of alarm for all to return to the fort. Scouting parties were sent out to hunt for the Indians.

Among the soldiers were two brothers, James and Benjamin Russell, who were selected as a scouting party to watch the movements of the Indians in the vicinity, but they seemed to have but little fear of Indians before their eyes, and spent their time in hunting for beaver and sable. The commander hearing this threatened to bring them into the fort, but they compromised the matter by promising to share with them one third of all the game. My narrator added, that it was very doubtful whether the commander ever received his share, as he could remember going into a room which was literally lined with the most valuable furs stretched on hoops as the reward of the chase.

The soldiers remained about two months and returned home. Another block house was erected in the lower part of the town, on the farm of Mr. Amos Young. It was two stories high and was occupied by a portion of the company. The last survivor of this company was Levi Dresser, of Lovell, who lived to an advanced age and died within a few years. I regret that I have not the names of the whole company. Their names should be recorded.

The effect of this incursion of the Indians on the town was disastrous. The lands became much depressed in value, and settlers were prevented from coming into the town until after the joyful news of peace. It is said that one of the original proprietors sold to Daniel Barker, for a mug of flip, that part of the village on Main Street from Gilman Chapman's House to Davis' Store including a half lot.

Chapter 10

Plantation Record

The following is the only official plantation record that has come into our hands, and is probably the only one now in existence. We insert it *verbatim et literatim*. For this we are indebted to Jedediah Burbank, Esq.

"We the Subscribers being a Committy for Settleing Accompts Beag leaf to Report that we have Examed the Following accompts and fiend them to be Jest Viz: Mr. Benj. Rusel accompt for going to Boston with a Pertition For Souldiers for our Defence last april it being for Thirty-three Days at 61 pr Day £9-18-0.

Jonathan Bartlet account for atending at Court at Boston two Day at 61 pr Day and Cash Paid to Simon Fry Esq. for his attending Court three Day at 81 pr Day and four Day work Don on the Road at 6 pr Day 3-0-0.

Mr. Moses Bartlet Six Day on the Road 61 pr Day 1-16-0.

Mr. Thadeas Bartlet three Day on the Road 61 pr Day 0-18-0.

Mr. John Grover account for going to Fryburg on an Express 1-10-0.

Jonathan Clark account for going to Bridgton and Fryburg to meet the Comittys of Bridgton and Fryburg to Choose an officer to take the Command of the Souldiers and 1, 1-2 Day on the Rhods at 61 pr Day 1-19-0.

Mr. John York account be alowed Eighteen Pence pr Day more for what work he Did on the Rhod last year it Beeing twenty-three & half Days, and Twelve Day the Present year on the Rod at 61 pr Day and 14 Days on the foort 61 pr Day 9-11-O.

Mr. Jesse Dusten 4, 1-2 Day on the Rhods at 61 pr Day and on the foort 9, 1-2 Day at 61 pr Day 4-4-0.

Mr. Josiah Been 9 Day on the Rhod at 61 pr Day and on the foort 14 Day at 61 pr Day 6-18-0.

Mr. Jonathan Been 6 Day on the Rhods at 61 pr Day and on the fort 9 Days at 61 pr Day 4-10-0.

Mr. Amos Powers 4 Day on the Rhods at 61 pr Day 1-4-0.

Mr. Daniel Been 9 Day on the Rhods at 61 pr Day and on the foort 1O Day at 61 pr Day 5-14-0.

Mr. Samuel Engalls on the Rhods 7 Day at 61 pr Day and on the foort 5 Days at 61 pr Day 3-12-0.

Mr. Isaac York on the foort 5, 1/2 Days at 61 pr Day 1-13-0.

Mr. Gideon Powers on the Rhods 4 Days at 61 pr Day 1-4-0.

Mr. Jermiah Andras on the Rhod 2 Day at 61 pr Day 1-10.

Mr. A Braham Rusel on the Rhods 5 Day at 61 pr Day 1-10.

Capt Eleazer Twitchel on the Rhod 11, 1/2 Day at 61 pr Day and three Day Servaing at 91 pr Day and 12 Day on the foort at 61 pr Day and 2 Schoutting at 6 pr Day for going to fryburg 10-0-0.

Mr. Eli Twitchel on the Rhod 17,-1-2 Day at 61 pt Day 5-5-0.

Mr. David Morshaall on the Rhod 13 Days at 61 pr Day 3-18-0.

Capt Joseph Twitchel account Eight on the Rhods at 61 pr Day and 12 Day for toowing from Sharburn here and home again at 61 pr Day 6-0-0.

Mr. James Swan account 4 Day on the foort at 61 Day 1-4-0. Total 83 - 0 - 0.

Sudbury Canada Nov. 8th. 1782.

November 18 1782 Voted to accept & allow the within and above account attest Jo. Twitchel moderator Petter Astin account for work on Road allowed by Com. 1-6-3.

Benj. Clark account for three & Half Days at 61 1-1-O."

Chapter 11
1785 Freshet

After the close of the Revolutionary War, settlers began to come into town, although not very rapidly till after 1790. The extreme poverty of the country incident to a protracted war prevented many from securing means to purchase lands. Several young men were encouraged by Capt. Eleazer Twitchell to come in, he having secured to each a lot and taking his pay in labor. The lower part of the town seemed to offer more inducements than the western portion, its broad intervales being very inviting to the new comers.

In October 25th, 1785, occurred what was known as the Great Freshet. The river rose to a height never known before nor since. The settlers had built their houses on the highest portions of the intervales which were supposed to be entirely secure from inundation. But the rain came on and poured down incessantly for two days and one night and carried away several of the houses. Lieut. Clarke's house was situated a few rods east of the barn on A. L. Burbank's farm. The water rose to the beams of his house and spoiled his books. He made a raft of his barn doors and took off with Mrs. Clark, and built a camp nearly opposite Mills Brown's dwelling house. Capt. E. Twitchell lived on the Island near the gristmill. The water rose to the garret and the family was taken off, who spent the night in a cabin made of boards. The upper dam on Mill Brook was swept away bringing down with it an immense amount of drift stuff, but fortunately it turned to the west of the house near Brown's Tannery, and the house was saved. Greely Swan had a house near Alder River Bridge; his wife was taken out of the chamber window in a boat, but the house, containing her web in the loom, was swept away. Benj. Russell's house near Alder River was also swept away. The houses on the lower part of the town suffered much in the same way. We suppose that the freshet must have risen more than twenty five feet. The freshet rose two feet above the level ground where Moses A. Mason's house now stands. Consequently, all that portion of the town was flooded. It is said that this freshet was higher than any other ever known, by four feet. The next highest was in Aug. 2d, 1825, when the Willey family were destroyed by the White Mountain slide.

This circumstance led the inhabitants to erect their houses on higher ground. Lieut. Clarke built the house known as the Frost House, while Mr. Swan built on the spot where Ayers Mason's house now stands.

Chapter 12
Notable Residents

We shall now give, from time to time, sketches of the early settlers so far as their descendants may furnish us with information respecting them. I trust that our citizens will respond to the call, for much of the real value of the History of the town will depend on these sketches of individuals.

North Yarmouth   March 11th, 1859
My Dear Sir: -- I saw in the *Courier* a notice asking information of certain persons to aid you in giving us the history of Bethel. I noticed among the names that of my Grand Father Stephen Bartlett (from whom by the way I received my name). Enclosed I give you in my own language as much of his life as I can gather from my Uncles who live in Bethel. You are welcome to make use of what part or all you may notice that will be of any interest to your readers. The facts you may rely upon. I have endeavored to obtain dates correctly.
STEPHEN BARTLETT KENNEY.

Stephen Bartlett, the subject of this chapter, had the honor of being born upon that year so famous in American history, the spring of the same year that Granville introduced into the British House of Commons his noted Stamp act, and Col. Isaac Barre made his noble speech in defence of American liberties, when the American people were first awakened to a scene of their situation, and rights, and nobly resolved to defend them; when the speck of liberty that now illuminates this mighty nature was first kindled; when the crazy George III, by signing this odious act, lost the most loyal part of his kingdom, and gave birth to this great Republic; the year that will be remembered to all ages as the most memorable of the past century. But to return to my narrative. Stephen Bartlett was born in Milton, Mass., April 21st 1765, where he lived with his parents until the year 1782 or until he was seventeen years of age. Following the example of his older brothers Jonathan, Moses and Thaddeus, who had already been attracted to the valley of the Androscoggin by its reputed beauty and fertility where they had erected cabins upon its banks, and began to clear themselves farms, Stephen bid adieu to the home of his childhood and resolved nobly to seek his fortune in the then almost unbroken wilderness of Maine.

Shouldering his axe, and taking his scanty wardrobe with a few provisions upon his back, he started on foot and alone upon his perilous journey, early in the spring of the above mentioned year. He accomplished the journey in safety, and engaged himself to work the season with his brother Jonathan who had commenced a clearing upon the eastern banks of the river, in the lower part of the town, and had built him a framed house low down upon the intervale; this was destroyed by the freshet of 1785 known as the Great Freshet. 'Twas with difficulty and but by the united and active exertions of the four brothers that they secured their cattle which they did in the following morning by pitching hay into the barn floor until they could drive their cattle upon the hay mow where they could keep above water. They also with difficulty secured their horses that were fast in their stalls where they could hardly keep their heads above the water. By this time Mrs. Bartlett was no longer safe in the second story of the house, from which she was rescued out of the chamber window by a boat in which she was taken across the river and intervale to the house of her brother Moses Bartlett who lived upon the upland on the north side. Stephen Bartlett, who was in the boat, used to tell this story often in after days, and point out an elm tree through the top of which the boat passed in safety on its passage across the intervale. The boat used upon this occasion was fashioned from a huge pine tree perhaps modeled after the one built by Crusoe, while upon the "lonely isle."

Jonathan Bartlett rebuilt his house the same season upon the upland on the east side of the river upon the farm now owned and occupied by Elias Bartlett, Esq., who lives in the old mansion still.

Stephen Bartlett then purchased land joining the farm of his brother Moses upon the north side of the river, where by hard work and perseverance he soon possessed a farm and buildings near his brothers. Being then about twenty-two years of age and as the saying was, "well to do," his thoughts were turned towards procuring him a suitable companion to share his labours and be mistress of his home. And as in those days working was not considered a pastime by either sex but a duty, Stephen sensible of his duty made it his business, and soon in the person of Miss Dorcas Barbour of Gray, he found one every way worthy to become the wife of a hardy farmer of those days. They were married Oct. 23d 1787.

Miss Dorcas Barbour, left Gray for Bethel in the winter of the year 1785 to live with her sister, Mrs. Moses Bartlett, who was then in declining health. She accomplished the journey as far as Paris Hill in the usual manner upon horse back behind her father where she bid him adieu as he could accompany her no farther. From this place she continued the journey on foot and on snow shoes accompanied by Mr. Josiah Segar who dragged after him a sled containing all her goods. They reached the Camp or halfway place just at night the first day; Mr. Segar hastened to light a fire which had to be obtained with a flint and steel but unfortunately his punk being wet he could not make it ignite, but remembering that they passed a stump on fire a few miles back, he resolved to go back and procure some. Leaving Miss Barbour alone in the lonely camp to rest upon a couch of hemlock boughs, he retraced his steps and procured some fire, after which they passed the night quite comfortably as she always testified. The next day they reached the house of Esq. Keyes who lived I think not far from what is now Rumford Point where she remained until the next day when the Esquire accompanied her to her sisters.

She commenced life with Mr. Bartlett in a rough log house where they lived until able to build a larger and more comfortable one, which is still occupied by his son Elhanan Bartlett, who has ever lived upon the old homestead situated in what is now Hanover. Stephen Bartlett had eight children, and he lived to see them all prosperously settled around him. He died in the year 1832 aged 67 years. His wife died in 1839, lamented by all who knew her. Elhanan Bartlett has in his possession the identical axe and a hammer that his Father brought with him from Milton, Mass.

Rev. Eliphaz Chapman. Among the early settlers was Rev. Eliphaz Chapman. He was born in Lee, N. H., in 1748. He was the son of Eliphaz Chapman, a respectable farmer in that town. He attended school in his earlier years and acquired some knowledge of the Latin and Greek languages when he studied theology under the Rev. Moses Bradford of Methuen, Mass. He was settled at quite an early age in Methuen, Mass., over the Congregational Church in that town where he remained for about fifteen years. His first wife was Miss Sarah Hutchins who died soon after their marriage. He then married Miss Hannah Jackman of Newburyport, from whom he had six sons and three daughters. Their names were Hannah, Eliphaz, Betsey, Abigail, Geo. W., Timothy, Samuel, Edmund, and Jonathan C. Betsey married John Swan of Bethel, and Abigail married James Walker, the first trader in Bethel. He owned a small farm in Methuen of about 20 acres, but having been dismissed from his charge, he resolved to seek the Androscoggin valley. He purchased the farm now occupied by his son Timothy Chapman, Esq., on the north side of the river. He came to Bethel in 1789, and secured a clearing and sowed it with winter rye, and returned to Methuen. The next spring he returned with his son Eliphaz and built a house and barn on the banks of the river on the spot where the Indians made their settlement. Here were the Indian cornfields, the hills of which were still visible.

This was the first opening on the north side of the river above Moses A. Mason's. Their oldest daughter, Hannah, was left behind till the next year for the purpose of learning the tailoress's trade, which would be absolutely necessary in a new country. She found abundant employment on coming to Bethel, which she did on horseback, the next year. The appearance of this portion of the town as it existed in 1790 is thus described by Dea. Geo. Chapman who came here that year at the age of ten years:

"The whole country was an unbroken forest, save where it was interrupted by small openings. On the north side of the river, Col. Eli Twitchell had a small clearing where Curatio Bartlett now lives, Dea. Ezra Twitchel, where Alphin Twitchell now lives, Capt. Eleazer Twitchell where Moses A. Mason now lives, and Rev. Eliphaz Chapman where Timothy Chapman now lives. On this side, the largest opening was that of Lieut. Clark where Mr. A.L. Burbank now lives. Then that of Abraham Russell on the Grout farm, so called, on the west side of Alder River, and Greely Swan where Ayers Mason now lives. These were the principal openings at that time."

The following description of their log house as described to me by Dea. G. W. Chapman, his son, may be novel to the young. The house was made of second growth poplars which grew on the Indian clearings to a great height and very straight. These were hewed on two sides and laid together. This consisted of but one room at first, but some boards were afterwards obtained and a room partitioned off for the girls. The father and mother slept in the principal room, while the boys climbed up the ladder into the garret. The fire-place consisted of some rocks placed in one corner. The chimney only came down to the chamber floor and was made by crossed sticks plastered with clay.

Some loose boards were laid down for a floor. These in a short time became so warped as to render it inconvenient for walking, and was the cause of a serious accident. Mrs. Chapman had brought with her from Massachusetts some beautiful crockery which was nicely arranged on the dresser; but accidentally while walking across the floor she stumbled and thereby threw down her crockery and broke the whole of it. She could not have been blamed if under such circumstances she did give vent to her tears. During the first winter they could get no grinding done at the mill, and they were obliged to live on hulled corn, stewed peas and bean porridge, of which the kind deacon thinks he ate too much that winter. As soon as they could have some cows they lived well. Their cows found a plenty of forage on the intervale, although the wild onion was so abundant as to affect their milk, whose unpleasant flavor they avoided by eating an onion before taking the milk.

They succeeded in raising bountiful crops, and by cutting timber and selling it they were able to purchase a yoke of oxen and two cows from Brunswick, after which they lived. They also obtained some sheep and put them on the islands in the river. After a few years he built the house where his son Timothy Chapman now resides.

At the incorporation of the town, Dea. Ezra Twitchell proposed that of Ai, but Mr. Chapman proposed that of Bethel, which was accepted. He was chosen as the first Representative to the Mass. Legislature. This was in 1808, and he was chosen for three successive years. He was a Justice of Peace and did considerable business in that capacity. He was evidently a man of considerable ability. He published two sermons on the Prophecies in 1799, which were characteristic of the theology of his day.

He died of consumption in 1814 aged 66, and lies buried on the north side of the river. He preached occasionally in the adjoining towns but was never settled over any society after coming into Maine. The numerous families of that name in this vicinity are his descendants.

Capt. Peter Twitchell, youngest son of Capt. Joseph Twitchell, was born in Sherburn, Mass., July 13, 1761. At the age of 17 he made a visit to Bethel, when there was no other house in the west part of the town except his brother Eleazer's on the island near the grist-mill. This was in 1778. He also visited the town in 1782 when the garrison was still standing. He was a man of uncommon strength. We have heard him relate an anecdote of his second visit here. There was a man at his brother's who was boasting of his skill at wrestling, when Capt. Peter told him that he could throw him over a house. The fellow rather jeered him, when the Captain caught his arms around him and ran up the shed roof of his brother's house and was about to throw him over when he cried, *enough*.

In the year 1784 he came to Bethel and commenced clearing land on the north side of the river on the farm now occupied by Mr. Alphin Twitchell. He cleared several acres of interval, and the next year secured a barn and sowed it with winter rye, but the great freshet that year carried the drift stuff on to it in immense quantities, that he lost one half of his ground that year, but the remainder bore a prodigious crop. About this time in consequence of his father's age, and he being the youngest son, he returned to Sherburn and took the charge of the homestead. He married for his first wife, Miss Sarah Bullard, May 8th 1783, who died Sept. 20, 1791, and for his second wife Miss Amy Perry, June 10, 1793. She was the daughter of Edward West Perry, of Sherburn. He had eight children; by his first wife, Almon, Eli, and Jonathan, and by his second wife, Eli, Julia, John A., Harriet, and Sarah. All settled in Bethel except the two eldest, who died young.

Capt. Twitchell kept a tavern in Natick, which in those days was of no small importance. He was an Assessor of the town at the time the Federal currency was introduced. He had quite a task in teaching the taxpayers how to reckon in dollars and cents instead of pounds, shillings and pence. He was a soldier under Gen. Lincoln and marched to quell Shay's Rebellion. He was afterwards chosen Captain of the Militia and did military honors on the death of Washington.

In the spring of 1810 he came to Bethel and commenced a farm on the Flat on Pleasant river, on the farm now occupied by his son, Col. Eli Twitchell. In 1816 he made a public profession of religion and united with the Congregational Church in Bethel, and till his death was a consistent member.

For 35 years of his life he was a vegetarian. Meat, tea and coffee were forbidden articles, and to this he attributed his long life. When over 90 years of age he walked four miles to church, stand in front of the desk leaning on his long cane, during the prayers and sermons on both parts of the day, and then walked home after services. This he did through choice for exercise, and this he was accustomed to do till a short time before his death.

Capt. Twitchell was a man of strong native powers. He was a man of a reflective and philosophic turn of mind. He prepared a manuscript of his own on Natural Philosophy. A favorite problem of his which he would propose to every educated man whom he met and which he seemed to meditate upon much of his time, was what he used to call his Philosophical Riddle.

The earth and the moon travel round the sun. If they travel one way, every time they go round the sun, there will be one day more than the earth revolves on its axis, and one more than the moon travels round the earth. If they travel they other way, the earth will revolve on its axis once more than we have days, and the moon will travel round the earth once more than we have moons. Question -- which way should they travel to have the extra day and extra moon?

It gratified him very much to have any one acknowledge that they could not solve it. He drew a small pension from the Government. He received an injury by being struck with a carriage while out on his walks and died Nov. 18, 1854, aged 94 years 5 mos.

Capt. Eli Twitchell was the son of Capt. Joseph Twitchell. He was born in Sherburn, Mass., Feb. 17, 1759. He marched with others to the vicinity of Bunker Hill immediately after the battle, and by carrying a very heavy gun on his shoulder he contracted a disease of the bone of the arm, a portion of which was removed. This unfitted him for severe bodily labor. He came to Bethel probably in 1782 and commenced operations on the farm now owned by his grandson Curatio Bartlett. He came on foot to Bethel in the winter, and was so chilled and exhausted that he was compelled to walk on his hands and knees for the last two miles before he reached his brother Eleazer's house. He built a comfortable farm house on the borders of the intervale below Mr. Bartlett's house. He kept bachelor's fare for some time, though it is said that the young ladies of the day were fond of visiting him every week and cooking up a week's supply of food for him, and receiving in return some of the West India goods, which he kept for sale. He was the first person in town who brought such things into town for sale. He married Miss Rhoda Leland of

Sherburn, who died in 1794. His second wife was Lucy Segar who died in 1844. In consequence of his lameness he directed his attention to mechanical pursuits in which he was very ingenious. He made brass clocks, and guns and repaired watches and jewelry. The Indians brought their jewelry to him from Canada to be repaired. During the great freshet in 1785 he stepped from his door in a boat and went over to the spot where Ayers Mason's now stands. At the organization of the town he was chosen Captain of the Militia. He built a large house on the spot where Mr. Bartlett's house now stands which was burnt about eleven years since. He had four children; by his first wife, Julia, Curatio and Lucia; by his second wife, Delenda.

Capt. Twitchell died Nov. 1845. He was a man of public spirit, and was much of the time in town office, as Collector, Treasurer, Clerk and Selectman. He also was a land surveyor and Justice of the Peace.

Dea. Ezra Twitchell came to Bethel about the same time with his brother Eli, and settled on the farm now occupied by his grandson, Alphin Twitchell. He was born in Sherburn, Mass., June 23, 1746, and married Miss Susanna Rice, of Framingham. He first resided in Dublin, N.H., and afterwards removed to Bethel. He was chosen deacon of the Congregational Church in Bethel, which office he worthily filled till his death. He had ten children: Susanna, Hannah, Anna, Calvin, Susanna, Calvin, Ezra, Eli, Thaddeus, and Nathan. The four eldest children died the same day of throat distemper leaving him at the time childless. This occurred in Dublin. So stupefied were the parents at the terrible stroke, that they could not shed a tear at the time.

The little settlement was thrown into quite a state of excitement in the year 1790 by the death of one of its citizens. Mr. James Mills removed from Dublin, N. H., to Bethel in 1785, and commenced a farm on Grover Hill. While engaged in felling trees for his brother-in-law he was struck by a tree and killed. They had been engaged in falling a jam which they finished just before dinner. While his brother-in-law, Walter Mason, went to the camp to prepare the dinner, Mr. Mills went into the jam to fell a tree that remained. As the tree fell it struck into a stump some ten feet high which threw the butt up and struck him, killing him instantly. He had married Hannah, daughter of Moses Mason, of Dublin, afterwards of Bethel, from whom he had five children. Some years after his death she married Mr. Elijah Grover of Bethel.

Capt. Eleazer Twitchell may be regarded the founder of the village at Bethel Hill. He was wont to look with jealous care at every thing that might serve to bring the Hill into notice. He had built his large house known as the "castle," fronting the present Common.

He gave the Common to the Parish on condition that the proprietors of the town would clear off the trees and build a church on it. This was about the year '97. The proprietors went so far as to clear the trees, stake out a lot for the meeting house and haul a portion of the timber, but as the other side of the river was quite as strong in numbers, opposition arose to the measure, and to settle it, Capt. Twitchell drew up a paper to secure subscriptions to have the house on the Common, while his brother Eli was to secure subscriptions to have it on the bank of the river. The latter succeeded and the house was subsequently built on the banks of the Androscoggin near the mouth of the Mill Brook. Capt. T. becoming dissatisfied at the course pursued, fenced the Common into a field, and raised wheat and potatoes for several years. Aged citizens still remember the Common covered with stumps and roots, and a crop of wheat out-topping them all.

The Capt. not only designed it as a location for a church but as a place for regimental parade, and after a few years still desirous that there should be Common he removed the fences. As he had not given any deed of the land, after his death his heirs, J. Ellingwood and Joseph Twitchell, all honor-to-them, generously deeded the land to the parish on condition that the stumps and rocks should be removed. This was done in 1823. The inhabitants voluntarily removed the rocks and stumps on the Common and on what is now Broad street, so that a regiment could and frequently did parade up the street and march down to the Common.

The following is a copy of the deed, which will be read with interest.

"Know all men by these presents that we, Joseph Twitchell, yeoman, and Jacob Ellinwood, cordwainer, both of Bethel, in the County of Oxford, and State of Maine, aware of the utility to the public from the conversion of a plot of ground into what is usually denominated a common, for the accomodation of the public on days of trainings and other popular collections: -- Convinced that the title to land appropriated to such use should be vested in the public: -- Desirous that the parcel of land in this town, generally called the Common, should be converted and accomodated to the public use, ease and convenience; and in consideration of one dollar and of certain labor, paid, done and performed thereon, by the inhabitants of the West Parish in said Bethel, the receipt and performance whereof we do hereby acknowledge, do hereby give, grant, bargain, sell and convey unto the said inhabitants, their heirs and successors the above named parcel of land situated in said Bethel as aforesaid, and being part of lot numbered twenty-three in the fourth range of lots on the south side of the Androscoggin river, and bounded as follows to wit: -- begining at the southeast corner of land situated in the said lot and deeded by Joseph Twitchel aforesaid to James Walker, Treasurer, thence running southwardly to the northwest corner of land deeded by Eleazer Twitchell to James Walker, Esquire, thence eastwardly on said land to the road leading to Norway. Thence northwardly on said road to southeast corner of land, deeded by the said Joseph to the said Walker, Trader, and thence westwardly on the said Walker's land to the first mentioned bound, be the same more or less for the purpose of using the same as a Common.

To have and to hold the aforegranted and bargained premises with all the privileges and appurtanences thereof, to the said inhabitants, their heirs and successors to them, their use and behoof forever so long as they shall not convert the same to any other use by erecting buildings thereon or other wise. And we do covenant with the said inhabitants, their heirs and successors, that we are lawfully seized in fee of the premises; that they are free of all incumbrances; that we have good right to sell and convey the same to the said inhabitants, to hold as aforesaid. And that we will defend the same to the said inhabitants, their heirs and successors forever, so long as they make use of the same as aforesaid, against the lawful claims and demands of all persons.

In witness whereof we have hereunto set our hands and seals this twenty-fourth day of April in the year of our Lord one thousand eight hundred and twenty three

JOSEPH TWITCHELL, { L. S. }
JACOB ELINWOOD.

Signed, sealed and delivered in presence of Amos Mason, Jr., and O'Neil W. Robinson.

Oxford S. S. Bethel April 25th, 1823. Personally appeared Joseph Twitchell and Jacob Ellinwood and acknowledge, the above instrument to be their free set and deed. Before me

Moses Mason, Jr.
Justice of Peace

About the year 1799, James Walker came to Bethel Hill, and opened a store in one of the rooms in Capt. Eleazer Twitchell's house. This was the first regular store in town, though Capt. Twitchell and his brother Eli had kept a few West India Goods to accomodate the people. In 1802 he built a large house and store on the S. E. side of the Common on the spot occupied by Dr. Fanning. This was the second dwelling house on the Common. He continued in the store a few years and subsequently studied theology and entered the ministry, about the year 1817. His brother Gardiner Walker built a store near where Ira Kimball's now stands probably near 1806. He was a single man and in a few years left the town and was succeeded by his brother Ezekiel. The building was afterwards occupied as a saddler's shop and is now situated in the door-yard of Phineas Stearns in this village.

In 1804, Jesse Cross occupied a small house in the front of I. C. Kimball's. Mr. Cross who is still among us, was born in Methuen, now Lawrence, Mass., April 20, 1779. When six years old his father removed to Andover, Mass., to take charge of a grist-mill, where his son remained till he came to Sudbury Canada, in 1800, where he married Lydia, daughter of Capt. E. Twitchell, and commenced clearing up a farm on the north side of the river where Ebenezer Richardson now lives. Capt. Twitchell having purchased a part of the town of Greenwood and feeling anxious to have settlers move into that town, Mr. Cross removed to that town where he remained till 1804 when he moved on to Bethel Hill making the third family in the village. On the death of Capt. Twitchell the grist-mill fell to him by inheritance, which he kept in his possession for many years. His wife died Nov. 29, 1849, aged 63 years. By her he had eight children: Moses, Aaron and Moses, twins, Abigail, Lydia, Frances, Jonathan and Caroline. He married for his second wife the widow Gray of Harrison, who still lives with him.

Moses Mason. It is always gratifying to the biographer to be able to trace back the ancestry of his subject as far as possible. Moses Mason, father of Dr. Moses Mason of Bethel, was the descendant of Capt. Hugh Mason who with his wife Esther came to this country in 1634 and settled at Watertown, Mass. He was a tanner by trade and was much employed in town affairs. He was commissioned as Captain in 1653, and was elected Representative to the Legislature for ten years. He died Oct. 10th, 1678 in his 73rd year; his widow died May 21st, 1692, aged 82. He left three sons and five daughters, of whom Daniel became a farmer by whose wife, Experience, he had five children. His youngest son by his first wife was Moses, who married in Boston, June 6, 1749, Lydia, daughter of Jesse, and Mary Knap and settled at Newton. He removed to Sherborn about 1757. In July 27, 1767 he sold land in Sherborn, and then removed to Dublin where he died Oct. 1, 1775. His widow removed with the family, in 1798, to Bethel, Me., and died there in 1802. He had four children, Martha, who married Eleazer Twitchell of Bethel. Lucy, who married David Marshall and settled in Bethel in 1781, but were driven away by the Indians the same year, and settled in Hebron. Lydia, who married John Morrison of Peterborough.

Moses, the subject of our sketch, was born April 26, 1757. He served as a soldier in the War of the Revolution, and fought under Gen. Stark at the Battle of Bennington. As he was marching to the assult, his fellow soldier, Absalom Farwell, who had seen hard service as a boat-swain on board a man-of-war, addressed him, "Moses," said he, "if they put my lamp out and don't yours, take my money out of pocket and carry it to my wife, and if they put yours out and don't mine, I will take yours and carry it to your mother." As they passed over the battle ground the next day, Farwell said to Moses, "Moses, you was afraid yesterday, when you came on to the ground." "No I wan't sir." "Yes you was, for if they put your lamp out you didn't care what they did with your money," showing the old veteran that he betrayed fear.

He picked up an elegant sword and powder horn on the next day, which he brought with him to Bethel and are still preserved in the family. An incident in the battle was related by him. While they were pressing upon the enemy in their retreat, his comrade threw his gun with the bayonet forward which stuck into the back of a retreating soldier and bent forward over his head. His son, Dr. Mason has in his possession the gun used by him in that battle.

June 20th, 1780, he married Eunice daughter of William Ayers, and settled in Dublin, N.H. In 1799 he removed to Bethel, and bought the farm occupied by Capt. Eleazer Twitchell, and now owned by Moses A. Mason, on the north side of Barker's Ferry. On this farm was originally a heavy growth of pine timber. So cheap was it that the fences were made of what would now be valuable pine logs. He was an industrious citizen and a good neighbor; was chosen Representative to the Mass. Legislature for five years, from 1813 to 1817. He died Oct. 31, 1837, aged 80. His widow died Feb. 4, 1846, aged 85. They had nine children born in Dublin, and two in Bethel. Thirza married Dr. James Ayer, of Newfield, Me. Suza married Richard Dunnells of Newfield. Moses, Aaron. Lydia married Eleazer Twitchell of Bethel. Eunice married Stephen A. Russell, of Bethel. Hannah, married Capt. John Pease of Parsonsfield. Charles, Ayers. Louisana married Dr. Baker Webster, of Newfield.

Mr. Mason was endowed with but a limited education, yet he was a man of correct judgment, and by his practical good sense often settled the difficulties among his fellow citizens without regard to the technicalities of law.

His remaining brothers and sisters were: Mary, b. March 22, 1760, m. Nathaniel Greenwood. She died 1825. Her h. m. again, and was living, 1840, at Farmington, Me. Descendants numerous.

Hannah, b. May 4, 1762, m. Feb. 7, 1782, James Mills, removed to Bethel, 1785, where her husband was killed by the fall of a tree, in 1790. She m. again, Sept. 10, 1792, Elijah Grover; and, in 1847, was the only surviving ch. of Moses and Lydia Mason. Mr. Grover d. 1805. Descendants numerous.

Betty, d. July 18, 1754, m. at Dublin, Benjamin Clark, of Newton, and d. at Bethel, Jan. 31, 1845. Her h. d. 1842. Descendants, in 1840, thirty-seven in number.

Walter, b. Oct. 10, 1766, m. Oct. 21, 1794, Esther Barker, of Waterford, Me.; d. June 30, 1840. She d. June 20, 1843. Ch. eight in number: 1. Esther, m. Eli Grover. 2. Elmira, m. Peter Grover. 3. Lawson, m. Anna Bean. 4. Walter, m. Charlotte Kimball. 5. Rachel, m. Andrew Grover. 6. John Barker, J.P. 7. Catharine, um. 8. Javan Knap, b. Sept. 20, 1817; graduated at Bowdoin College; studied theology at Bangor, Me.

John, b. May 2, 1769, m. in Dublin, Jan. 16, 1789, Bethiah Houghton, dr. of James H., re. to Bethel about 1790; to Gilead, Me, 1793; d. Sept. 19, 1844. She d. April 21, 1846, ae. 74. Eleven ch., one born at Dublin (John), one at Bethel, and the rest at Gilead.

Thirza, b. April 10, 1772; d. at Dublin, Oct. 2, 1775, ae. three and a half years.

Chapter 13

Hunting

HUNTING. Game appears to have been quite abundant in this vicinity. The numerous small streams running into the Androscoggin furnished fine situations for the beaver to construct his dam and pond. Remains of their dams may still be traced out and specimens of wood gnawed by them, are still dug out of the peat bogs. During one spring, James Swan, Benjamin Russell, John Perkins, and a man by the name of Wadleigh, killed sixty moose. They tried out the fat, and saved the best pieces for food, and left the rest to be devoured by wild beasts.

When the garrison was built after the inhabitants were carried off by the Indians, James and Benjamin Russell, brothers, belonging to the fort, were selected as a scouting party to watch the movements of the Indians in the vicinity, but they seemed to have but little fear of Indians before their eyes, and spent their time in hunting for beaver and sable. The commander, hearing of this, threatened to bring them into the fort, but they compromised the matter with him by promising him one third of all the game. My narrator added that it was very doubtful whether the commander ever received his share, as he could remember going into a room which was literally lined with the most valuable furs stretched on hoops, as the rewards of the chase.

As the earliest settlers could not raise beef or pork, the products of the chase must have been most acceptable. The territory in the vicinity of Locke's Mills, Sunday and Bear Rivers, seem to have been favorite haunts for game. The last beaver caught in town was in 1825. He had made a dam on Alder River, a trap was set for him, and he was caught by the fore leg. This he gnawed off and escaped. He was again caught by the other fore leg which he also gnawed off. The third time he was secured by the hind leg and caught. Moose, deer, loup cerviers and others, are occasionally taken.

The bear was one of the greatest depredators in the cornfields. One was caught by Eleazer Twitchell by setting a trap composed of a pan of new rum, molasses, and milk, of which they are excessively fond. Bruin was as fairly caught as his more civilized neighbors sometimes are. On waking up he found himself completely secured by a chain, and against which he manifested a great deal of spite. Bears still find their way occasionally from the mountains. One was shot within a mile of this village in 1858.

In 1791, the wild pigeons pitched upon the territory, we believe, in the vicinity of Isaac Cross's farm as a brooding place. In accordance with their peculiar habits they assembled by thousands. They hatch two to a nest and just before they are able to fly they are fatter than ever afterwards. By felling the trees the inhabitants carried off immense numbers of the *squabs* as they were called. The more particular account of them, I accidentally find in the *N. York Journal and Patriotic Register* for July 20th, 1791, which I transcribe:

"The following discovery has lately been made at Sudbury, a new settlement on Amaroscoggin river:

'A Mr. B. Russell, was hunting in the woods in the beginning of last May, and found a large extent of ground where the trees were universally covered with pidgeon nests, containing the young. On his return home, his account was not credited by his neighbors. About a fortnight after, several of them accompanied him, and found his account did not equal what they there beheld! On a large extent of land of several miles, through which they passed (how much further they knew not) the trees were entirely covered with pidgeon nests. The young were mostly in their nests, but ready to fly. There was but one in a nest, still they took four dozen from a tree. They took from 50 to 100 dozen in a day.

The scene was admirable to behold! The young were hovering on their nests, and calling for food, while the old ones darkened the air with a continual motion, to and from the nests, busily employed in feeding their young.'"

Chapter 14

Act of Incorporation

As the town increased in population the inhabitants began to agitate the question of securing an act of incorporation. A petition was circulated and sent to the Mass. Legislature and an act of incorporation was granted as follows:

COMMONWEALTH OF MASSACHUSETTS,
In the year of our Lord one thousand seven hundred and ninety-six.
An act to incorporate the Plantation called Sudbury Canada, in the County of York, into a town, by the name of Bethel, and for dividing the same town, and establishing therein two Parishes.

Be it enacted by the Senate and House of Representatives in General Court assembled, and by authority of the same, that the tract of land called Sudbury Canada, bound, as follows, viz: Beginning at a beach tree marked S. Y., one mile from Amarescoggin river, and on the north side of Peabody's Patent, thence running south twenty degrees east; four miles and one half on Peabody's Patent, and Fryeburg Academy land, to a hemlock tree marked -I-I-I- III. Thence east twenty degrees north, nine miles on Oxford and State lands to a beach tree marked I-- Thence north twenty degrees, west four miles one quarter and sixty rods on Newpennicook to Amariscoggin river; thence west two degrees south, three miles and three quarters on Howard's Grant to a beach tree; thence west, thirty four degrees south on Thomastown to the first mentioned bound. Together with the inhabitants thereon, be and they are hereby incorporated into a Town by the name of Bethel. And the inhabitants of said town are hereby invested with all the powers, privileges and immunities which the inhabitants of towns within this Commonwealth do, or may, by Law enjoy.

And be it further enacted that Benjamin Russell, Esq., is hereby authorised and empowered to issue some suitable inhabitant of said Town of Bethel, directing him to notify the inhabitants of said town qualified to vote on town affairs, to meet at such time and place as he shall appoint, to choose such officers as other towns are empowered to choose, at their annual meetings in the month of March or April, annualy.

Be it further enacted, by the authority aforesaid, that the said Town of Bethel be, and the same is hereby divided into two distinct Parishes, to be designated, "The East Parish and West Parish," and the following shall be the dividing line between said Parishes, viz: Beginning at the south line of the town at a tree marked sixteen seventeen, standing on the line between the sixteenth and seventeenth ranges, to the north line of the town; and all the lands in said town with the inabitants thereon, east of said dividing line, be and hereby are, incorporated into a separate Parish by the name of the East Parish in Bethel. And all the land in said town with the inhabitants thereon west of the said dividing line, be and hereby are incorporated into a seperate Parish by the name of the West Parish in Bethel:

And that each of said Parishes be and are hereby possessed with all the powers, privileges, and immunities which other Parishes within this Commonwealth are entitled to or do by law enjoy.

And be it further enacted by the authority aforesaid; that Benjamin Russell, Esq., be and is hereby authorized to issue his several warrants directed to some sutable person in each of said Parishes requiring him to notify and warn the inhabitants wherein he lives to meet at the time and place expressed in such warrant for the purpose of choosing such Parish officers, as may be chosen in the month of March, or April, annually, and also to transact any other business that may be legally transacted in Parish meetings.

From the House of Representatives, June 10th, 1796. This bill having had three several readings passed to be enacted.

        Edw. Robbins, Speaker.

From the Senate, June 10th, 1796. This bill having had two several readings, passed to be enacted.

        Sam'l Phillips, Pres.

June 10th, by the Governor approved.

        Sam'l Adams.

True copy attest:

        John Avery, Sec.

The first Town Meeting after its incorporation was held at the house of Gen. Amos Hastings. It may be noticed here that it was the custom of that day to bestow the office of Hogreeve on the young men who had married within the year.

ACT OF INCORPORATION

COMMONWEALTH OF MASSACHUSETTS.
York SS -- To Eli Twitchell, of Bethel, in said County of York.
Gentlemen --   *Greeting.*

You are hereby authorized and directed forthwith to notify and warn freeholders and other inhabitants of said Town of Bethel, qualified to vote in Town Meetings, viz: such as pay to one single tax besides the poll or polls, a sum equal to a single dollar tax; to meet and assemble at the dwelling house of Mr. Amos Hastings in said Town on Monday the fifteenth day of August next, at one of the o'clock in the afternoon, giving fifteen days notice, at least, of said meeting, for the purpose of choosing officers as other towns are empowered to choose, at their annual meetings in the month of March or April, annually. First, to choose a Moderator to regulate said meeting, 2d, a Clerk, 3d, Selectmen, 4th, a Treasurer, 5th, Assessors, 6th, a Constable, 7th, a Collector of Taxes, and any other officers that the town may think proper to choose. And you are hereby directed to make return to me of your doings in consequence of this warrent to you directed. Given under my hand and seal, this twenty-third day of July, in the year of our Lord one thousand seven hundred and eighty-six -- by order of the General Court.

BENJ. RUSSELL, Justice of Peace.

Persuant to the above warrant I have notified and warned the inhabitants of said town qualified as therein expressed, to meet at the time and place, and for the purpose within mentioned.
ELI TWITCHELL.

At a legal meeting of the inabitants of the town of Bethel, opened on the fifteenth day of August, A. D., one thousand seven hundred and ninety-six. Made choice of Lieut. Jonathan Clark, moderator of the meeting, and by a vote made choice of Benj. Russel Town Clerk the ensuing year. Then voted that there be three Selectmen chosen the ensuing year. Then by written votes made choice of John Killgore, for the First Selectman the ensuing year.

Voted, That Lieut. Jonathan Clark be the Second Selectman for the ensuing year.

Voted, That Jonathan Bartlett be the third Selectman for the ensuing year.

Voted, That Lieut. Jonathan Clark be Town Treasurer for the ensuing year.

Voted, That Mr. Joseph G. Swan be Constable for the ensuing year.

Voted, That the person that will collect the Town, County, and State taxes for the least sum on the dollar, be the Collector for the ensuing year. It was bid off to Mr. Joseph G. Swan at three cents on the dollar.

Then voted for Tythingmen for the ensuing year. Made choice of Messrs. Jedediah Grover, Gideon Powers.

Surveyors of Lumber -- Mr. John York, Lieut. Jonathan Clark.

Hogreeves the ensuing year -- Messrs. John Stearns, James Swan, Jr., Silas Powers.

York ss -- in the month of August, 1796. Personally appeared all the above mentioned Town Officers and were sworn to the faithful discharge of the duty of their respective officers before me --

BENJ. RUSSELL, Justice of Peace.

York ss -- August 15th, 1796. Personally appeared Benj. Russell, Esq., and was sworn truly to record all votes passed in this meeting and at other town meetings during the year and until another Clerk shall be chosen and sworn.

Before Jonathan Clark, Mod.

Chapter 15
Ecclesiastical History

The inhabitants of the town early gave attention to the establishment of religious instruction. Ministers frequently came among them and gave them that instruction which their situation demanded. I have not ascertained the name of the ministers who first visited the town. Previous to 1798 there had been to the plantation the names of Taft, White, Rev. Dr. Coffin, of Buxton. Taft was a candidate for settlement, but died at an early age. Rev. Wm. Fessenden of Fryeburg also came among them occasionally.

The town was divided into the East and West Parishes. The first meeting in the West Parish was held Sept. 8th, 1796. In 1797, the Parish voted to raise one hundred and twenty dollars to hire preaching the ensuing year, and twenty dollars to defray expenses.

In 1798, Caleb Bradley preached a few months as a candidate for settlement, and taught school. In 1799, Rev. Daniel Gould was also a candidate for settlement. A divided opinion seemed to exist respecting the candidates, but the majority of the votes favored Mr. Gould. A few became disaffected in consequence and united with the Calvinist Baptists. After the Rev. Daniel Gould had preached some time in the West Parish of Bethel, they proceeded to pass the following votes, viz:

1. To give Mr. Daniel Gould a call to settle with them as their gospel minister.

2. Voted to give Mr. Gould one hundred and sixty dollars, the first year as a salary; and to rise ten dollars a year and so to continue so long as he shall be the their minister. One third part to be paid in money, the other two thirds to be paid in produce.

3. Voted to give Mr. Gould one hundred and fifty-dollars to be paid in labor.

Chose Esq., Russell, Mr. Amos Gage & Lieut. Ezra Twitchell a committee to treat with Mr. Gould on the above proposals.

A true copy attest,
JOSEPH GREENWOOD,
Parish Clerk.

Mr. Gould accepted these proposals requesting the Parish to furnish in addition a few cords of wood.

Previous to installing Mr. Gould, the following persons were organized into a church:

BETHEL, Oct. 7th, 1799.

Joseph Greenwood, James Grover, Ezra Twitchell, Zela Holt, Eleazer Twitchell, Asa Kimball, Benj. Russell, Sarah Greenwood, Susanna Twitchell, Mary Greenwood, Mary Russell.

Voted unanimously to give the Rev. D. Gould a call to settle and to take the pastoral charge of the church in this place.

EZRA TWITCHELL, Moderator.

RESULT OF COUNCIL.

At an ecclesiastical council convened at the house of Benj. Russell, Esq. The Rev. Wm. Fessenden, was chosen Moderator and the Rev. Nathan Church, Scribe.

1. Voted, That Mr. Daniel Gould's confession of faith is satisfactory; and that nothing appears at present, to prevent his installation.

2. Upon the Rev. Mr. Gould's exhibiting his church standing, an account of his ordination as an evangelist; and after considering the opposition, unanimously proceed to the Installation.

3. Voted to recieve the Church in the West Parish in Bethel, organized by the Rev. Daniel Gould as a sister church.

This therefore is to certify that the Rev. Daniel Gould was this day settled over the church and people in said Parish according to gospel order.

A true copy attest:

NATHAN CHURCH, Scribe.

BETHEL, Oct. 9th, 1799.

This day the Rev. Daniel Gould was admitted into the church and installed over the church and people of the West Parish in said Bethel. The Rev. Nathan Church of Bridgeton, made the introductory prayer. The Rev. Wm. Fessenden of Fryeburg preached from Heb. 13, 17. The Rev. Joseph Robey of Otisfield made the installing prayer and gave the charge.

The Rev. Nathan Church gave the right hand of fellowship and the Rev. Wm. Fessenden made the concluding prayer.

BETHEL, April 25th, 1800.

Lieut. Ezra Twitchell, and Mr. James Grover were made Deacons.

Mr. Gould continued as pastor of the Church and Parish till 1809 when it was thought advisable to dissolve the relationship existing between them. A council was called May 3d. 1809, consisting of Rev. Nath'l Porter, Nathan Church, Lincoln Ripley, and Lieut. Robert

Andrews, Dea. Stephen Jewett, Dea. Ephraim Chamberlain, and decided to that effect which was adopted by the Church, May 7th 1809.

From 1808 to 1819, the church was without a pastor. Money was raised every year and the people supplied with preaching a portion of the time. Among these were Rev. Valentine Little, and Rev. Timothy Hilliard. In 1817 there was quite an addition to their numbers and in Jan. 20, 1819, an Ecclesiastical Council was held to Install Henry Sewall as Pastor. Rev. David Thurston preached the sermon. Rev. Noah Cressey made the consecrating prayer. Rev. Wm. Ripley, the charge. Rev. Samuel Sewall expressed the Fellowship of Churches, and Rev. Wm. Thurston made the concluding prayer. The sermon was afterwards printed, a copy of which I now have in my possession. His relation with the people did not prove the most happy, and he was dismissed May 11th 1820.

Soon after, Mr. Charles Frost, a young man, came to the place as a candidate for settlement and on Feb. 20th, 1822, a Council was held consisting of the following: Rev. Daniel Gould, Dea. Hezekiah Hutchins, John W. Ellingwood, Bro. Ammi R. Mitchell, Rev. Josiah G. Merrill, Wm. Spurr, Rev. Asa Cummings, Jacob Mitchell, Rev. John A. Douglass, Moses Treadwell, Rev. Joseph Walker, Daniel Stowell, Rev. Allen Greely, Martin Bradford, John T. Smith, Aaron Beamer. Rev. Mr. Merrill made the introductory prayer. Rev. John W. Ellingwood preached the sermon. Rev. Allen Greely made the ordaining prayer. Rev. D. Gould gave the charge. Rev. Joseph Walker gave the right hand of Fellowship. Rev. Asa Cummings gave the charge to the people. Rev. John A. Douglass made the concluding prayer. The sermon was printed, of which I have a copy.

Mr. Frost commenced his ministry under favorable auspices, and he continued its successful pastor till his death in 1850, a period of 30 years. During his ministry 166 persons united with the church. The church and society as soon as convenient made arrangements for a successor to Mr. Frost. An invitation was extended to the Rev. John H. M. Leland of Amherst, Mass., to become their Pastor. A Council was held July 2nd, 1850, for that purpose, and on the following day Mr. Leland, was installed. The following was the order of exercises: Rev. J. S. Gray, invocation and reading of the scripture. E. S. Hopkins, introductory prayer. Wm. T. Dwight, D. D., sermon. J. W. Chickering, D. D., installing prayer and charge. G. F. Teuksbury, right hand of Fellowship. G. E. Adams, D. D., address to the people. D. Garland, concluding prayer. Benediction by the Pastor.

Mr. Leland continued Pastor for nearly three years during which time the church became better organized and efficient as a body, but for various reasons he concluded to ask a dismission which was granted by a council, May 10th, 1853.

In March following the Church and Society extended an invitation to Rev. E. A. Buck to become their Pastor, which being accepted, he was ordained May 31st, 1854. The order of exercises was as follows: Invocation and reading of the scripture, Rev. David Garland. Introductory prayer, Rev. L. Rood. Sermon, G. E. Adams, D.D. Ordaining prayer, Rev. Mark Gould. Charge to the Pastor, Rev. D. Sewall. Fellowship of the Church, H. D. Walker, E. Abington, Mass. Address to the People, A. S. Loring. Concluding prayer, D. Goodhue. Benediction by the Pastor.

Mr. Buck commenced his labors as pastor under favorable auspices. He labored earnestly to advance the interests of his church and people. His pastoral visits to which he devoted much time were made over a large extent of territory. During his ministry forty-one persons united with the church, mostly by profession. His labors here were too severe for so slender a constitution, and he received a dismission from an ecclesiastical council held Sept. 21, 1858, and is now settled in Statersville, R. I. During the present year, 1859, the desk is supplied by Rev. J. B. Wheelright.

Number of members admitted to the First Congregational Church, in West Parish, Bethel:

1799, 11　1800, 9　1803, 2　1808, 4
1809, 6　1810, 8　1811, 1　1814, 4
1815, 7　1816, 5　1817, 18　1820, 1
1822, 3　1824, 4　1827, 3　1828, 1
1830, 21　1831, 1　1832, 22　1833, 4
1835, 4　1836, 2　1837, 1　1838, 11
1839, 72　1840, 2　1841, 1　1843, 3
1844, 3　1845, 2　1846, 2　1852, 2
1851, 3　1852, 6　1853, 6　1854, 3
1855, 6　1856, 5　1857, 6　1858, 11
1859, 6

DEACONS OF THE CHURCH
(from its organization to the present time)

Ezra Twitchell, James Grover, Samuel Barker, Timothy Carter, Robbins Brown, Leonard Grover, Elbridge Chapman, Joshua Fanning.

The church in which the Society had worshipped since its erection, having become much dilapidated and a desire being felt to secure a location in the village, the last sermon was preached in the house February 1848, by the Pastor, Rev. Charles Frost. It will no doubt interest our readers as exhibiting a specimen of the simple and clear style of the author as well as the historical incidents related by him.

1ST SAMUEL -- 7. 12.
HITHERO HATH THE LORD HELPED US.

Human life is filled up with a great variety of incidents, some of which, from their intrinsic importance, or from their relations to other events cannot fail to awaken our attention, and bring a high claim to serious consideration and regard. The same is true in regard to the history of communities and States. Like a landscape its history will be adorned with events and parts of an almost infinitely varied and diversified character. Yet there will be some which stand out prominently to the view, and demand more than ordinary attention. And in all ages and among all nations, barbarous as well as civilized, pagan and christian, a custom has prevailed of commemorating the more prominent events in history, by monumental inscriptions. This custom so frequently referred to in the scriptures and sanctioned by them, is attended with advantages it cannot fail to recommend it to the regard of all who seek to promote the promotion of the institutions, civil, literary and religious, that lie at the foundation of human society.

As a devout recognition of God's hand, in the dispensation of his providence, it is adapted to awaken emotions of gratitude to him -- to cherish a sense of dependence and thus to give a new impulse to the emotions and exercises of piety. In this dark and distant world in which Christians live so much by sight and sense, they need often to be reminded of the Lord's goodness, and of their vows and obligations to him. And in seasons of despondency and gloom, on which faith is weak and wavering, it is good to recur to the dealings of God; and resolve, with the Psalmist, that we will remember the years of the right hand of the Most High.

The pious Samuel no doubt cherished an *habitual* acknowledgment of God; and offered to him the gratitude of his heart for daily mercies; but in view of the deliverence which the Lord wrought for him and his people, from the land of the Philistines, he felt that something beyond the ordinary expressions of gratitude were due to the great deliverance. Young Samuel took a stone and set it between Mizpeh and Shen, and called the name of it Ebenezer, saying: *Hitherto hath the Lord helped us.*

These words have an appropriate meaning which applies to *us at any period of life.* But there are times which, from some special interest, they seem *peculiarly* adapted to give utterances to the emotions of a devout and humble heart.

A period has occurred in our history, as a religious community, when it seems proper for us to pause and survey the past, and which duty to God and our generation requires us to erect our monument of gratitude to his goodness saying, *Hitherto the Lord hath helped us.*

I propose this afternoon, to glance at some of the more prominent events and facts in history, that we may understand what reason we have to adopt the language of the Lord's prophet, *Hitherto hath the Lord helped us.*

I will begin with the history of the Church. From the records in my posession, I learn that the church in this place has existed a little short of fifty years. Just before the close of the last century a little band of Christian disciples, consisting of seven males and four females, organized and entered into visible Covenant with one another and with God to keep his statutes and attend on his ordinances. Most of these brethren previous to their removal to this place had been connected with Christian churches, and brought with them the spirit of the Puritan fathers, who felt it incumbent on them to provide for themselves and their offspring the means of religious instruction. They had previously procured a man to labor with them, in word and doctrine and two days after the organization of a church he was installed over them as their Pastor.

This seasonable movement to secure a proper regard for the institutions of religion, while the elements of society were in a forming state, evinced not only their piety toward God, but their benevolent regard for the good of their fellowmen, and their farreaching views in regard to the welfare of their descendants. In days still more remote than the present, there will be occasion for gratitude to God, that he put it into the hearts of *all* pioneers in the wilderness to erect for him an altar and a sanctuary in this place, whose beneficial influence will continue to be felt in all coming generations. The pious efforts were approved of God, and during the next year, in addition to the aid of a Pastor, they received an accession of seven more to their number, two of whom still survive.

Additions were made to the church from time to time, and although they were sometimes tried, they increased in numbers and strength; and during the years of 1817 and 18 they were blessed with an interesting revival of religion, which brought a larger number of persons in the flower and strength of their days into the kingdom of Christ, and who have since been the substantial friends of his cause; and with others have been so ready to co-operate in efforts and sacrifices for its promotion, who have stood shoulder to shoulder, through every emergency and trial, breasting the storms of life, to the year 1820. When the labors of the present pastor commenced, the church had been furnished with preaching a large part of the time either by settled Pastors or stated supply. My first acquaintance with this place commenced in the autumn of 1820. I spent a few weeks here as a missionary, and in the following spring entered on what has since proved permanent labors in this place, although my ordination did not take place till the beginning of the next year.

In more respects than one, *it was* a day of small things; religion was at a low ebb in the churches in the vicinity. At the time my labors commenced here, there were but three churches in the county supplied with pastors, and but little interest felt in many places to enjoy the stated ministrations of the gospel.

Of our own church nothing worthy of special note is recorded till the year 1830. This year commenced with unusual seriousness and solemnity. Christians had been awakened to a view of our condition, and had begun to wrestle with God in prayer, for a revival of his work. The impenitent too gave indications from time to time, that which was far from peace and joy. The stillness of the sanctuary, the solemn conversation, the breathless attention, the falling tear from eyes unused to weep, told plainly that truth and conscience and the spirit of God, had found access to their hearts.

An interesting revival commenced in which other denominations participated. As the fruits of the revival, more than 20 persons, a majority of whom were the heads of families, were admitted to our church the same year. In 1832 twenty-two more were admitted into the church, most of whom became interested in the revival. Another short season of refreshing was enjoyed in 1836 and 7. But I have not time to detail these events which were regarded of such surpassing interest at the time, and will only just advert to a single manifestation of the divine power and grace, during the winter and spring of 1839.

The season is so *recent*, and so impressive and interesting in its character and results that I need not dwell upon it a moment. By those which witnessed and enjoyed it, it can never be forgotten; when this house was filled with the glory of God, so obviously that the bare entrance of it was almost sufficient to overwhelm the soul with reverence and awe, and make the trembling sinner cry out as the persecuting Saul did when met by his insulted Lord. What wilt thou have me do? This was emphatically the year of the right hand of the Most High. I love to call to mind these manifestations of his mercy; and refresh my spirit by dwelling upon these fruits and evidences of his tender compassion and care; and renew the pledge of fidelity to him by acknowledging in a public and manner, the work of his greatness. *Hitherto the Lord hath helped us.*

This revival brought a large accession of strength to the church, and we trust of active and consistent piety. Seventy-two persons in the course of the year connected themselves to us; and several others united with evangelical churches, making in all more than 100 hopeful conversions in the space of a few months.

But I might not dwell on these points; suffice it to say, from the best information I am able to obtain, there were gathered into the church, since its organization, two hundred and fifty members. There have been upwards of 70 deaths, and dismissions have been more then 30 mostly in the prime of life, including 5 pastors of churches, 8 deacons &c. Of 100 which still retain the connection with the churches, more then 30 are residents in other towns in this and other states.

I feel unwilling to dismiss this topic without adverting briefly to the covenant faithfulness of God, to his people. His promise is to them and their offspring. It is interesting to know that the present generation of those which sustain a visible relation to the church are the children of those who have loved the gates of Zion and labored and prayed from its prosperity and enlargement. That honored land, which almost 50 years ago erected their banner on this frontier of civilization, have each their descendants among the followers of Christ and I know not of any parent who has deceased, not having one or more of his offspring enrolled among his disciples.

I advert next to the cause of education among us, and draw some further witness of the divine power toward us.

It seems to be the design of God, that religion and learning should exert a reciprocal influence upon each other. It is true that knowledge may be prevented and abused: the infidel and the licentious may employ it for the base purposes of darkening council by words without knowledge, and leading away the unwary into the paths of error and vice. But it seems the principal friend and ally of virtue; and is most generally found in connection with purity of moral sentiment, as well as refinement in taste and manners. Accordingly, the friends of order and religion have always aimed to sustain and promote the cause of education: and endeavored to employ it likewise, as an auxiliary in the work of spreading true religion over the world. Our fathers watched with sleepless vigilance, the progress of learning; and next to the sanctuary, they regarded the influence of the common schools as an indispensable agency for the promotion of good order and sound morality in the community. And enlightened Christians know that for all the substantial purposes of life, a well educated mind is unspeakably more important to the young than treasures of gold and silver.

It is probable that the circumstances of the place have contributed some thing toward the cause of education among us. Our youth is removed from those scenes of temptation and amusement, which have such a demoralizing influence in many places, and are furnished with leisure. It seems to invite them to the cultivation of the intellect and the heart, almost as a recreation.

Accordingly, unusual attention has been paid to the subject of education among us. Through the efforts of a former Pastor, an impulse was given to it; and a class of men were raised up to fill, with honor and usefulness, the most important offices in society; and through their influence as teachers and professional men, there has been a wide and almost universal diffusion of the benefits of education through the community.

No one, I think, can better appreciate the advantages of education among all classes of persons, than a minister. It is to him a source of high satisfaction, that he speaks to those who can appreciate motives, can weigh arguments, and feel the force of rational conclusions; that he has not to contend with jealousy and bigotry and fanaticism, which are the never failing attendants of ignorance. Beside the interest felt in the common school education of our youth, considerable attention has been paid to the higher branches of education. During the period under review, more than twenty persons have been raised up among us for the learned professions. Fifteen have graduated at College, and two are now pursuing their studies in College. Of which number, five are now pastors of churches in three different States. One has just received license to preach, and another is laid aside by ill-health.

Some of our young men are filling honorably, the responsible stations of teachers, physicians, and ministers, in the most prosperous cities and towns in our country.

These and similar facts furnish no inconsiderable proof of an enterprising, humble spirit; and of a good degree of prosperity in worldly pursuits. It has been said, with how much truth I have not the means of knowing, that this small territory embracing a population of not more than ten or twelve hundred inhabitants, has, for the last ten years, furnished more students for college, than any other town or city in the State. And, now, while each is ready to ascribe his success in these enterprises to the unseeing hand of God, and to say, "Hitherto the Lord hath helped me:" allow me to call your attention for a few moments to some facts in relation to the present state of society, in a pecuniary point of view, compared with what it was 25 years since. Who can look out upon the improvement in your farms, your dwellings, your equipage, your flocks and herds, without being constrained to acknowledge the good hand of God upon you?

There is probably more than double the amount of available property now in the hands of the church, than at the time of my ordination, and a much larger proportion of persons are, by providence of God, brought into a situation to hear and be benefited by the preaching of the gospel. It is remarkable how brief God in his providence has prepared the way when our prejudice, sectarian bigotry, and jealousy have subsided: and families and individuals are throwing themselves open to our influence; and seem desirous of casting in their lot with us, that they may share in the privileges and blessings conferred upon us. It may, indeed, increase our labors and trials; but we should rejoice in such a state of things, and as furnishing us with opportunities of contributing to the welfare of our fellow men. This is just such a state of things as is desirable to the benevolent heart. It shows clearly the widening influence of religious institutions, and invites the Christian laborer to enter a field with most ample encouragement that in due time, he shall reap if he faint not. Thus my hearers, from every aspect in which we review the past, we are furnished with most decisive evidence of our obligations to God; and with abundant reason to erect our Ebenezer, saying, *Hitherto the Lord hath helped us.*

The time has arrived when the providence of God seems to indicate that it is our duty to leave this house as a place of worship, and to occupy one recently erected for that purpose. Before retiring, however, my hearers will allow me to make a few remarks expressive of my own feelings, with all frankness and fidelity, and pardon any allusions which I may make of a personal nature.

To me this house has been a most interesting and delightful place. No other spot on earth has ever been endeared to me by such sacred relations and such hallowed associations and influences. The first Sabbath my youthful voice was ever heard in the public worship of God was in this house, and for more than 27 years, with comparitively few exceptions, when I have had strength to visit the Sanctuary, my Sabbaths have been spent here.

But this is not all that I wish to say. The kindness and patience of my people, and the manner in which they have received and treated me, have rendered my labors in this house comparitively light and easy. I came among you at a most critical period of life, with no other claims to your regard, than those which grew out of a commission to preach the Gospel, in the hands of an inexperienced youth. And yet parental tenderness and fidelity seemed but the natural expression of feeling flowing out towards me, from many hearts. It is this that has endeared my people to me; and in connection with a sense of duty has operated as a motive to fidelity and perseverance in the service. And knowing something of the feelings of a stranger, and the advantages of a friend in youth, I resolved to afford all the aid in my power to the young, and take them by the hand and encourage them in every lawful and praiseworthy pursuit.

But more than all, the scenes I have witnessed in this house of surpassing interest and joy, will cause my thoughts to linger with delight about the consecrated spot, long after it has ceased to be a place of worship. This is a birth-place of souls. Of Zion it shall be said, this and that man was born in her. When the Lord divideth up the people, he shall count, that this man was born there. Here, Christians have been fed with the bread of life, and have enjoyed seasons of delightful fellowship with God and one another; and beholding the exhibitions of the divine glory and partaking the pledges of His affectionate regard for them, they have seemed reluctant to depart. Here, Christians have mourned for sin, have wept and prayed, and had their minds softened and subdued by the power of divine existence and love. Here we have confessed and received pardon from the divine head; and heard as it were His voice addressing us: -- *Go in peace and sin no more.*

Here they have wrestled and prayed for the conversion of their fellowmen; with an importunity it seemed, willing to receive no denial; and taking him by the hand, they have endeavored to convert and place him beneath the droppings of His most precious blood that cleanseth from all sin. And here, having wept with those that wept, they have also had their souls filled with joy unspeakable, in consequence of the joy of those who were brought to believe in Christ.

But God dwells not in temples made with hands. We would cherish no superstitious veneration for any object or place on earth. God may be worshipped with acceptance, if circumstances require it, in the open air, or in the most rudely constructed edifice. It is not so much the place, as the feeling that renders our worship right and acceptable. God looks on the heart, he requires truth in the inward part; and they that worship Him must worship Him in spirit and truth. We should be grateful to God, however, that He condescended to record His name on earth, and has graciously promised to be with His people, and to aid and accept them in their attempts to worship Him.

While here, I love and desire to cultivate a grateful sense of obligation to my people; my first acknowledgment is due to God. Hitherto has He helped me: and He has employed an agency that was preeminently adapted to awaken emotions of gratitude to Him, and to cement, stronger and stronger the bonds of affection to my people.

Retiring now, as we do, from this spot, as a place of worship -- let us call to mind the delightful seasons we have here enjoyed -- the benefits we here received -- the vows we have here made, only to tighten our sense of obligations to God, and aim to enter upon His service hereafter with more fidelity, meekness, faith, and Christian affection; and the more entire consecration of all our professional talents to Him. In what way can we better honor the cause of Christ what is dearer to every Christian heart, in what way can we better evince our gratitude and love to Him, who died for us, than thus endeavoring to walk worthy of the vocation wherewith we are called; with all lowliness and meekness; with long suffering, forbearing one another in love; endeavoring to keep the unity of the spirit in the bond of peace? In what other way can we secure the approbation of our own consciences; or enjoy the favor of God? In what other way can we be prepared to meet the realities of the future, or enter on the possession of those pleasures reserved for *all* who love God, and look for His appearance and kingdom.

How soon, brethren, shall we be done with earth. If Christians, how soon will our heavenly Father call us away from every earthly sanctuary, to enter upon the pure and holy worship of the sanctuary above, where there will be no more removals, no more mistakes, or separations; and no more charge, except from glory to glory by the spirit of the Lord. AMEN.

The Congregational Church early engaged in the benevolent enterprises of the day. In 1815, A Female Cent Society was organized which has been in operation to the present time. Silently its members collected their weekly contributions which were devoted to the spread of the

Gospel. Many a more imposing name has accomplished far less good for their fellow men. The First Sabbath School was organized in 1817. The first teachers were Col. Samuel Chapman, Dea. Robbins Brown and Jedediah Burbank, Esq., with three scholars each. This has always been an efficient organization. From this have colonized the Sabbath School on the North side of the river, and many left to form another in the Universalist Society at their organization, and still the numbers are quite respectable, embracing most of the young people in the society.

In 1828 a Temperance Society was formed consisting of seven members, viz, Dr. Timothy Carter, Dea. Robbins Brown, Leonard Grover, Jedediah Burbank, Esq., James Walker, Esq., John A. Twitchell and Rev. Charles Frost. Wm. Frye, Esq., delivered an address on the occasion. This society increased rapidly in numbers and excited a wide spread influence for good in the community. It is believed that but few communities can be found where the evils of intemperance have been so lightly felt as in this. To this fact may be attributed much of our material prosperity. In 1835 a Maternal Association was formed composed of the mothers in the Church. They remained an active body for thirteen years. From their records one may learn an important lesson, that the most powerful influences that are made to bear on society are often the most silent in their operations.

In 1842, a Martha Washington Society was formed by the ladies of the Congregational Church, which was in active operation till 1849, when it was changed into the Ladies Sewing Circle. Since the formation of another society in the village its efforts are chiefly confined to the members of the Church and Society.

The Church has, through most of its history, maintained weekly social prayer meetings, which especially on Sabbath evenings have been well attended. One Sabbath in the month is devoted to the monthly Concert for Missions, and another the Sabbath School Concert, which has for several years past been universally flourishing.

The various benevolent operations of the day have received a share of attention from the church by monthly contributions. The Church has for most of the time during its history supported preaching without foreign aid, especially for the last 40 years.

After the church was erected in the village, the inhabitants on the north side of the river felt that it was too inconvenient for them to cross the river in a ferry boat, and come so far to Church. Whatever may have been the feeling at that day, time has proved it to have been a wise arrangement in thus establishing among themselves the means for religious instruction.

In September 1848 the members of the church living on the north side of the Androscoggin River petitioned the church to grant them leave to be organized into another church.

At a meeting of the church held the 10th day of the same month it passed the following vote:

"Voted, That the members of the church on the North side of the river, who desire it, have leave to be organized into a separate church, when a council called by them for that purpose, shall so advise."

An ecclesiastical council was called in accordance with the vote taken, on the 31st day of January 1849.

The council was composed of the following persons: Ministers, Rev. Isaac Rogers, Joseph Smith, Simeon Hackett, Carlton Hard, Jotham Sewall, Jr., and Calvin Chapman. Delegates, John Barker, Stephen Cobb, and Benjamin R. Page. Rev. Isaac Rogers was chosen moderater and Rev. Calvin Chapman Scribe. The council complied with the request of the petitioners and organized them into a separate church.

At the meeting held by the church on the 10th day of Feb. Mr. Leander Jewett was chosen Moderator of the meeting. Mr. Barbour Bartlett was chosen clerk of the church. Mr. Nathan F. Twitchell and Edmund Chapman were chosen deacons.

Rev. David Garland, son of Dea. John Garland of Newfield, was their first minister. He graduated at Amherst College in 1843, and at Andover Theological Seminary in 1846. After leaving the Seminary he labored in the ministry six months in South Solon, one year in Sweden and one year in Burlington, Mass. He commenced his labors with the second church in Bethel the first of April 1849. He was ordained pastor of the church on the 15th day of Aug. the same year. The council called to advise and assist in the services of his ordination was composed of the following individuals: Bethel, Rev. Charles Frost, and Br. Josiah Brown; Rumford, Rev. E. S. Hopkins, and Bro. O. C. Bolster; Norway, Rev. Charles Packard; Turner, Rev. John Dodd; Albany, Rev. C. F. Tewksbury and Br. I. H. Lovejoy; Sweden, Rev. John Foster and Br. Nathan Bradbury; North Bridgton, Rev. L. W. Harris, and Br. Moses Gould; Waterford, Rev. John A. Douglass and Br. Amos Gage; Portland, Rev. John W. Chickering. The following persons performed his ordination services: Invocation and reading the scriptures, E. S. Hopkins. Introductory prayer, C. Packard. Sermon, J. W. Chickering. Ordaining prayer, J. A. Douglass. Charge to the Pastor, C. Frost. Fellowship of the churches, L. W. Harris. Address to the people, I. Dodd. Concluding prayer, J. P. Foster. Benediction, the Pastor. On the 17th day of Sept. 1849 he was married by Rev. J. J. Carruthers D.D. of Portland to Miss Mary E. Twitchell of Bethel. He is still the Pastor of the Church.

CALVINIST BAPTISTS

Among the earliest settlers were a few who sympathized with the Baptists. Ministers occasionally came among them. Among them were ministers from Paris and Hebron, who visited the town as early as 1792.

A church was organized in 1795. They engaged the ministry of Rev. John Chadbourne, but had no increase. At the end of seven years their number was reduced to two members. Benj. Cole came from Pejepscot, and preached to them in 1800. In 1802, assisted by travelling preachers, they received an addition of three by baptism and in May 28, 1803, one more; and on the following day for the first time they partook of the Lord's Supper. Elder Tripp of Hebron occasionally visited them.

In 1804 the church enjoyed a special revival and were made to forget their days of adversity. Ebenezer Bray was ordained as pastor in 1807, and continued as such till 1812. Twenty-nine united with the church under his ministry.

The church was now without a pastor, but prospered by occasional supplies from neighboring ministers, among whom was the Rev. Arthur Drinkwater, who frequently preached to them from 1812 to 1817. The next year Rev. Daniel Mason was elected pastor, and devoted the remainder of his life to the cause of the church. He died in 1835. Mr. Mason was indefatigable in his efforts, laboring with his own hands the most of the time for the support of his family and preaching on the Sabbath with but a trifling compensation. He was succeeded in 1836 by Rev. Benjamin Donham, who was ordained pastor in October. On 1845 the whole number was one hundred and thirty two.

The present pastor is Rev. Wm. Beavins, under whose ministration the church is enjoying a good degree of prosperity. The larger portion of the members reside in the East Parish, and their place of worship is located at the Middle Intervale.

THE METHODISTS

The following extract from the Records of the Protestant Episcopal Church in Bethel was made by Rev. Joshua Taylor who recently died in Portland at an advanced age.

"The rise of Methodism on Bethel circuit was as follows: -- About the beginning of the year 1798, Nicholas Snething (who was then stationed on the Portland circuit) came and preached a few times in Rumford and Bethel, and in the following spring John Martin, a local preacher, came up the river and preached a few times and returned to me with a request from the people that I should visit them, which I did with a degree of satisfaction, as there appeared to be some tenderness among a few of the congregation. After this they were visited by myself and Bro. Martin a few times, as they requested to have a preacher among them, and a prospect appeared of doing good. I strove for it, but could not obtain my end, till towards the close of the year 1796. They were then connected with the Portland circuit, and during that winter they were visited about once a fortnight by Bro. Merritt, Bro. Becker, and Bro. Merrick, who rode on the circuit. On the spring following, Bro. Joseph

Middle Intervale Meetinghouse, 1816

Baker came and staid with the people, and at the Conference at Lynn, July 1800, this was set off as a separate circuit, and Joshua Baker was appointed as their preacher. The following September the first Society was formed at which time about 14 only were admitted. It now appears that from the time in which they were visited in the spring of 1798, there have been some awakenings. But there was nothing of great note in general till a preacher was stationed among them, and although at some times the prospect has been gloomy. Glory be to God there has been a good work for several months past, and I trust a number have been truly converted. May God bless and prosper the circuit.

May 22d, 1801.   JOSHUA TAYLOR, *P. Elder*.

The following is a list of circuit preachers in the town: -- 1800, Joseph Baker; 1802, Daniel Jones; 1803, David Stinson; 1804, Allen H. Cobb; 1805, Dan Perry; 1806, Clement Parker; 1807, Allen H. Cobb; 1808, Jonathan Chaney; 1809, Joshua Randall; 1810, Wm. Hinman; 1811, Ebenezer Blake; 1812, Daniel Tilmore; 1813, Benj. Jones; 1814; John F. Adams; 1815, Joshua Randall; 1816 John Pain; 1820, Job Pratt; 1821, Elijah Spear; 1823, John Shaw; 1824, True Page; 1825, Daniel Wentworth; 1826, Ebenezer T. Newell; 1829, Caleb Fuller, Isaac Downing; 1830, W. T. Farrington; 1834, Dan Perry, in charge, Huse Dow Assistant; 1836, Dan Perry in charge, John Cumner; 1838-9, Isaac W. More; 1840, Geo. Child; 1841, Aaron Fuller; 1842, Marcus Wight; 1843, Daniel Whitehouse; 1845, Jonathan Fairbanks; 1847, C. Fairbanks.

This closes the catalogue so far as recorded in the Records in our possession. Could the early ministers of this denomination be permitted to tell the simple story of their labors it would unfold a series of events now almost lost to the present generation.

The following facts have been kindly furnished by the present circuit preacher, Rev. Mr. Davies:

"Mr. Editor: -- I see by the minutes of last year that the Bethel circuit reported 170 members, 40 probationers beside some 20 or 30 in Bethel on the other side of the River which belong to Hanover and Newry circuit. The Methodists own the greatest part of Locke Meeting House, and a small part of the Meeting House at Bean's Corner. Since I came to the circuit I have started a subscription paper for a meeting house at Bethel Hill, and at Walker's Mills. But neither place will suit a sufficient number of our people to warrant an effort to build at present, though more than 30 persons were secured for a house at Walkers Mills. We have 7 classes and 7 prayer meetings in the town weekly. This includes one of each at Bethel Hill which Div. we hope will be a good society in that growing place. Some 19 have been converted and some 13 reclaimed, 26 have joined on trial, 11 have joined the Church, 28 have been baptised this conference year, this includes 8 baptised at letter B. From the above facts you will see that Methodism in the Town is in a

somewhat prosperous state, though its society is scattered far and near, and without boasting we may truly and safely say, Methodism is doing as much for the salvation of the town as any other society.
Yours Truly,
E. Davies."

THE METHODIST EPISCOPAL CHURCH

I find by reference to the minutes that Rev. W. Summersides came to preach on Bethel Circuit in 1847, and continued through 1848. 1849, Rev. T. Jones came and remained two years. 1851, Rev. Joseph Hastings came and remained two years. 1857, Rev. Seth B. Chase came and remained two years. 1855, Rev. Joseph Gerry came and remained two years. 1857, Rev. W. C. Stevens came and remained two years. 1859, Rev. E. Davies came who is now the present pastor.

A Camp Meeting has been held in the town for several years past, at which there is usually a large number of people assembled. Their present grounds are very favorable and pleasantly situated in a grove a short distance from the Town House, at Middle Intervale.

NOTE. In our last article we inadvertently described it as the Protestant Methodist Church. It should be Methodist Episcopal. Ed.

THE UNIVERSALISTS

Individuals had been known for many years as partial to the opinions of the Universalists, and occasionally ministers, came to the town and preached, but no regular organization was effected till Dec. 1847, when Joseph Twitchell and seven other persons associated to form an incorporated religious society in the Town of Bethel. From the Constitution framed at that time, the first article reads as follows: This Society shall be called the first Universalist Society in Bethel. The object of this Society shall be the promotion of *Truth*.

During the next year the Rev. George Bates preached a few Sabbaths at the Academy, but they did not establish public worship for want of a suitable house. In 1854 a church was erected at an expense of $2342.00, and the Rev. Zenas Thompson was chosen Pastor. He labored with the society till the winter of 1857.

Rev. A. G. Gaines of Kentucky was next chosen Pastor, and entered upon his duties in June, 1857. Under his ministration the society has sustained preaching through the year, and in Autumn of 1859, a church was organized consisting of 43 members. The comparitively recent history of the society gives us but few incidents of an historical nature. The society have been harmonious in their operations and have induced many to attend public worship on the Sabbath who might not have been brought under the influence of any other religious society.

Chapter 16
Physicians

In the early settlement of the town the inhabitants were compelled to go to Fryeburg, a distance of thirty miles, for a physician. Few persons can appreciate the hardships which this class of men have to undergo in traversing a new country. To ride on horseback 25 or 30 miles on a winter's night regardless of the weather is no trifling effort; yet such was the frequent situation of the physicians in this portion of the State.

A short time after the Revolution, a Dr. Martin made a visit to Bethel. He had come to this country with Baron Steuben, but became a vagabond and soon left the town. The first physician who made his residence in town was Dr. John Brickett of Haverhill, Mass. He came here in 1796. He studied medicine under his father, John Brickett, of the same place. He lived on the spot now owned by Samuel Cross. The limited number of families did not afford him much, and in 1798 he removed to Newburyport, where he had an extensive practice, and I believe, died in that town.

Molyockett visited the families of the town, and exhibited considerable skill in collecting roots and herbs and bark, from which she could make poultices, salves and drinks to meet the exigencies of the case.

The position of the inhabitants was such that they could not be expected to remain long without a physician, and the town was most fortunate in having move into it the subject of the following sketch.

Dr. Timothy Carter was born in Ward, Mass., Nov. 27, 1768. At the age of eleven years, his father, who was a house-carpenter, fell from a building and was killed. Timothy being the oldest of the family went to live with a man in Sutton, Mass., who was an oil dealer. From what few hints I have been able to gather respecting his youth, he was largely dependent on his own resources for an education, but like most men who are thus situated, he made the best use of his time in preparing himself for his future profession. He studied medicine with Dr. James Freeland of Sutton, Mass., and for several years, practiced medicine with his teacher. He was married to Miss Fanny Freeland, daughter of Dr. Freeland, July 28, 1792. She was born Sept. 9th, 1771, and died in Bethel, Nov. 14, 1815. Dr. Carter removed to Bethel in 1799 at a time when there were about 80 families in the town. He settled on the spot now occupied by his son, Elias M. Carter, Esq., at Middle Intervale. This section of the town was at that time regarded as the centre of influence as it had increased more rapidly in population than the West Parish. Dr. Carter soon had an extensive practice. His rides on horseback extended from Dixfield to Shelburne on the river, a distance of nearly 50 miles, while he was constantly called to visit families among the mountains and in places where no carriage could possibly enter. Much of the time his only guide was the spotted trees! In 1800, the next year after he came to Bethel, he was chosen Town Clerk & Treasurer, which offices he filled for twelve years.

His plain hand-writing stands very conspicuous on the town records. He was Selectman in 1801, 20, 21, & 23. He was a Justice of the Peace for many years. He was also the Superintending School Committee for many years of his life and visited the schools all over the town year after year without a cent of compensation. Probably he did as much to raise the standard of our Common Schools as any other man. I find a little discrepancy in the Church Records in regard to the time of his admission into the Congregationalist Church. The records say that he was admitted Dec. 8, 1817, while the same record says that he was chosen Deacon in July of the same year. I am inclined to think he must have united with the Church in 1816. He held the office of Deacon till his death. He married June 25th, 1818, for his second wife, Miss Lydia A. Russell, who was born in Bethel, July 16, 1790.

Few men have succeeded in rearing a family of children who have so generally arrived to positions of honor and responsibility as Dr. Carter. His eldest son, Lawson, was born in Sutton, Mass., Nov. 20th, 1793, graduated at Dartmouth College in 1816, and studied theology in N. Y. City, and entered upon the duties of a clergyman at Ogdensburg, N. Y., and is now Rector of Grace Church, in Cleveland, Ohio.

Galen was born in Sutton, Mass., June 19th, 1795, and graduated at Middlebury College in 1818, studied medicine with Dr. Stearns in New York City, and first practiced medicine in Monson, Mass. For 30 years past he has been a practicing physician in New York City. James T. Carter was born May 12th, 1797. He was a merchant in New York City at the time of his death in Nov. 1840.

Timothy J, was born in Bethel, Aug. 19, 1800. He attended the Law School at Northampton, Mass., and opened an office at Rumford, and afterwards at Paris, Me. He was elected Representative to Congress in 1836, and died at Washington, March 14, 1838.

Luther C. was born in Bethel, Feb. 25. 1805. He has been a merchant in New York City for 35 years, and for many years he was Supervisor of Schools in that city, and in 1859 was elected Representative to Congress.

Dr. Carter's "Brick-end House," 1816, Middle Intervale

Frances Carter was born in Bethel, Sept. 1st, 1809, and was married to Robert A. Chapman, Esq., of Bethel, Mar. 28, 1833.

Elias M. was born in Bethel, Sept. 11, 1811. He was a member of the Governor's Council in 1847 and 8, and has been engaged in town affairs most of the time for twenty years past.

Lydia D. was born in Bethel, March 22, 1823. Sarah W. was born May 8th, 1823. She died June, 1843. Abigal A. was born April 9, 1821, and married Rev. Mark Gould, now of Standish, Me.

Theodore R. was born July 12, 1827, and is a merchant in New York City. Benjamin was born in Bethel, July 4, 1832, and is in company with Theodore in New York.

Dr. Carter stood high as a physician and as a man. Under him several prominent physicians received their medical education. Among these were Dr. James Ayer of Newfield, Dr. Cornelius Holland of Canton, Dr. John Barker of Wilton, and Dr. John Grover of Bethel. I well remember his appearance in 1835. His head was white as snow, yet his form was erect and he was a handsome old man. Probably no man in this town ever more worthily deserved the title of an old school gentleman. He was well fitted as a pioneer in laying the foundations of an intelligent and virtuous community. No man in his profession in this community has been more highly and more universally respected than he. He had no physician as a neighbor till 1813, when Dr. Moses Mason commenced practice at Bethel Hill, and Dr. John Grover in 1816. He acted well his part through a long and useful life and died suddenly of disease of the heart, Feb. 25, 1845, at the age of 77 years.

DR. MOSES MASON

Dr. Moses Mason was born in Dublin, N.H., June 2, 1789. When he was ten years old, his father moved into the town of Bethel, and settled on the farm on the north side of the river owned by Moses A. Mason, so that the subject of our sketch may fairly commence his biography with the present century. Having but few privileges for an early education, he was engaged on the farm with his father during his minority, but having an inclination to pursue the study of medicine he entered the office of Dr. James Ayer, of Newfield, with whom he acquired his practical education, and commenced practice at Bethel Hill in 1813. There were but few houses in what is now the village. The lot on which the Doctor's house now stands was a dense forest and bore the representation of a swamp, and to most men would have presented a most forbidding aspect, but he had the good fortune to marry Miss Agnes Straw of Newfield, June 15, 1813, who came to the new town, and with willing hand and heart aided her husband in her appropriate duties towards establishing a home. The doctor soon had a respectable and lucrative practice, and won the confidence of a numerous class of citizens. Still the doctor was never wedded to the practice of medicine. He had early, partly by the force of circumstances and partly from choice, engaged in public affairs which from year to year increased upon him till the year 1833, he was elected to Congress, when he laid aside the practice of medicine entirely. He was appointed the first Post Master in town Jan. 1814. Previous to that time the inhabitants had to go to Waterford for their nearest office. I have often heard the Doctor say he was scarcely ever more excited in his life than while he stood listening to the postman's horn sounded in the distance, announcing the important fact that the mail was coming to Bethel for the first time. The first arrival of a train of cars created no such an excitement. He held the office till 1834, a period of twenty years, when he resigned. He was commissioned Justice of the Peace in 1821, which office he has held most of the time to the present. He has united in marriage some eighty-six individuals for which he never received a cent, invariably giving the fees to the bride. He was appointed County Commissioner in 1830. In 1833 he was elected Representative to Congress for the Oxford District, and was re-elected in 1835. He was in Congress during the exciting administration of Andrew Jackson, where he was familiar with Wright, Clay, Webster, J. Q. Adams and others who took a prominent part in the public affairs of that day. Few men can better entertain a visitor with the congressional history of that period than Dr. Mason. He was a member of the Governor's Council in 1843 and '45. In 1844, he was appointed a Trustee of the Insane Hospital. For fourteen years he was chosen a Selectman of the town. He was elected President of Gould's Academy in 1854, which office he now holds. For several years past the Doctor has had but little connection with public affairs, but lives in quite retirement on the spot which he first chose for a home, where he employs his time in reading, and in some mechanical employment in which he is quite ingenious. He has spent much time in adorning the Woodland Cemetery, in which he exhibits excellent taste. He is the oldest proprietor in the village, having lived on the same spot forty-seven years.

Though decided in his political preferences, he has the good sense to respect merit wherever it may be found. As a counsellor, especially in political affairs, he was unusually sagacious, as long as he was engaged in public life, pretty surely predicting the result of any given course of action. May he live to enjoy the comforts of a serene old age.

DR. JOHN GROVER

It is quite probable that the most prominent members of society have their origin in the remotest parts of a town as in its villages. Dr. John Grover was the son of John Grover, one of the early settlers in the town. He was born in Bethel, Nov. 22, 1783, and engaged in agricultural pursuits during the greater part of his minority. But he had a

Dr. Moses Mason

Dr. John Grover

strong desire to improve his mind. I once heard the late Jedediah Burbank say, that he employed him about some work, and going out to visit him, found him engaged in solving a mathematical question on a post which he had hewed smooth for the purpose. Such a mind can never be arrested in its onward course, and accordingly John found his way to the study of Rev. Daniel Gould, who was at that time in the habit of giving instruction in the English and classical studies to the young men of the town. He also went to Monmouth and Hebron Academies, which had been recently established. Having a desire to study the French Language, he went to Montreal where he pursued the study under Messrs. Roi and Jobin for eighteen months. This rendered him able to speak and read fluently in that language. Having acquired an extensive knowledge of the French, Latin and Greek Languages, and the mathematics, he commenced the study of medicine under Dr. Timothy Carter of Bethel, and subsequently under Dr. John Merrill of Portland. He also attended a course of lectures at Harvard University.

During the war with Great Britain he was hospital steward at Portland in 1814 and 15. Having thus had advantages, especially in surgury, much superior to most young men in a newly-settled country, he commenced the practice of medicine in Bethel in 1816, where he has been in constant practice of his profession to the present time, a period of forty-four years.

Dr. Grover's practice has been very extensive, and often of the most difficult and trying character. For many years it has been very much as a consulting physician and surgeon. Few men have spent their leisure hours to reading and study so unremittingly through a long life as he, and now at the age of 76 he is constantly making himself familiar with all the improvements in medical science, and in new and valuable medicines. I render it no unmeaning compliment, that I have not met more than three or four men in the State of Maine, who could talk so understandingly on so great variety of topics as Dr. Grover. When visiting the Academy as a Trustee he could throw out some valuable suggestion on every topic presented which was worthy of thought by teacher and student. He was for thirty-five years surgeon of the Militia.

He was a member of the convention that met at Portland to frame the Constitution of Maine, and was elected Representative to its first Legislature. In 1829 he was elected a member of the Senate. For many years he was President of Gould's Academy, and has taken a more lively and active interest in its prosperity than any other man. During the last year he made a tour through the western States where he took careful notice of everything that came under his observation.

The Doctor spends the most of his time in his office where he has a large and varied stock of medicines, and where he is ready to be consulted by all who need his services.

In 1819, he was married to Miss Fanny Lary, who has done well her part in rearing a family. They have had six children -- Abernethy, who graduated at Bowdoin College and resides in Albany; Prof. Talleyrand, who graduated at Bowdoin, and was Prof. of Ancient Languages in Delaware College, and died in June, 1859, in Upsala, Sweden: Lafayette, who pursued his studies at Bowdoin College, and at Philadelphia, is a resident of Salem, Oregon, and first represented that new State in Congress: Cuvier, who graduated at West Point, is now Captain in the U. S. Army: Philophrene, who died at an early age; and Philophrene, their only daughter now living.

PROF. JOHN LOCKE, M. D.

Although Dr. Locke was never a practising Physician in this town, yet he came to the town in his infancy and ever after considered it his home; I consider it appropriate to introduce his history here. I shall therefore republish an address delivered soon after his death before the Cincinnati Medical Society, by his colleague, Prof. M. B. Wright, M. D., of Cincinnati.

It will be read with deep interest, not only by his surviving friends but by the general reader.

ADDRESS

Members of the Cincinnati Medical Society:

From motives of kindness I have been intrusted with a mournful, and yet, in view of the object, an agreeable duty. When I remember, that for twelve long years, Dr. John Locke and myself were associated as teachers in the same Medical Institution, and that during this entire period not an unkind word had ever fallen from the lips of either -- when I review his repeated manifestations of friendship and confidence, I become doubly anxious to render as full justice to his memory as the materials before me and the extent of my ability will allow.

The great luminary disappearing beneath the horizon sends back his rays upon the celestial arch, that they may be reflected in brightness and beauty upon us; but they are gone too soon for the easel and canvas of the painter. Another light, in going down behind the curtain of time, has left indelible rays upon the firmament of science, yet they are so scattered, it seems equally difficult to transfer them to paper. It shall be our effort, however, to concentrate them, here and there, that you may trace, more plainly, the pathway that leads to the grave of fallen greatness, and keep the sod upon it fresh and green, by the dews of memory and affection.

Samuel Barron Locke, the father of the subject of our sketch, had acquired reputation as a mill wright, far in advance of most of his contemporaries. In consequence of this, his services were in great demand, and his engagements required him to reside successively in

Vermont, New Hampshire and Maine. In 1796 he removed permanently to Bethel, in the latter State, where he erected some mills, still known as "Locke's Mills."

John Locke was born February 19, 1792, in Leominster, N.H., and was, therefore, about four years old when his father removed to Bethel. His mechanical taste and ingenuity were manifested at an early age, and some interesting anecdotes have been related and published, illustrative of his skill in handicraft. It is probable, that in boyhood, he learned the use of tools, and the construction of machinery, under the direction of his father. And it is easy to imagine, that during this period, while calculating the velocity and motive power of water, and the resistance to be overcome -- the velocity of the floatboards of the wheel -- the number of turns of the wheel in a given time -- the size and turns of the mill-stone proportioned to the wheel -- the number of staves in the trundle, and the number of cogs in the wheel, his young mind became fascinated with investigations in philosophy, and calculations in mathematics.

Bethel was not noted for the castle of a gouty Baron; nor for her Abbey, containing in its gloomy apartments the tombs and ashes of Kings; nor for her Elysian fields, in which the multitude could congregate to witness and admire the newest fashions; but, better than all these, she had a living oracle, bespeaking pleasure, prosperity, and happiness to those who might partake of its counsels -- a *Circulating Library*.

Among the works of the Library was the *Minor Encyclopedia*, by Rev. Thaddeus M. Harris, of Mass. This book, although brief, contained some sketches and definitions of Sciences not common in those times. Those relating to Botany especially arrested young Locke's attention. He could not understand the terms used, for the book did not contain an explanation of them; but he made a successful appeal to nature to supply the deficiency. For instance, he found the term *filament*, and from its common meaning he suspected the part of the flower to which it applied. Again, he found that the filaments were surmounted by anthers. Here was illustrated another term. Thus, by guessing at the meaning, and observing every point of consistency, he found substantial illustrations of much of the language of Botany. In the years 1808 or '10 his studies in Botany were thus prosecuted; soon after which he entered an academy in Bridgeport to study languages; but even there he could not withdraw his attention from those pursuits for which he had so strong a propensity. Through the kindness of a most excellent preceptor -- B. Cushman, A.M., a class-mate of Nathaniel Wright, Esq., of Cincinnati -- he obtained Adam's Philosophy, distinguished for the perfection of the illustrations of apparatus, and the descriptions of its use, for the author was an instrument maker, at Holborn-hill. These volumes were read by him with eagerness and attention, and their facts were preserved as so many rare treasures. The representations of instruments were so perfect, that he used them at once, with great facility, in his manipulations.

About the year 1816, after returning from the academy to Bethel, young Locke commenced the study of medicine. At this time he obtained access to Gregory's *Dictionary*, then just published, by the aid of which he acquired knowledge with rapidity. Mrs. B____'s *Chemistry*, a book highly attractive to those engaged in the elements of chemical science, arrested his attention. He had never seen a chemist, nor a piece of chemical apparatus, but his inventive genius led him to the construction of his own instruments, and the performance of a series of experiments, in all of which he was successful.

It may be stated, however, that a few years previous to this time the experiments of Galvani and of Volta became known, and the results were so wonderful that the young philosopher could not rest satisfied until he had tested the experiments, and verified the results. For this purpose he chiseled out a mould in a soft brickbat, and cast a set of dishes of zinc, about the size of a silver dollar. Twenty of these, with as many silver dollars, were constructed into a "pile" the dollars being used for the negative element and cloths wet in brine for the imperfect conductor. No shock could be perceived by touching the poles of this instrument with the wet hands, but by thrusting pins under the skin, a decided and powerful effect was experienced. Thus began his acquaintance with that wonderful agent, which was afterward to occupy so much of his attention. Some of those zinc plates, cast in the brickbat, are now in existence.

Bethel, it will be perceived, was not calculated by its attractions to retain the ardent searcher after knowledge. He must needs acquire a profession, and was induced to visit Dr. Nathan Smith, justly celebrated in his time, from whom he received great encouragement in the prosecution of his studies. Subsequently he became the pupil of Dr. Twitchell, of Keene, New Hampshire, accomplished and successful as a surgeon. Anatomical preparations in abundance and a good library captivated the mind of the now medical student. Still he could not relinquish the pursuit of general physics, and was frequently engaged making barometers and other instruments, and such experiments as were suggested.

A copy of *Silliman's Travels in Europe* fell into the hands of the restless student, and by him the fascinations of the book were transferred to the author. He resolved to overcome all obstacles and proceed at once to New Haven. Here, for the first time in his life, he found satisfactory means for acquiring knowledge. He could call to his assistance books, teachers, apparatus, experiments, and was surrounded by men qualified and ready to answer any of the numerous inquiries which were continually rising in his mind. Great, indeed, was the contrast between this and the lonely, destitute condition of his earlier efforts. Still, it may be a question whether his scanty means did not lay the foundation for future success. Originality and self-reliance became a necessity, and at a period in life unusually early, he was led to attempt and accomplish much more than the mere absorption of other men's ideas.

It is not surprising that the student of botany, at the present day, should admire the beauty of the flower and the delicacy of its structure, but that he should also become anxious to learn the classifications and every word in the vocabulary of Botanical Science; for, now, books, teachers, and means for illustration are abundant. At the time of which we speak it was far different with young Locke, and no one except an enthusiast could have pursued his way in defiance of all obstacles as he did. Such books as were within his reach limited his information to something like the following:

"Pentandria -- The name of the fifth class of plants in the Linnaean system of Botany." It was, doubtless, gratifying to find some plants having this character, but it was not enough. In this way, however, a hint had been obtained that Linnaeus had written a book. An effort was made to obtain it, but it was not to be found even in Boston. Miss Wakefield's little book on Botany was speedily and profitably read. As yet our student had not seen anyone possessed of botanical knowledge. And, doubtless, many amusing comments were made by those who saw him engaged in gathering and dissecting clover heads and dandelion flowers.

From this time the clouds that had obscured his botanical prospects began to disperse. Passing through Hanover he learned that Dr. Solon Smith was studying botany. Now he felt that he was near a congenial spirit, ready to extend to him aid and encouragement, and without delay he sought an interview. Young Smith had also received so many jeers and gibes that he had become misanthropic, and distrusted the sincerity of the seeming intruder. A few interchanges of sentiment, however, secured mutual confidence and co-operation. They were soon on their homage to Flora, and in constructing bright garlands for the enchanting goddess. They did not appear before her as jealous rivals, but with the feelings of worshippers at the same holy shrine. *Bigelow's Plants of Boston* had been published, and was in the hands of Smith. No treasure could be seized with more avidity than was this book. Its teachings were immediately applied to practice. A plant was in flower, and the diagnostic description of it leading to the discovery of the name, great satisfaction was felt and joy manifested.

These twin enthusiasts were together not only in the green fields and woodlands and blooming gardens of summer, but in cold mid-winter they climbed to the top of "East Rock" to study buds and frozen evergreens.

They separated after a close intimacy of two years, each to pursue his own line of duty. The subject of our sketch returned to Keene, New Hampshire, not as a medical student but as a teacher of Botany. A correspondence had been opened between himself and Professor Bigelow, of Boston, and through the influence of the Professor he became procurator of plants for the Botanical Garden of Cambridge. In this situation, under the patronage of the Agricultural Society, and with Professor Bigelow as his teacher and his counselor, his many golden dreams were realized, and, in his own language, he "reveled in the Hesperides of Botanical felicity."

During the year 1818, he delivered his first public lectures in Portland, Maine. In Dartmouth College, in Boston, Salem, and in several academies and schools he lectured upon his favorite topics. A spirit of inquiry and examination spread from the teacher to the auditor and pupil, and woods and fields were trodden by nimble feet and filled with the sounds of happy voices.

Presidents and Professors are often censured for bestowing favors upon some one in a class without considering, in any degree, the circumstances surrounding the parties; without advocating it as a principle we think the justice of it at least, in one case, may be made apparent by the relation of the following incident:

On a certain occasion Dr. Kirkland, the President of the University of Cambridge, sent word to the Curator that he wished to see him. The summons was obeyed, yet with that internal feeling of dread which a country boy, a modest curator, might be supposed to have approaching one occupying so dignified and distinguished a position. The meeting, however, was not one of embarrassment. The case of manner and graceless attitude of the President forced upon the visitor the sensible reflection "a man's a man for a' that." The student need not be told what this attitude was for the President has already been pictured, in his imagination, leaning back in his chair with his feet high on the mantel piece. His salutation was jocose and without formality, and ran into the following conversation:

"Locke, I understand you are endeavoring to learn something."
"Yes, sir, it is my desire to learn all that I can."
"But, Locke, you do not seem inclined to go through College."
"I am unable, sir."
"Indeed! Out of several hundred students how many know anything of that they profess to have studied?"
"I can not answer that question."
"Well, I suppose about one out of ten. The nine prefer the diploma without the knowledge, while you, Locke, are satisfied with nothing but the knowledge."

This interview ended with as high a compliment as was ever extended to a humble curator by the President of a University.

"Come to me, Locke," was the earnest request; "at stated hours bring with you fresh specimens of flowers, and instruct me in the science of Botany."

Notwithstanding these individual tokens of reward and encouragement, the devoted student found himself in unequal competition with those young men who accommodated themselves to the fashions and religious doctrines of the day. He had a decided repugnance to the dominant religious sect, on account of the efforts which they openly made to become the controlling party in the halls of legislation. They had obtained a majority in the Legislature of Massachusetts, and passed an act compelling all persons to pay a tax for the support of the settled clergyman of the parish, unless they produced certificates of payment for the support of a minister of some other denomination. Large numbers refused to procure the certificate, and suffered themselves to be drawn in carts to the jails by the parish collector. The young Botanist saw the cattle of his own father, who was attached to the Methodist Church, driven away by force, and they were sold for the maintenance of a clergyman he had never heard and had no desire to hear. Those who knew Dr. Locke in the maturity of his intellect can easily imagine what he would say and do in resistence of such tyranny, when the fire and energy and determination of his young manhood were being fully developed.

The Botany of New England had all been learned, and like one bent on the accumulation of wealth he wanted more, more! His mind turned to the Pacific, as thousands of others have done since from different motives that he might acquire a knowledge of Botany as it existed along her coast. He obtained an appointment in the navy as Assistant Surgeon, and sailed in the Macedonian frigate, with bright and buoyant hopes. A West Indian tornado dismantled the ship, and she put back into Norfolk to repair. While there orders were given to open her at Valparaiso, and thus her final destination was rendered uncertain. Disappointment thus far in the accomplishment of his object, and with nothing to inspire confidence in the future, the Assistant Surgeon asked and obtained leave to withdraw from the service. He returned to New Haven, entered upon a second course of medical lectures, passed an examination and received the degree of Doctor of Medicine.

Previous to entering the Navy, he had commenced a treatise on the elements of Botany, and after his return in 1819, completed the work. It professed to be chiefly an abridgement of Smith's *Botany*, but in truth it contained more originality than many of those works issued as entirely new. While it was in progress he employed an engraver in Boston to execute one of the plates. The execution was bad, and the charge high. The author was dissatisfied, and, having purchased some tools and sheet copper, made his own engravings afterward. These representations were so close to the original that Mr. Nuttall used them in a work subsequently published by himself.

Scarcely four years had elapsed since he left the valley of the Androscoggin a plain country boy, and yet, within that time, he had secured the favor of distinguished men, had received the appointment of Assistant Surgeon in the Navy, had become a Doctor of Medicine, an author of a popular scientific work, a teacher and lecturer in colleges, not only to pupils, but to professors. All this was accomplished without one dollar of patronage or support, except that created by his own exertions. His father, although not destitute of means, nor of intelligence, could not fathom his designs, nor appreciate the tendency of his labors sufficiently to induce any pecuniary outlay. Perhaps, if the son had pursued the slow, even tenor of his way, had trudged along the old beaten path, and had been satisfied with teaching and correcting the young urchin in the country School-House, the parent would have been mindful of his necessities. And it may be, the parent reasoned, "If the boy can summon courage enough to appear before learned men, and, by his unaided efforts, has acquired knowledge enough to impart to them instruction, he needs no assistance from me; his own *will* seems destined to achieve that which money can not purchase."

Men of science are national men; that is, they are ever mindful of the good of the people, and endeavor to promote it, so far as it may fall within the line of their respective pursuits. This principle was engrafted upon the mind of the botanist whose career we are endeavoring to sketch at a very early period in life. He gazed admiringly upon the tiny flower, but he examined, with a view to their utility, plants and trees of large growth. Nearly forty years ago he called the attention of the public to several matters of interest, and among them the value of the river maple, compared with sugar maple in the production of sugar, and as a shade tree. I can not refrain from quoting a few sentences from his communication. "I never contemplated," he says, "a picture or a landscape with more delight than I have the banks of some of these streams (the Androscoggin, Saco, etc.), when viewed from the opposite shore. The tops of the trees present one continued range of foliage, which rises like a fleecy cloud, changing beautifully in the wind, as the upper green, or under white surface is presented to view. This cloud of leaves is supported by the clusters of trunks, like so many Gothic pillars, forming a variety of deep-shaded arches, and avenues beneath. I mention its beauty, because I think it deserves attention as an ornamental tree."

Dr. Rush had expressed the opinion that a sufficient quantity of sugar might be obtained from the maple to exclude, in a good degree, the West India article. This he advocated, not only as a system of national protection, but with the remote prospect of lessening the value of slave labor, and thus to ameliorate the opressed condition of the slave himself. Although not embracing these sentiments to their full extent, the Botanist suggested that by the preservation and culture of the maple, the country could have means at home on which they could rely in time of war. Since that time the great West has been opened to full view. Where now is that beautiful tree, which rose so majestically along our rivers, and in the solitude and silence of our forests? Beneath its branches the sugar-making groups of the early settlers were busy and happy. It enabled them to sweeten the cup of refreshment after the day of toil, and to secure a degree of independence in the far off cabin. Where is it now? It has fallen under the stroke of the wood-man's ax, and commerce has destroyed almost every trace of the landscape, of which it made so conspicuous a part.

Later in life, indeed, after he had become prominent as an original investigator in the field of general science, Dr. Locke felt great delight in the investigation of botanical subjects, and in rendering the labors of the study easy. He invented a Botanical Press, which in part is thus described in Silliman's Journal: "Although this press is so portable as to be packed in a common traveling trunk, it will exert a force, by the application of one hand, of half a ton. When neatly made of mahogany, and polished, it is not unsightly in the parlor; and the pressure being applied to the pile of papers containing the specimens, the click holding the last force, the lever may be removed, and it may be set on one end, at the side of the room, scarcely incommoding any other operations. It is peculiarly adapted to the purposes of traveling Botanists. It is capable of being applied to other uses than those of pressing plants for an herbarium. On a large scale it would be an excellent cheese press, and it has been already adopted for some parts of book-binders' operations. Printers will find it convenient to apply to their paper in wetting it down."

After having graduated, Dr. Locke attempted to establish himself as a physician. He found patients, but they could give thanks more easily than money. They were acceptable as a means of increasing his knowledge of disease, and skill in its treatment; but current expenses had to be met, and how was this to be done if he received no remuneration for his services? It is not surprising that in after life, his sympathies were so strongly drawn out in behalf of the indigent student, and unrequited practitioner.

All those bright prospects that had been seen in the dIstance, during his medical studies, and that seemed to be more and more within his grasp, in proportion as the time for his receiving the Doctorate grew near, were speedily dissipated under the weight of pecuniary engagements. His debts were, comparatively, a trifle; yet to a man of his sensibility and strict honesty, all debts are large which he has not the means to pay. Under feelings of discouragement and despondency the practice of medicine was abandoned, and a place accepted in a female academy, in Windsor, Vermont, as assistant teacher. This academy was under the superintendence of Col. Dunham, who subsequently removed to Lexington, Ky. The assistant had agreed to accompany him. The time for their departure had arrived, but the principal being detained, it became necessary for the assistant to proceed alone and organize the school in contemplation. In June, 1821, he reached Lexington and entered speedily upon the task before him. Much to his surprise, the classes were to be composed, not of romping school girls, but of young ladies of beauty and fascination, whom he had already seen in the midst of those brilliant social parties for which Lexington has been so distinguished. And no man could have felt more keenly the delicacy and responsibility of his new position.

Dr. Locke had, in good time, discovered, that he too had an important study before him. He had not emigrated to the West with any fixed ideas of intellectual superiority, nor with any predetermined models to whom he expected his pupils to conform. Western character was here before him, and he examined it like a sensible, unprejudiced man, encouraging it in the full development of its excellencies, and modifying other points, as circumstances might indicate. He gave instruction, heard recitations, and endeavored, by every possible means, to facilitate the study of the pupil, and give stability to his laudable purpose. By and by, it was deemed necessary to attempt a change in the habits of some of the pupils by an appeal to their judgments and pride of character. The form of the appeal was as follows:

"Young Ladies: -- I perceive there are two parties in this Academy, and I shall not offer any objections to it; for it seems in this country there are two parties in everything. I shall not interfere with your arrangements in this respect, further than to give a description of your two parties, and my opinion of the course or destination of each."

"One party draw their seats near each other, and seem to enjoy themselves very much in conversation. They are evidently very happy in each other's society. Enjoyment and happiness are the legitimate pursuits in life; so I can say nothing against the occupation of that party, so far as immediate enjoyment is concerned. The other party separate themselves, solitarily, and are mostly engaged silently in study. Although cheerful, they are not flushed with excitement, and, unless we take into account other remote results, they would seem, comparatively, to be engaged in a kind of self-sacrificing occupation. They are certainly the losers, unless we can find some result which, hereafter, will be to their advantage."

"Let us look now, to what will occur by and by. Your parents have sent you here, with the desire that you will improve yourselves in the attainment of useful knowledge, and that you will acquire reputation and honor by so doing. There will be an examination at which your parents, and the public, will be present. The sociable party will then appear to disadvantage; parents will be disappointed, teachers mortified, and individual members deeply chagrined. All this may be more than the equal of the merry sociability which has consumed so much precious time.

"The studious party will acquit themselves with distinction, and receive the admiration of all. This will be their reward for former sacrifices. It is for you to decide, whether such a reward is worth seeking. Now, I will not urge you to join either of these parties, but I desire to 'divide the house,' that we may understand to which of these parties you rightfully belong."

What followed Dr. Locke must describe.

"During this short appeal there were flashes of light from beautiful eyes, that told eloquently the strong emotions of ingenuous hearts. And when I asked, 'Who will join the studious party?' a tall, elegant girl, a member of the Breckenridge family, leaped literally into the air, and exclaimed, 'I will!' Another, and another followed, while I looked on the scene with admiration and astonishment. Not a soul but kept her pledge, and the results of order and study were most delightful. The circumstance was told to the parents, and for many years, after I had removed to Ohio, I had the affections, the confidence, and the patronage of that frank and generous people. Ever after I abandoned coercion in the government of youth, and appealed to better motives than those of fear, and all with the most gratifying success."

In 1822 Dr. Locke left Lexington and came to Cincinnati. As he emerged from the woods of Kentucky, on horseback, and rose over the hill south of Newport, the valley surrounding the now Queen City opened to his admiring view. On approaching the city the rattling of drays, the clink of hammers, the smoke of factories, the rush of steamboats, the firing of signals of arrivals and departures, acted upon his mind with all the force of enchantment, and he determined to make it his abode during life. He had met with a cordial and open hearted reception in Lexington, and he had supposed that his introduction into the society of Cincinnatians would be no less easy and agreeable. In this, however, he was mistaken. His letters of introduction received little or no attention, and just as he was becoming disheartened, and on the point of abandoning his projects, Ethan Stone became interested in his views and welfare, and requested his nephew, now a Judge D. Stone, to interest himself in making the stranger known to the people. Through his kindness Dr. Locke became acquainted with the late Rev. Dr. Wilson, a man whom many of you know to have been a model of this kind, strong in intellect, decided in character, and deservedly influential throughout community. From him Dr. Locke received encouragement and the promise of his laughter as a pupil. The Rev. Dr. Ruter also became his friend, and thus he was enabled to lay the foundation of an institution, the success of which equalled his most sanguine hopes.

In the establishment of his school Dr. Locke did not conceal his views in respect to moral and religious instruction. The business of teaching he considered secular, to be sustained without a shadow of sectarianism. Yet he deemed it important, on all suitable occasions, to impress upon the minds of his pupils the great principles of religion -- the existence and attributes of Deity -- the expediency and necessity of cultivating social virtues. "Open your school, then, that it may be patronized by all denominations," said Dr. Ruter, "and great good will be the result."

"Dr. Locke's School" very soon acquired high reputation. With him teaching was less an occupation that a pleasure. He was always ready with an explanation. His instructions were given with conversational ease and perspicuity that seldom failed to remove timidity and to reach the dullest comprehension. He was singularly gifted in illustrations, and with the faculty of selecting those which captivated the feelings while they convinced the understanding. When least expected a question outside of their studies would be put to the scholars and an immediate answer requested. This plan was adopted with a view to cultivate quickness of thought. On one occasion he addressed the scholars in a seemingly hurried, impatient manner, with this interrogation:'Young ladies, on what day of the month does the Fourth of July come?' Not one of the entire school answered the question. All had gone beyond the near and simple fact, and were exercising their minds upon some imaginary abstruse problem.

For some months preceding his fatal illness Dr. Locke gave instruction to some classes in the Wesleyan Female Institute. To him this was a happy period, and in singular contrast with the exciting and distracting scenes that had been constantly passing before him during three or four previous years. His connection with this college not only afforded means of partial support but occupation to a mind that could not be idle. He was forcibly reminded of the youth, and beauty, grace and gentleness, quickness of perception, and refinement of thought, the vivacity of girlhood and the dignity of maturer age, that existed at that time when so many of the intelligent mothers of Cincinnati were his own pupils.

Dr. Locke was among the earliest instructors and lecturers in the Mechanics Institute. At an early period it had no commodious and attractive building to designate its location and reflect its character, for then the plastic hand of a Greenwood with its energies and munificence, had not been laid upon it. In his own private apartments Dr. Locke gave his first instruction to classes of young mechanics belonging to the Institute; next in a building on Walnut street occupied by a congregation of Baptists; and, at a more recent period, in the building known as the Bazaar. Some of those who constituted the classes at the Institute were inspired by the enthusiasm of their teacher, and are now among the most intelligent and skillful of our artizans. All might have been benefited if that mistaken school boy idea had not been cherished that labor and study contribute more to the good of the scholar. Like a true philosopher Dr. Locke was not satisfied with explaining the reason of things, but with his own hands assisted in the construction of tools and machinery. The clockmaker may construct with most exquisite skill wheels and pendulum, without knowing anything of the principles governing their movements. When Dr. Locke found such an one he derived great pleasure in imparting to him instruction, and very recently several have expressed their gratitude to him for having given them a more thorough understanding of their own daily occupation.

In 1835 Dr. Locke was elected Professor of Chemistry in the Medical College of Ohio. He had been liberally patronised, he had been successful as a teacher, his associations were adapted to his sensitive nature, and all around were daughters, wives, and mothers, sustaining by their intelligence and accomplishments, his self made reputation. Under these circumstances he must have accepted his new appointment with great reluctance. He was, however, deeply engaged in the investigation of scientific subjects, requiring both labor and leisure, and a place in the college seemed to open the way for a more speedy and sure accomplishment of the great ends in view.

The newly elected Professor entered upon his duties with the zeal of one having no thought of failure. He found the chemical department of the college almost destitute of the necessary means of illustration. Many obstacles were overcome, and deficiences supplied by his own ingenuity and handicraft. Still his liberal views, and the increasing intelligence of the profession, required something more. To meet every possible demand, he visited Europe and purchased apparatus at an expense of several thousand dollars. On his return he was introduced to an almost entire new set of colleagues, most of them untried men, Drs. Cobb, Cross, Eberle, and Smith having resigned their professorships. In addition to these discouragements the very able Faculty of the Cincinnati College, then in existence, were contending manfully, not to say fiercely, for supremacy. But his will and his efforts were unfaltering, although large pecuniary guarantees were offered as an inducement to join a Medical School in a neighboring State. The college gradually gained in reputation and patronage, and much credit was due his name and influence for a large size of the classes.

There were but few men who possessed more of the elements essential to success, as a teacher, than Dr. Locke. With a perfect knowledge of his subject, ample means for illustration, unfailing resources as an experimentalist, he combined animation and fluency of speech, which removed all dullness and obscurity from the mind of the student. Extemporaneous, rather than written lectures are best adapted for the instruction of most intellects. And this would apply with great force to the lectures of Dr. Locke. While *reading* a lecture, his enunciation was guttural and indistinct, and in any other man would have been called affectation. When his attention, however, was no longer directed to the cold, attenuated ideas spread out upon paper, and his mind was permitted to have free scope, his voice became clear and expressive, more and more as he progressed in the elucidation of his theme. Indeed, when his ideas became, as it were, a part of himself, they were thrown off like rays from an immense luminary, and kindled a fixed glow upon the understanding of his hearers.

Although Dr. Locke expended such an amount of labor and thought on electricity, galvanism, and magnetism, their nature and relations, their advantages to science and uses to man, he was no degree inattentive to those subjects appertaining more immediately to his chair. Every new suggestion, every new element, every new compound in chemistry, received the test of examination, and especially valuable, these suggestions, and elements, and compounds, became a part of his lecture. If proven false, or useless, they were with out any ado rejected.

An idea has become somewhat prevalent, that men, advancing in years, have adhered so long to old ideas, that they are not qualified to progress with the spirit and discoveries of the age. Lazy men, whether young or gray headed, are alike in this particular. The first has the advantage of not being over-burdened by the present, and knowing nothing of the past. The latter has the advantage of being able to compare what he knows of the past with what he knows of the present. A man with Dr. Locke's capacious intellect, devotion to science, and untiring habits of investigation, could not be otherwise than perfectly acquainted with every fact in Chemistry, and if any one has ever attempted to depreciate his qualifications as a teacher, on the ground of deficiency in knowledge, we may conjecture the true motives without any feelings of uncharitableness.

No man, perhaps, had a more accurate acquaintance with Geology in general, and especially the Geology of our country, than Dr. Locke. Most of his studies and explorations were conducted from a desire for knowledge, and the pleasure they afforded; but, at one period, we find him engaged in behalf of the government, in exploring the mineral lands of the United States, especially the *physical department*, including the barometrical observations, the measured altitudes, and the geological sections. At another time he was engaged in making a geological survey of Ohio, under the patronage of the State. During the latter survey he found the largest Trilobite known. The Trilobite species of the extinct fossil family is interesting from the fact that it "is supposed by Naturalists to be one of the first animated beings of our earth, called into existence by the Great Author of Nature." As fragments only of the Trilobite were found, doubts were expressed in both American and European journals respecting the correctness of the measurements. A Trilobite to measure nineteen and a half inches, and twelve inches broad, was too monstrous for ready belief. Other portions, in different localities, were subsequently found by Mr. William Burnet, Mr. Carley, and Mr. George Graham, and that the *"Isotelus megistos"* once had fossil life, is now considered a verity. It may be mentioned here, that Dr. Locke has also described another new Trilobite, under the name *"Cerausus crosotus,"* as being "one of the smallest, and at the same time one of the most elegant of this family of extinct crustaccaus."

A professional friend who has devoted much time to the study and investigation of Geological subjects and whose long continued friendly intercourse with Dr. Locke has enabled him to form a very correct opinion of his character as a Geologist, has given us his views in the following letter:

Cincinnati, Ohio.

M. B. Wright, M. D.

Dear Sir: -- Dr. Locke's taste for Nature early led him to the cultivation of the department of Geology. To the period during which he lived, the first half of the nineteenth century, belongs the merit of having given form and character to this Science; previously to this, it scarce had a place among the Natural Sciences. Many facts had been obtained, many observations made, but the material which had accumulated wanted arrangement, classification; new fields were inviting research, a vast store of knowledge lay hidden beneath the surface, ready to yield up its wealth to the magic influence of an intelligent industry. At such a period in the history of a science, the labors of such a man were of incalcuable value; his strong powers of mind, combined with his laborious habits, contributed largely in developing and defining those great principles which are now recognized as connected with the "earlier history of the earth," its primitive condition, the various changes which it has undergone, and the successive races which inhabited it previous to man's appearance. He employed most of the time devoted to this subject to the investigation of its great principles, and the practical application of them to the useful purposes of life; yet, when opportunity offered, he was not unmindful of the beauties of Palaeontology -- the *"flora* and *fauna* of the ancient world" -- and some of his contributions to this department are not only remarkable for their originality, but for their accuracy. For the restoration of one of the most remarkable animals which inhabited the earth during its first sustaining period, are we to him indebted, and with which his name must ever be associated.

Located, as was Dr. Locke, at Cincinnati upon the *Silarian* formation, the first of the fossiliferous series, a rare and rich field surrounded him, and in its cultivation, he displayed an earnestness worthy of all recommendation. The strata here he studied carefully, and by an intimate acquaintance with them, he was enabled to identify and classify formations in distant localities, when in after years he was employed in the service of the government.

In 1838 he was engaged in a Geological survey of Ohio, and his report to the Legislature upon the Geological structure of the southwestern part of the State must ever be regarded as a paper of much value -- essentially scientific, yet written in a pleasing style, so divested of technicalities, and abounding with so much of practical importance, it will be read by all classes with equal pleasure and profit. It is much to be regretted that provision was not made for the continuance of the survey, from year to year, until the work should have been completed. But although engaged but one season, the labors of Dr. Locke have thrown much light on the Geology of our State, and have greatly facilitated the development of that of the great Mississsippi valley.

He was next in connection with David D. Owen, called to the service of the United States government, for the survey of the mineral lands of the Northwest, and while engaged at this work, he had advanced after studying faithfully the "Blue Limestone" at Cincinnati: viz., that it was the characteristic strata of the *silurian* system, continuous underlying the entire valley. This theory was confirmed when he found this same strata, with its peculiar physical properties and organic remains, cropping out in Iowa in the West, and at Lake Superior in the North.

During his labors in the mineral lands, his familiarity with Electricity and Magnetism, and the accuracy of his Magnetical observations, were singularly useful in indicating the depth and course of veins of ore, and in defining the situation and extent of mineralogical deposits.

I have thus endeavored to merely indicate the character and tendency of Dr. Locke's accomplishments in this department, and to show some of his readings in this section of the great Book of Nature. To do the subject full justice would require much more space than could be here allowed.

In conclusion I may make this remark, that every Geologist who reads Dr. Locke's Geological writings, and sees what he accomplished in so little time, must regret that he could not have spent his whole life in bringing forth the beauties, and elaborating the principles of a science, for which he was so admirably adapted.

Very respectfully,
W. W. Dawson.

I have recently had the pleasure of reading an exceedingly interesting report, somewhat in the form of a traveler's journal, made by Dr. Locke, of the regions about Lake Superior, and I can not restrain my pen from giving a few extracts. The facts they contain, the eloquent manner in which they are presented, and the deep poetic feeling exhibited may lead many persons to form a more correct knowledge of some of the traits in Dr. Locke's character than any description I can give:

"The Sault St. Mary's is a rapid or fall of the river over a barrier of sandstone, by which the waters in the course of a mile descend from eighteen to twenty-one feet, obstructing entirely the navigation of the stream with the exception of the batteau and birch canoe. The subject of a ship canal around this fall has very justly attracted the attention of our government. With the idea of such a canal in my mind I passed several times over the ground. The circumstances are the most favorable possible for the accomplishment of such an undertaking. The foundation rock is a soft sandstone, easily excavated, and yet having consistence to withstand the effect of hydraulic pressure and the abrading of the currants. The lower part of the line, along which the canal must be extended, presents loam, sand, gravel, boulders, and other loose materials to an unknown yet undoubtedly moderate depth. Most likely the same sandstone, in place at the head of the rapids, would be found in the bottom of the excavation, forming a very desirable foundation for the whole work from beginning to end.

The loose materials already named at the surface, have evidently been brought to their present place by the rapids themselves, which occupied the place proposed for the canal, and which then, as now, undoubtedly had the sandstone beneath them. Boulders of granite, gneiss, and sienite are still lodged abundantly on the present inclined plane of the rapid, serve to tear the descending waters into an agitated form. As fast as these boulders are undermined and removed by currents, by ice, or otherwise, new ones are brought down by similar causes and take their places. Thus these huge rocks, some of them from four to ten feet in diameter, as well as the waters of the St. Mary, are moving by bits down the stream, only at a slower rate. It has not escaped the notice of those who have reported to the Secretary of War on the subject of this canal, that the boulders may be used in the construction of the canal itself. They are of sufficient size, and some of them of suitable quality, for such a purpose, but a large portion of them will be found difficult to be wrought. But the want of materials for such a work need not be any impediment, as the limestone of Drummond's Island would be easily transported to the Sault. The hasty observations which I was enabled to make are consistent with what has already been communicated to the United States Senate by the War Department, with a single exception. I doubt whether vessels drawing more than six feet of water can at all times navigate the St. Mary's river, on account of the two bars already named: one rock at the Nebish rapids, and the other of mud in Lake Huron. This, if true, would not require the proposed canal to be so deep as twelve feet, the depth which has been suggested.

The advantages which would arise from connecting the navigation of Lakes Huron and Superior are at many points self-evident. The commerce of a coast of fourteen hundred miles In extent, although the region may be uncultivated, ought not to be lost for the want of a canal only one mile in length. The development of the unexplored mineral resources of a region which has so far given very favorable indications, would be encouraged and facilitated by the measure, and our means of benefitting the native tribes, both by commerce and by the more efficient exercise of active benevolence, would attach them to our interest, and present those depredations which, in case of war with any foreign power, they have always been but too ready to commit. Besides these kinder influences, the consciousness of the facility with which we would be enabled to reach the heart of their country, and keep them from the chief source of their supplies, the fisheries of the lake, would cause the savages to hesitate in any policy which would not meet our approbation.

There remains another consideration which, although not immediately connected with wealth, is still important as furnishing that without which wealth can not be enjoyed. We venture to urge the opening of Lake Superior to steam navigation in order to facilitate the access of thousands of invalids to a region so picturesque, so novel, and so invigorating, as can scarcely be equalled on the globe. What is the object of all the wise plans and devices of government, or of individual enterprise, but human happiness, and how can it be better attained than by the dissipation of intellectual suffering and bodily disease? There is a lassitude, a debility, and with it a weariness of life, created by the miasmata of the Mississippi, and by the calm, dry heat of a summer in the Southwest, which no ordinary remedial means can arrest, and which too often proceeds gradually, yet steadily, to a disorganization of the solid tissues of the body, and which must necessarily terminate fatally. For such a state of suffering, an early escape to the pure water, the clear atmosphere, the temperate summer climate, the rugged fir-clad rocks, the piney glades carpeted with Reindeer moss, and hung with the dangling usnea, and above all to the holy solemn stillness of the natural solitude of Lake Superior, must all act as they have heretofore acted, as a rapid restorative.

The canal being opened, the citizen of New York escaping from dust and ennui, and the resident of New Orleans fleeing from the pestilence of the summer months, may be speedily wafted to a meeting at Porter's Island at Isle Royal, or at La Point, and there enjoy most of Borean wonders of which they have read in the voyages and travels of Ross, Franklin and others, and there, in the day, admire the delusive mirage of the distant shores, and, in the night, the portentous streamers of Aurora.

The loon, or diving bird, very common on Lake Superior, almost always flies against the wind, and the Gibewa Indians have a superstition that she has power to bring the wind from any point she pleases, or from the quarter to which she flies. Hence, when she meets them in their canoes, they address to her the following prayer: 'Nodin nadin, nodin nadin, nodin nadin,' which means, go bring us wind, or more literally, wind bring us, wind bring us."

As the voyagers were gliding over the surface of the lake in their canoe, a diving bird flew by, when Dr. Locke composed an impromptu boat song. It was sung to the tune of "Hail to the Chief," and the chorus was constructed of the foregoing and other lndian expressions. By its wildness it suited the scene, and being cheerily sung with their united voices, the Indians and voyagers were excited to the utmost of their enthusiasm. The sketch continues:

"I took lodgings with the Missionaries and never did I see the Christian religion appear more lovely than in this sequested spot, where sectariamism dies a natural death, and the Christians almost, or quite forget to which denomination they belong, further than that are Christians; and where, beside the poor Pagan idolatry, or fanatical fears of the Aborigines, Christianity stands strongly contrasted, in simple, unaffected, graceful, benevolent majesty.

From the slight sketches I was able to obtain from Missionaries and Indians, I came to the conclusion, that their traditionally and religious opinions, which are entirely blended with their ideas of Medicine and Necromancy, had no settled form but were the machinery by which their artful ones obtained an ascendancy over the more simple and credulous and that it admitted every latitude or variation which suited that purpose."

To escape the dangers of a fearful storm, the voyagers landed, and turned their canoe bottom upward, as shelter. The journal proceeds: "We found ourselves just above the mouth of Garlic river. The shore at this place is a level plateau, shaded by tall Norwegian pines, and carpeted by whortleberries, arbutus, and other lowly plants. In the center of this plain, highly picturesque in itself but rendered enchanting by overlooking the broad, deep, clear waters of the great lake, is a solitary grave, covered by a monumental log cabin, with an ample cedar cross overgrown with long Usnea moss, waving and sighing mournfully in the breeze. Peeping into this little house of death, I saw the sand had sunk down on the decayed body."

There was to Dr. Locke, "something so touching in the simple, rude monument which pure affection had reared," he was inspired with sentiments of true poetry, which were partially expressed in the following:

APOSTROPHE.

Stranger, another stranger calls to see thy sacred dwelling place,
Where, for years, thou'st slept alone in this sequestered spot.
No unhallowed foot of sauntering idler
Comes to spend a vacant hour
In fashionable, fantastic cemetery;
But a heart-thrilled stranger,
Persecuted by Superior's relentless waves.
Is cast by Fate, upon the sand-chafed shore,
And with holy breast, and tearful eye,
Leans o'er thy rude built monument,
And by the ills of life, as by Superior's wave,
Would fain lie down beside thee,
To share this envied place.
Thy comrades, laid thee gently in the sand,
Reared up this cabin-monument,
And o'er thy lowly head have placed
This ample cedar cross, on which
The tangled moss has grown, to mark
The unlettered time.
The spring fir tree greens around,
And spreads its balmy fragrance;
The lofty pine tree bends its boughs,
And breathes Aeolian murmurs;
The river glides its winy waters;
The lake sends up its billowy cry,
And here, amid God's holy temple,
Which he himself has made,
The stranger kneels, and breathes a prayer,
That both our souls may rest in Heaven.
Sleep on -- I leave thee now, but soon
Must sleep in earth more rudely trod.
Like thine, my breast too must yield
To earthly pressure, and the sand,
The cold, sharp sand, must fill that chest
Where, now so long, the lungs have heaved,
And heart has throbbed, and ached,
And throbbed and ached again.

The report of Dr. Locke concludes thus:

"The mountains about the lake are not high -- one thousand to fifteen hundred feet -- but the scenery is picturesque, and interesting beyond description; and with the cool invigorating climate, must be an attraction for invalids, and for the curious, not surpassed by Niagara itself. To be sure, Niagara is a grand unit, but Lake Superior is a constellation of curiosities, and the cascade of the pictured rocks has double the height of Niagara itself. To the Philosopher it will ever be interesting as the region of greatest terrestrial magnetism, the head quarters, the high abode of that invisible, almost spiritual power, which, with heat and light are in the hands of the Almighty, the Soul of the Universe."

The strong reference to electricity in the closing paragraph of the report would seem to make it proper to introduce here a more extended notice of Dr. Locke's labors, discoveries and inventions in the great field of Electricity. In the *American Journal of Sciences*, vol. 33, is a description of an instrument called *Thermoscopic Galvanometer*, invented by Dr. Locke. Of it he says:

"The object which I proposed in its invention was to construct a thermoscope so large that its indications might be conspicuously seen on the lecture table by a numerous assembly, and at the same time so delicate as to show extremely small changes of temperature. How far I have succeeded will, in some measure, appear by a very popular, though not the most interesting, experiment which may be performed with it. By means of the warmth of the finger, applied to a single pair of bismuth and copper disks, there is transmitted a sufficient quantity of electricity to keep an eleven inch needle, weighing an ounce and a half, in a continued revolution, the connections and reversals being properly made at every half turn."

In January, 1838, Dr. Locke addressed a letter to Prof. Silliman, explaining an apparatus he had constructed to illustrate the principles of magneto electricity -- a subject he was then investigating with great earnestness and labor. The letter has for its caption, "*Magneto*-Electricity, and *Electro Magnetic Machines*." Experiments were made showing the following points:

"1. *The Dip by Electro magnetism.*

2. *The Dipping Needle made to move by Terrestrial magnetism.*

3. *The North end of the earth shown to be virtually a magnetical South pole.*

4. *The South polarity of the North end of the earth still more strikingly exhibited.*

5. *Magneto electricity produced by Terrestrial magnetism.*

6. *Electricity produced by motion, and motion produced by magnetic electricity.*"

The subject of Terrestrial Magnetism received the attention of Dr. Locke among the earliest of its investigators in this country. A commmittee of the American Philosophical Society, to whom a communication of Dr. Locke's was referred, say in their report, that "the interest of this paper is much increased by the circumstance, that no accurate experiments on the intensity and dip of the needle have heretofore been made in the United States, west of the Alleghany Mountains."

During the five years Dr. Locke was engaged in his magnetical investigations of terrestrial magnetism, his enthusiasm never abated, and he felt "almost irresistibly compelled to prosecute the subject, but the economy of his domestic affairs rendered it inconsistent with his duty."

In 1837 Dr. Locke made a journey to Europe, as already mentioned, partly to procure the necessary instruments with which to prosecute his investigations in magnetism. The points of interest examined embrace an area from Massachusetts, east, to the western limits of Iowa; and south, from the center of Kentucky to the northern boundaries of Lake Superior. Many thousand miles were travelled in determining the various questions of interest, from time to time presented. The heavy expenses incurred during this long period of labor and investigation were defrayed mostly by himself.

Dr. Locke discovered "that the point of greatest magnetic force is at or near Lake Superior. Thus there are three important poles, or points, nearly on the same meridian, nearly equally distant from each other, and directly north of the United States, being between the longitudes 85° to 90°: first, the true North, or Astronomic pole; second, Ross's pole of perpendicular dip, and of magnetical convergence, twenty degrees south of the Astronomic pole; third, the pole of maximum intensity of magnetic force, twenty-one and a half degrees south of Ross's pole, forty-two and a half degrees south of the North pole: viz., in 471-2° of North latitude."

The discovery of the point of greatest magnetic force was deemed by scientific labors of vast importance, and Dr. Locke received, in Europe as well as in America, a due need of praise. Before me is a letter to Dr. Locke, from Col. Sabine, dated Woolrich, England, November 20, 1843, from which have been taken the following extracts:

"I hasten to acknowledge the receipt of your very obliging and agreeable letter of the 25th of October, I am very glad to learn that the 'Report on Magnetism,' which I took the liberty of sending you, in 1840, reached you in safety, and I can not but be most highly gratified to hear it, in any degree, contributed to induce you to undergo the labor and fatigue of making the series of magnetical observations, over the extensive and important district of which you speak. I can not doubt that so valuable a contribution to magnetical science, bearing so immediately on one of the critical points of magnetical theory, will be most warmly welcomed by one of your own national institutions, and will be published, as it is so desirable it should be, among the scientific records of the nation.

Permit me to express the hope that not less for the interest of science, than for your own sake, you will spare no endeavor to obtain a very early publication of your observations. Both what they accomplished and what they leave unaccomplished will be a guide to those engaged in similar undertakings. The Magnetic Survey, which is now in progress under the direction of Lieutenant Sepoy, in British America, is making a very rapid and successful advance and promises to furnish ample materials for maps for the three magnetic elements north of the United States frontier. It is much to be desired that the survey should be met at the frontier by researches of citizens of the United States, conducted on their own grounds. I learn from your letter that you have yourself achieved already a very considerable part of this undertaking. The field of operation is thus greatly narrowed on the one hand, while on the other a full knowledge of the results which are obtained, may be expected to indicate the direction in which further researches can be most profitably made.

It will be desirable to have a well assured comparison of the force at Cincinnati and Toronto, Upper Canada. If there should prove a difficulty causing a serious delay in the publication of your discoveries in the United States, I can not doubt that either the Royal Society of the British Association would be very proud to receive and print them."

The very flattering manner in which Dr. Locke's investigations were received by Colonel Sabine, were highly gratifying to his feelings. His devotion to Science were for its own sake, and his energies were renewed by the encouragement of one of kindred spirit. The generous commendations of Colonel Sabine were no less acceptable, coming from a European savant. Still, like a true patrion, he preferred the approbation of his own country-men and the approbation of his labors to the renown of his native land. In a manuscript paper I find some very appropriate comments upon this subject, a part of which I am tempted to transcribe:

"By what means let me now ask has the Western devotee to Science so far had of becoming known, or of putting into circulation, for the common benefit of mankind, the results of his researches? So isolated and so retired has been his lot that some might smile at the idea of his existence; and yet such entities are to be found not unfrequently in that great garden included between the Alleghanies and Rocky mountains, a region eminently calculated to elicit that enthusiasm which the Creator has seen fit everywhere to infuse into the hearts of a few, whom for his wise purposes he has destined for the accomplishment of special duties. Being thus unknown the scientific man of the West has stood no chance, however deserving he may be, of receiving any share of that small patronage which our government had power to bestow.

Generally in the United States perhaps there is no class of society whose interests are more neglected than those of the men who devote themselves to the cause of Science. This applies more especially to those who engage in original researches, and who by their occupation are most likely to bring honor and profit to the country. Let me ask the simple question: What must the man do who has the talent and the will to engage in the toil of research, desirous of nothing more than the means of accomplishing his object without any special advantage to himself? Is there any means by which he can procure the needful instruments? -- by which he can pay the expense of a journey? When his researches have been made are there any means by which he can publish them for the honor of his country and for the benefit of mankind? I know of none. It is true we have periodicals which will receive some light and unimportant articles, requiring little expenditure to bring them out, but when a paper containing the results of a great deal of labor and requiring expensive engravings is offered it will be rejected -- it must be rejected, as the periodical itself has not the means of executing it. What then must the savant of the United States do that his researches may be made and published? He must, in the first place, purchase instruments at his own cost, conduct his own experiments at his own expense, travel if his subject requires it, paying a small tax for correspondence and postage, and finally, to save himself the credit of his labors, must pay all the expenses of publication. In how many cases under these circumstances does it occur that foreign countries are the first to know and publish what of value has been achieved among us, and transfer to their own credit that which should have appeared as the grace, the ornament of our own country, merely because they are willing to publish in a handsome and creditable manner without cost to the author? How is such an evil to be remedied? It is, I conceive, to be achieved by the establishment of the National Institute, an event which marks a new epoch, and commences a new era with learned men and with the nation. It can not fail to receive unqualified popular favor, and to be ultimately fostered by public munificence."

During Dr. Locke's extensive journeyings and examinations, he was induced to examine the "connection between Geology and Magnetism." In a paper upon this subject is this explanation: "It was but natural that I should note the geology of the substratum, at each station; and on reducing my observations, and putting them into tabular form, I examined the properties of each group, extending over rocks of a similar kind, and found, so far as I had examined, some general indications by which classes of rocks might be distinguished, although concealed at considerable depths; the magnetical instrument in this respect answering the general purpose of a mineral, or divining rod."

Prof. Wheatstone, Sir David Brewster, and Prof. Locke, were engaged, about the same time, in interesting and curious experiments "on single and double vision, and on optical illusions." Their experiments and results were somewhat similar, each one, however, being entitled to the credit of originality -- the experiments of one being conducted without any knowledge of the other.

Dr. Locke invented an instrument for the purpose of making experiments under the head of what he had called "binocular vision." This instrument, and the researches into "binocular vision," serve to extend, considerably, our knowledge of the anatomy physiology of vision -- nor is the subject by any means exhausted. It will illustrate many important points in optics, and especially the physiological point of single vision by two eyes. It shows, also, we do not see an object in itself, but the mind contemplates an image on the retina, and always associates an object, of such a figure, attitude, distance, and color, as will produce that image by rectilineal pencils of light. If this image on the retina can be produced without the object, as in the phantascope, then there is a perfect optical illusion, and an object is seen where it is not. Nay, more, the mind does not contemplate a mere luminous image, but that image produces an unknown physiological impression on the brain. It follows that, if the nerves can by disease, or by the force of imagination, take on this action, a palpable impression is made without either object or picture. As this would be most likely to occur when actual objects are excluded, as in the night, we have an explanation of the scenery of dreams, and the occasional "apparitions" to waking dreams. The murderer, too, has a picture stamped on the sensorium, by the sight of his victim, which ever wakes into vibrations when actual pictures are excluded by darkness."

In vol. XXIII of the *American Journal of Sciences*, is a description of a Microscopic Compass, invented by Dr. Locke. His own language will best convey the general objects of the instrument. He says, "I do not propose this as a substitute for the surveyor's compass, but merely as an instrument exactly suited to amateurs and scientific travelers, to whom it is inconvenient or unpleasant to carry a back load of machinery to take the bearing of an object. I have, for several years, been carrying on a trigonometrical survey of the beautiful valley of Cincinnati, in which I reside. This I have done for the recreation, both physical and intellectual, which it affords. It invites me to exercise in the open air, and is the best antidyspeptic I have tried. I have managed the several points of the valley much to my satisfaction with the sextant; but nothing answers so well for "meandering" the ravines and ridges of the hills, as the Microscopic Compass. I take the angles with equal accuracy with the surveyors, and with ten times the convenience."

A practical engineer speaks thus of the instrument: "Several engineers to whom I have shown Dr. Locke's hand-level, all concur with me in the opinion, that it is an invaluable instrument for the civil engineer.

No one, acquainted with its merits, would be without it; and I have heard many express their disappointment at not knowing where to procure them ready made."

This pocket instrument was patented to Dr. Locke, in 1850, and is kept on sale by Mr. James Foster, Philosophical Instrument maker, in this city. This invention was patented, not with any hope of pecuniary reward, but, simply, that he might secure to himself the claim to which he was entitled -- the credit of having rendered some service to science, and lessened the wants of his fellow laborers. It was a trait in Dr. Locke's character to be scrupulously exact. He was always ready to award to every man just merit, and always willing to labor for public benefit; but he was not willing, that his original thoughts and inventions should be claimed as the exclusive property of those who had no brains to think for themselves. He did not wish to deprive any one of the pleasure of seeing and feeling, and even using these jewels in his crown; but those jewels were his, obtained at great cost, and no other mortal had any legitimate claim to that crown. In a few instances then, he appealed to the government to sanction his claims through the medium of a patent.

The examples which have been presented to us, of Dr. Locke's genius, or his great powers of origination, seem to have arisen from a happy combination of mechanical skill and scientific knowledge, so that he could individually adapt the means to the end. Some of our mechanics, possessing great skill in the construction of delicate machinery in conformity with models and instructions, are destitute of all knowledge of the principles involved in the adaptation of that machinery. This to Dr. Locke has been a source of great perplexity, and to the mechanic of regret and mortification. The doctor improved an Astronomical clock, by adapting dentets to hold the movements, while the pendulum, which is the time keeper, swings independent of everything, except the point of suspension. I called upon a clock maker, who made the mechanical part of the improvement, for an explanation of the new principles introduced into the clock. He replied that he had to work entirely under the instructions of Dr. Locke, and had not a sufficient amount of scientific knowledge to appreciate the principles associated with the above improvement, and consequently could not give me the information desired.

Another illustration may be given, not only of the enthusiasm with which Dr. Locke pursued his investigations, but the effect of his mechanical ingenuity and scientific knowledge combined.

Soon after he had commenced his investigations in electricity, and its associate subjects, depending for results mainly upon his own tact and resources, he was informed by Mr. Wells, of this city, that he had seen a magnet, of great superiority, made by a rude, unlettered blacksmith. The latter offered to communicate to Dr. Locke the method by which he imparted to magnets such immense power for the sum of twenty five dollars. An agreement was entered into between them, but the blacksmith was dilatory, and neglectful of his appointments. At length a scientific London journal was received by Dr. Wells, describing the manner in which the force of the magnet was increased by electricity. This journal was carried by Mr. Wells straightway to Dr. Locke, who became almost wild with excitement, and together they wrought out, and experimented with a magnet, hour after hour, during the night, and until day dawned. This led, step after step, to inventions and discoveries, until he brought forth the improved Galvanometer, the results of which have already been mentioned. This Galvanometer he took with him to Europe, and exhibited it to those engaged in the production and examination of electrical phenomena, and after an interchange of sentiments the enthusiasts united their labors. And here the ability of Dr. Locke shone forth conspicuously, and to great advantage. His knowledge of mechanics enabled him to use instruments with astonishing results, which were comparitively useless, even in the hands of those by whom, and for whom they were constructed.

If Dr. Locke could express his wishes respecting the future greatness of Cincinnati, one prominent wish would be that all her young artizans should avail themselves of the incalcuable advantages now before them for acquiring scientific knowledge. Then, like himself, they could not only work to order, but could order work; or could, if need be, at the same time plan and execute.

Other inventions must be passed by, for a brief consideration of his great achievement -- his crowning glory -- the "*Electro Chronograph*," or "*Magnetic Clock*." Some of the facts connected with this invention may be given in Dr. Locke's own language. He says, "My attention was first drawn practically to the subject of the combination of clock and electrical machinery, for procuring useful results, in 1844, '5. I was delivering a course of popular lectures in Cincinnati on Electrology. My object was, not so much to reduce anything to a complete system in actual practice, as to show the essential elements of what was actually practicable. Having commenced and continued my studies of Electrology, under what was called 'disadvantageous circumstances,' viz., without the usual aid of instruments, or instrument makers, I was under the necessity of devising and making my own apparatus. Under these circumstances, I had accumulated in the shop room, contiguous to my laboratory, a very efficient and perfect set of tools, among which are the lathe and other shop tools made by the distinguished sculptor, Hiram Powers, and used by him while he occupied himself as a mechanic in Cincinnati. Whenever a new principle was announced, I found it better to devise and make the apparatus suited to its illustration, than to purchase the stereotyped models imperfectly planned, and worse manufactured. Thus avoiding all servile copying, and venturing almost to avoid the trodden path pointed out by books, we drank as much as possible from the fountain, itself, by appealing directly to nature. This course gave a freshness to popular instruction which evidently excited an interest, and produced an effect proportionate to the intense toil which the prosecution demanded."

The following is the language of the late Sears C. Walker, who ranked among the first scientific men of our country. "Dr. John Locke, of Cincinnati, has invented a very cheap and simple instrument, which can be attached to the same pivot with the second hand of any clock, and which will, when put in connection with the telegraphic circuit, make the clocks beat at the same instant, all along the line. The hours, seconds, and minutes may be registered on a fillet of paper, and by striking on the telegraphic key, at the instant of any occurrence, the date of it is recorded on the same paper, to the hundredth of a second. This invention will be useful for many practical purposes. It makes the current of time visible to the eye in a permanent record. It does not change the rate of going of the most delicate clock. It will doubtless be applied, hereafter, to many purposes for the advancement of science -- such as the determination of geographical longitude, in connection with transit instruments; the measurement of the velocity of sound; perhaps, if the circuit be long enough, of the lightning itself. The most expert clockmakers and mechanics, and the most expert telegraph operators, and inventors, including Dr. Morse himself, had been consulted. None had succeeded in a mode that was absolutely satisfactory. It required the union of all the arts of electro-magnetism, of clock making, and of telegraph registering, in the same person, in order to insure success. Dr. Locke had all the requisites. He made the invention. His son made the model. It was attached to a clock made by himself. It was tried on a register of his own invention and handicraft. He is, therefore, in every sense, the inventor of the attachment. The utility of the invention to the coast survey is so great, that one night's work with the new apparatus, and such accompaniment as will necessarily be provided, may, perhaps, be worth as much, in practical results, as a whole campaign would be without it."

Lieut. Maury's letter, announcing officially Dr. Locke's invention to the Hon. John Y. Mason, Secretary of the Navy, from the *National Intelligencer*, of June 8th, 1849, and dated, National Observatory, Washington, January 5th, 1849, reads thus:

"I have the honor of making known to you a most important discovery for astronomy, which has been made by Dr. Locke, of Ohio, and asking authority from you to avail myself of it, for the use and purposes of this Observatory. The discovery consists in the invention of a magnetic clock, by means of which seconds of time may be divided into hundredths, with as much accuracy and precision as the machinist with rule and compass, can subdivide an inch of space. Nor do its powers end here. They are such, that the astronomer in New Orleans, St. Louis, Boston, and any other place to which the magnetic telegraph reaches, may make his observations, and at the same moment cause this clock, here at Washington, to record the instant with wonderful precision. Thus, the astronomer in Boston observes the transit of a star as it flits through the field of his instrument, and crosses the meridian of that place instead of looking at a clock before him, and noting the time in the usual way, he touches a key, and the clock here subdivides his seconds to the minutest fraction, and records the time with unerring accuracy. The astronomer in Washington waits for the same star to cross his meridian, and as it does, Dr. Locke's magnetic clock is again touched; it divides the seconds, and records the time for him with equal precision. The difference between these two times is the longitude of Boston from the meridian of Washington. The astronomer in New Orleans, and Saint Louis, and every other place within the reach of the magnetic wires, may wait for the same star, and as it comes to their meridian, they have but to touch the key, and straight away this central magnetic clock tells their longitude. And thus this problem, which has vexed astronomers and navigators, and perplexed the world for ages, is reduced at once, by American ingenuity, to a form and method the most simple and accurate. While the process is so much simplified, the results are greatly refined. In one night the longitude may now be determined with far more accuracy, by means of a magnetic telegraph and clock, than it can by years of observation according to any other method that has ever been tried. It is therefore well entitled to be called a most important discovery. It is a national triumph, and it belongs to that class of achievements by which the most beautiful and enduring monuments are erected to national honor and greatness."

After the observations of Dr. Locke in magnetism had been published, the English government forwarded and presented to him a full set of magnetical instruments as an evidence of their high appreciation of his labors.

The great amount of knowledge acquired by Dr. Locke, and his marvelous success at invention, were attributable, not only to the strength, and activity, and expansion of his intellect, but from a belief that he could accomplish whatever he undertook, from his tireless industry, and from his almost exclusive devotion to a subject, until thoroughly understood. While in Europe he purchased a transit instrument, and not long after his return, placed it in a small observatory, erected by himself, east of the Medical College of Ohio. Night after night his astronomical observations, and day after day his calculations were made, until his series had been completed, and some great object attained. He was not sustained by patronage, nor encouraged by applause. In the still hours of the night we have often found him, with nothing to disturb the monotony of silence, save the tick of his chronometer, and his own voice, repeating one, two - one, two - one, two. While gazing through space, and watching the movement of some heavenly body, his face became as radiant with devotion as that of a saint before an object of worship. His astronomical knowledge having been made as perfect as the claims of science generally, upon his time, would justify, he turned to other subjects with equal ardor and energy. Not a space was left, not a link was broken out of his long, and varied, and invaluable chain of action.

Following this, perhaps, his thoughts became concentrated upon some important invention. Once engaged, he allowed nothing to interrupt him until the work was molded at least in his own mind, or completed. He had devised a galvanic battery, upon a new principle, and during the period he was engaged in constructing it and experimenting with it, he was almost constantly in his laboratory. I visited him at different hours in the night and found him at work. Several days and nights were required to finish the apparatus and to bring it into good working order, and nothing but the highest state of mental and nervous excitement could have sustained his physical energies for so long a time and with so little sleep. Prostration followed, but as soon as possible he was engaged in unraveling some mystery, improving some machinery, or elucidating some useful and interesting subject.

In the application of principles Dr. Locke's mind was amazingly suggestive, and he was never satisfied with his own inventions until they had been submitted to every possible test, and by comparison deemed perfect.

This concentration of thought was with Dr. Locke a habit; and often subjected him to the charge of absentmindedness. Traveling by public conveyances, and surrounded by strangers, he generally found it most agreeable and profitable to commune with his own thoughts. He invented the microscope compass while riding in a stage coach.

A man of genius whose mind is embracing admiringly and lovingly some of its own creations, or who is aspiring to perfect something still more new and beautiful, may be unmindful of things around him until indifference becomes a habit. I have sat at my own table with Dr. Locke when it seemed that he ate more from the demands of his system than from choice of taste, and this peculiarity was so fixed that he never asked for any article of food at his own table although he seldom refused any dish handed to him.

It was but seldom that Dr. Locke was seen carrying an unbrella even as a protection from the rain. In his botanical and geological excurions and in his out-door labors generally he found it more an encumbrance than a protection. Thus the umbrella with him fell into disuse. His appearance therefore, in the rain without any other protection than an old cloak thrown over one shoulder, was rather from the force of habit than from absent-mindedness.

When Dr. Locke became intently engaged in the investigation of some abstruse subject, he was unmindful of the hour or day, while a single question remained unsettled. After his mind had been placed upon the track of thought it seemed to advance with such velocity and power that although it could be guided it could not be suddenly stopped. Still, the fixed laws of nature being violated, the penalty is almost sure to come.

"Six days shalt thou labor and do all thy work," is one of the commands of the Almighty. Within that period he had created the heavens and the earth, and was not only willing to dignify his creatures by stamping his own likeness upon them, but by bestowing upon them power, in weak imitation of himself, to accomplish, within a given period and for the time being, all their temporal purposes. The seventh day opened upon a newly created world, the sun reflecting grandeur and glory, the moon and stars moving in their appropriate orbits through space. It was a hallowed day -- the soul of the great Architect was taking repose, and silence pervaded the universe.

There is a voice speaking through nature which appeals to the intelligence and feelings of every man. And the power of faith controls him, as it were, in spite of himself. He sees more beauty in the landscape, impressed by the serenity of the Sabbath, than on any of the busy, bustling days of the week. The summer forest seems to be robed in a deeper green, and the mellow leaves of autumn have brighter and more various hues. The wild flowers, skirting the woodland, open their petals wider and exhale a sweeter fragrance, while the willow by the brook bends his head in more profound homage. The crack of the hunters rifle sounds louder through the forest, and rolls a more prolonged echo along the hillsides. The noise of the hammer has an unwelcome sound even to the workman himself.

The command to labor six days and to rest on the seventh was not only designed to test the faith and to inculcate a moral obligation upon man, but to enforce the practical truth, that he should appropriate one-seventh of his time to mental and physical repose. Man is in a certain sense and to a limited degree self-regenerating, yet there is a limit to his powers of endurance. The inroads upon Dr. Locke's strong physical organization forcibly illustrate this truth.

Dr. Locke was not a man of the world, as the expression is commonly received, hence he was not a man for the world. In his feelings as well as in his habits, he was modest and retiring; yet when he did mingle socially with his friends, he was animated and joyous, his conversation abounded in wit, sweetly flowing truths, and beautiful imagery.

He did not carry his taper that he might be seen, here and there of men; but in the solitude of his laboratory he kindled the fires of his genius, and sent out rays as from a grand mirror, that the whole world might be illuminated. He did not mount the rostrum and harangue the multitude, as a leader in some fierce contest; but he summoned the spirits of nature from the mountain, and forest, and prairie; from the caverns and mines of the earth; from the streamlet on the mighty ocean; from the firmament, and from the spheres far beyond unaided vision. While thousands upon thousands were playing with a bauble, a useless toy, he was chaining light, heat, and electricity, "the soul of the Unlverse," to the chariot of science, and propelling her onward, full freighted, for the good of mankind.

If a mind, that can fathom and comprehend deep and abstruse things; if genius, that can originate, and skill, that can execute; if will to labor, and patience to endure, constitute greatness, Dr. Locke was, truly, a great man. He had the inspiration and language of a true poet; he understood music as a science; he could sketch the landscape with the accuracy of a practised artist; he was a mechanic, a mathematician, an astronomer, a chemist, a philosopher, a logician, a physician. He had studied all things upon the surface of the earth, had penetrated into its hidden depths, and had formed an intimate, every day acquaintance with the beauty and glory that surround it.

The following letter, written by one who, it will be seen, was long acquainted with Dr. Locke, and whose zeal has been equalled only by his refined taste in the investigation of natural science, we are induced to present entire.

CINCINNATI, Ohio, 1857.

Doctor M. B. Wright,

My Dear Sir: -- You have asked me to state what I knew of our lamented friend, Dr. John Locke.

It is thirty-four years since I made his acquaintance, and during the greater part of that time our relations, brother naturalists, were of the most intimate character -- our sympathies and tastes being congenial. Many a pleasant ramble have I enjoyed in his company, in search of Botanical or Geological specimens, for these were his two favorite branches in natural science. It was amusing to witness his earnest enthusiasm, when holding up some new specimen which he had found, and exclaiming "treasures! treasures!" to the inquiry, "What have you got there, Doctor?"

On one of his Botanical rambles, among the hills back of Covington, with his tin case under his arm, he was watched, followed, and came very near being arrested for a counterfeiter, by some of the police, who had kept an eye on his walks to the hills and ravines for months before -- the tin box looking very suspicious. And it was only after a thorough examination of its contents that they dismissed him for a "fool yarb Doctor." He always took a friend with him, after that, for fear of accidents and mistakes.

The Doctor had a slow and deliberate walk -- it might be termed a *mathematical* walk. This greatly annnoyed a sprightly, nervous little girl, of some four or five years of age, whom he passed at her door on Fourth street, every day as he went to the Post-Office. It was in strong contrast to the hurried and rapid walk of those who thronged that busy thoroughfare. At last the child could stand it no longer, and one day came out on the pavement, stamping her little foot, and calling out to him, man, why don't you walk faster? Walk faster! Hurry man! Every body walks faster than you!" The Doctor used to tell the story with great relish.

It would make this letter too long to state all I know illustrative of the character of this remarkable self-taught, self-made man. But his acts, while living, will keep his name in bright remembrance long after his death, for they were all of a practical and useful kind. As a teacher he was successful and beloved by his pupils, both in his Female Academy and in the Medical College of Ohio. As a Naturalist he was accurate and discriminating, and his judgment in matters of science was much respected by his associates.

Of his character as a Medical laborer in the College of Ohio, especially in Chemistry, you, having been associate professor, are better able to judge than I am.

His knowledge of the mechanic arts was wonderful, taking into view his various other studies. But he appeared to have a natural taste for them. He once told me, that for years he had made it a duty to learn as much as he possibly could of some one trade every year. His workshop was a perfect museum of materials, tools, and specimens of his handicraft in the several trades he had studied. These hobbies sometimes cost him more than he could well afford.

He was connected, for a time, with the Coast Survey, but left it as it took him away from his family too long.

The Directors of the Cemetery of Spring Grove engaged him to lay down a true Meridian, or base line, from which an accurate survey of all lots was to be made, on a system of triangulation. This work he accomplished in the most satisfactory manner.

Upright and honorable in all his dealings, simple in habits, and economical in his expenditures, he lived strictly within his limited income at first, until his earnings in after years enabled him to leave, at his death, a handsome property to his family.

Very respectfully,
R. Buchanan.

It is not unusual for a portion of the public, at least, to consider those who are earnestly and successfully engaged in the cultivation of science, as destitute of those affections which come naturally and purely from the heart. They would have love always dancing, and on tip-toe --

always softening the eye, and furnishing the tongue with melodious accents -- in a state of effervescence -- always with *rouge* upon the cheeks, and rightly perfumed. The deep, quiet, clear, unsophisticated fountain of affection brings from them no tokens of approval.

Is the mind and the heart placed in such opposite extremes, that when one is admiring the beautiful creations of Spring-time and Summer, the other must endure the long night and icy chains of the Artic circle? When the mind goes down into deep caverns, roams over broad oceans and is amazed at the number and magnitude of other worlds -- must that tie, which bound the heart in its early love, become broken? When the mind becomes dazzled by the brillancy of those scientific lights which genius may have kindled, must the heart be insensible to the warmth of that flame which is ever bright and beautiful on the altar of kindness and love? It was not so ordered by God, and constitutes no part of the true nature of man.

Dr. Locke's seeming disregard of surrounding objects, and his intensity of thought when engaged in the investigation of some pleasing or important subject, may have given to the exterior man a degree of formality and coldness. But the deep feeling manifested on proper occasions, gave full assurance that the inner man retained its sensibilities and hallowed associations. A very few years before he died, Dr. Locke visited his New England kindred, and in an ode of eleven stanzas, written on that occasion, he has given us the sweet flowings of his sensitive nature. A portion of it may be here repeated.

1. We came from distant lands
    To join our frienily hands,
    With those we love;
    And here mid, friendship's flow,
    We've all been blest below,
    With joys which angels know.
        In realms above.

3. Here, where the rocks and hills,
    The groves, and leaping rills,
    In beauty shine;
    And lofty mountains rise
    Up tow'rd their kindred skies,
    With which their grandeur vies.
        In looks sublime!

8. And now, again we part,
   While ev'ry throbbing heart
   Beats high and warm;
   And though the leaf be sere,
   Be this, our meeting here,
   To mem'ry ever dear,
     Not time shall harm.

There is always a degree of curiosity in the public mind, to know something of the religious sentiment of its distinguished scientific men. Aside from a willingness to gratify this curiosity, there are other and more weighty reasons for announcing on the present occasion the sentiments of Dr. Locke on this all important subject. His own thoughts can be expressed in his own language. A few short paragraphs, therefore, will be transcribed from a lecture on Natural Theology, delivered by Dr. Locke, in the Medical College of Ohio. It comes to us, increased in value from the fact that it is among the last, if not the very last published record from his own pen. He says:

"The term 'Natural Theology' means the study of the existence and attributes of God, as evinced in his visible works in the created Universe. I do not propose this study as a substitute for revelation, but as an auxiliary; and, although it does not teach the attributes in which salvation has its foundation -- *mercy and power*. To the greater part of mankind, religious faith obtains a place by education, feeling, and habitual exercise. To them religion is an emotion, never questioned by any attempt at rational objections. But to those whose professions, pursuits, or tastes lead them to a study of nature, the conclusions of Natural Theology are especially important. It is a great work, too, when we have established in the mind of a young person, a full and impressive belief in the existence of Deity, and that too, by an authority of the 'Elder Scripture,' written by God's own hand; that autograph of the Almighty, which has not been copied; the unspotted mirror which reflects the image of the Almighty.

We can not comprehend a blade of grass, a drop of water, or a grain of sand, how much may we profess to know with respect to any of the attributes of the Creator, and how dare we undertake to judge and condemn a brother upon that supposed knowledge. And let us not in our pride felicitate ourselves upon our mercy to a brother thus condemned by us, that we do not take his life while we cut him off from our kindness, and blist and destroy his reputation by calumny. By some means or other this state of strife, disputation, uncharitableness, and persecution is to disappear, and the happy time is to come when all shall see alike, when backbitings shall cease, and the tongue of the slander shall be forever still. The study of God's works, so magnificent, so infinite indeed, and therefore so humiliating to the beholder, is to contribute to this millennial result.

The Scriptures have an ultimate, and our object ought always to be to discover that ultimate truth, by all the lights which our Creator has given us. As the study of nature, in a right spirit, is one means of arriving at such truth, that study recommends itself by no ordinary consideration. We are commanded to consider the lilies of the field, how they grow; they toil not, neither do they spin, yet Solomon, in all his glory, was not arrayed like one of these! And is any one an infidel because he studies the things that are made? And especially when he studies those things with a sincere desire of learning, by that study, the invisible things of Him that made them -- even his eternal power and Godhead! The things that are made! What a study! What a source of pure, holy heavenly happiness to those who will study those things attentively, and industriously! It were a fault to present the heavenly principles of moral feelings, and moral duties in a garb so sombre, so cold, so forbidding, as to repel and chill the natural vivacity of youth. But, when we turn our attention to the things that are made, how inviting! how persuasive! how eloquent! The flowers of the garden, the lilies of the field, the violets and anemonies of the woods spread their charms, not so much to invite the bee to their nectaries, as to attract the intelligence of unsophisticated youth to the study of the excellencies of the Creator; every flower acquiring a tongue, and speaking in music, as sweet as their odors, the lessons of wisdom.

While we have these vast demonstrations, resting as it were on our very senses, who is there that does not feel a delightful awe? Who is there that does not spontaneously, and before he is aware of it, find himself prostrated in intellectual humility, before his Maker, in the essential act of adoration and worship. These emotions may be transient, may be stifled, but still they must have darted, at happy moments, through the hearts of almost every one of us."

In early life Dr. Locke was partial to the doctrines and modes of worship of the Quakers. He never attached himself formally, however, to any church; nor do I know that he ever determined on doing so, until about the period of his last illness, when he had decided upon joining the Episcopal Church. He had been impressed with a belief that he had a mission to perform for himself and others; and that was, to exhibit the power and goodness of God, through His works, in aid of revalation. We have seen how faithfully and ably he performed his allotted duty. But when he found that his energies were failing, and that his mission could no longer be efficiently continued, he decided upon resigning all into the hands of his Maker, knowing his own delinquencies would be canceled by the spotless perfections of One, to whom his soul could render unceasing glory.

Would to God he had lived and enjoyed health, long enough to have united himself with the church, and to have given to the world practical evidence of pure joy, associated with true, active piety. He had been a worshipper of every thing bearing the impress of an almighty hand, and should he have concentrated all his thoughts and feelings upon God, and his mediatorial sacrifices alone, how ecstatic and uncontrollable would have been his enjoyment. We have tried to appreciate the character of his mind, the goodness of his heart, and the value of his labors; we have had confidence in his integrity; we have sympathized with him in difficulty; and we should have rejoiced to have heard him depict his foretaste of heaven.

Already have I trespassed upon your time and patience; but still you will not be satisfied, unless I describe, briefly, the causes and nature of his illness.

The time he was inventing and constructing his magnetic clock may be considered his palmy days, although he had had, previous to that time, following severe and long continued mental labor, attacks of high irritation, or slight inflammation of the brain.

During the winter of 1849-'50, while the internal affairs of the Medical College of Ohio were being conducted quietly, harmoniously, and successfully, she was dragged into the arena of political warfare. The elements of attack became more deadly, and the asailants more numerous; in proporation to the nearness of triumph, Dr. Locke was removed from his professorship, and notwithstanding he was subsequently re-elected, the circumstances attending his removal preyed upon his spirits, weakened his energies, clouded his hopes, and he was never himself again.

In the sadness of his heart, and amid the gloom surrounding him, he wrote a letter declining an acceptance of the chair from which he had but recently been removed; but your speaker urged a re-consideration of his decision, and finally induced him to re-enter the school. Beyond this nothing was seen calculated to prevent his utter prostration.

He yielded to the persuasions of those whose best judgments and good wishes he had secured, but he remained unhappy. He has visited us at a late hour in the evening, and remained until he had unburdened himself of his deep grief, which was, frequently, not until after the hours of another day had been counted. He spoke of the college as of a froward child, to whose interests he had devoted all his faculties, and to whom he had given, without stint, his time, his means, and his kindest wishes; and there was a contagion in those bitter tears as they were seen coursing down his furrowed cheeks.

He resigned his professorship after about two years additional service, and removed to Lebanon, the academy in that place having been placed under his management. He had been induced to think that he might elevate the character of the school, by the introduction of some new branches of education, especially those adapted to the interests of the agriculturist. It seemed necessary, also, for the restoration of his sinking powers, that he should secure a degree of quietude, freedom from the excitements of a medical professorship, and a withdrawal from those scenes to which he could not recur without painful and depressing emotions. At different periods, during his residence at Lebanon, he visited our city. At one of these periods he was seized with a paroxysm of fever, associated with a high degree of cerebral and nervous excitement. After having been restored partially to health, he returned home; but the pure country atmosphere did not exert upon him its wonted invigorating influence.

In October, 1855, having resided in Lebanon about eighteen months, he returned with his family to the city. His increased failure of mind and body was apparent. He was pale and thin, his step was tremulous, exhaustion followed moderate exercise, and he became subject to severe and alarming paroxysms of asthmatic breathing, the action of the heart being greatly interrupted, and the whole subsiding in a degree of stupor.

From the time his health became permanently and perceptibly impaired, he would frequently fall asleep, for a moment, while in conversation, without seeming conscious of it on awaking.

Being deeply interested in his welfare, his medical adviser urged him to withdraw from care and labor, and seek advantage from traveling, and from sojourning for a time on the Atlantic coast. On former occasions he had derived benefit from Geological excursions, and, instead of following the above advice, decided upon going to Virginia, to complete an examination and survey of some coal lands he had undertaken some time previously. The weather was unfavorable; the streams were high, the earth was wet and muddy, good lodgings could not always be procured, food was mostly unsuitable, and hunger was often the only friend near. Under these discouraging circumstances it is not surprising that after an abscence of five weeks, making his examinations on foot, Dr. Locke should have returned with indisposition greatly increased.

At first, after his return, his condition seemed to be that of exhaustion, following excessive mental and physical effort, although the volume and strength of pulse might have led to other inquiries. His general appearance was that of anemia, associated with paucity of blood. For a week, perhaps, after his return, he made occasional calculations from his field notes, wrote a few pages, examined some specimens he had recently collected in natural history, and recorded, for his own satisfaction, and for future use, the prescriptions of his medical attendants.

A very distressing condition now became a leading one -- an inability to keep awake longer than a few minutes at a time whether engaged in conversation, or in taking food. During the sleeping periods, breathing was labored and irregular, or wholly suspended. He was roused by a sense of suffocation, as in extreme asmatic conditions, or dropsy of the chest. The liver was greatly enlarged, and prominent even to the eye, and continued so more or less, until within a few days before his death. His inferior extremities became very much distended by dropsy, but returned to nearly their natural size toward the close of life. The remembrance of names became gradually obliterated, faces were not recognized, vision grew dim, paralysis disabled the upper and lower extremities of the right side, unconsciousness supervened and continued four or five days, when, July 10, 1856, and at the age of 64, death terminated his sufferings.

An examination was subsequently made. His brain was much above the average in size, weight, and depth of its convolutions. A portion of the left hemisphere was softened, and without decided evidences of active inflammation; water was found in both cavities of the chest; but, from the fact that the respiratory murmur was distinctly and loudly heard, from the base to the apex of his immense lungs, and that not a spot of dullness was indicated by percussion, it was inferred that the deposit took place a short time before death. The fullness and strength of pulse, which continued during the almost entire progress of the case, was accounted for by this examination. The heart and its blood-vessels were free from disease, but larger, much larger, naturally, than any ever before observed by those engaged in the examination. One, whose opportunities for observation has been extensive, exclaimed, "His aorta is as large as that of an ox."

Laying aside technical expressions, and technical interpretations, it may be said, that there had been such a breaking up, as it were, of the great nervous centers, such a weakening of the very essence of vitality, the great machine could no longer be kept in motion. And thus, day after day, was it our melancholy privilege to behold a widely expanded intellect gradually fading away from earth, to enter a brighter eternity.

In the death of Dr. Locke the world has lost a philosopher, science a tireless and original thinker, the medical profession a cautious and wise observer, and the Queen City a bright jewel from her diadem. May his virtues and worth be cherished in our hearts forever.

DR. ROBERT G. WILEY

Dr. Robert G. Wiley was born in Fryeburg, Nov. 11, 1811. After attending to the studies pertaining to a profession, he commenced the study of medicine under Dr. Ira Towle, of Fryeburg, and subsequently under Dr. John Grover, of Bethel. Under their instruction he had an excellent opportunity of becoming familiar with the different phases under which disease constantly presents itself and under which the experienced physician is instantly called upon to express his judgment. He was thus prepared to enter at once upon the duties of his profession.

Having attended the medical Lectures at Brunswick and there being an opening at Bethel, in consequence of the election of Dr. Moses Mason as a member of Congress, he commenced the practice of medicine in Bethel in 1835.

Earnest in his profession then, as now, he could be seen at that time on horseback, with his saddlebags behind him wending his way into every inhabited recess within his circuit of practice. Dr. Wiley has been more exclusively devoted to his profession than is the lot of most men. When not in duty he is always at home in the enjoyment of his family. He engages in no public matters. His horse is harnessed wherever a call is made for his services and away he rides, and so it has been incessantly for a quarter of a century. It would seem as though he had had enough amid the storms of wind, snow and rain to wear the hair off from a bear, but the Doctor still holds good apparently for another quarter of a century.

A large book filled with incidents of domestic life could be written from the doctor's experience as a physician. In consequence of this devotion to his profession he has secured an extensive practice and enjoys the confidence of a large circle of friends.

In Oct. 17th, 1835, he was married to Miss Abigail B., daughter of the late Col. Thaddeus Twitchell of Bethel, with whom he can soon enjoy a silver wedding. Their course of life has been shaded by the sudden death of several of their children. The Doctor has resided for many years on the pleasant spot formerly occupied by Dr. John Grover, a mile and a quarter west of the village, where he has a small lot of excellent land which he keeps in the highest state of cultivation, and from which he obtains a bountiful annual harvest.

WM. WILLIAMSON, M. D.

Dr. Wm. Williamson, son of John Williamson, was born in Manor Hamilton, Ireland, Sept. 22, 1812; at the age of nine years his parents came to America, and have resided most of the time in Bethel.

William, manifesting an inclination for study, was sent to the High school in 1835 and subsequently to the Academy in Bethel and then commenced the study of Medicine under B. C. Mulvey of Saco, and graduated at the Medical School in Brunswick in 1847. He practiced medicine about two years in Saco, and then removed to Bethel and settled at Middle Intervale where his father resides. Since that time he has been deeply engaged in agricultural pursuits. The practice of medicine has never seemed to be congenial with his feelings, and he has given his services of eight years only when he could avoid it.

DR. JOSHUA FANNING

Joshua Fanning, son of James Fanning, was born in Suffolk Co., Long Island, N.Y., March 9th, 1797. For several years he attended school with an eminent teacher, L. E. Eidenbrott, where he acquired a good English and Classical education. Having determined on the choice of the medical profession, he entered the office of David Hozack, M. D., an eminent physician and professor of N. York City, and graduated at the Columbia Medical College in 1819. His opportunities for witnessing hospital practice were excellent. Under such Professors as De Witt, S. T. Mitchell, David Hozack, W. Post, Valentine Mott, J. W. Francis, names familiar to the profession as household words, the student could not fail of receiving such lessons as would prove of the greatest value to him in subsequent life. He commenced practice at Sag Harbor on Long Island, where he remained till 1854. After spending a year in Ohio, he was engaged in lumbering operations in Oxford Co., Maine, in which we suspect he was not so successful as in the practice of medicine. In 1857 he settled at Bethel and entered upon the practice of his profession. In Jan. 1820, he was married to Miss Alma Tuttle of River-head, Long Island. Dr. Fanning is enjoying a good practice and has acquired the confidence of a large number of patrons.

DR. OZMON M. TWITCHELL

Son of Joseph Twitchell, was born in Bethel, June 29th, 1819. After attending school more or less during his minority at Gould's Academy, he entered the office of his brother, Dr. Almon Twitchell. He also attended lectures at the Medical College in Hanover, N.H., and Woodstock, Vt.

He settled in Milan, N.H., in 1846. There being no physician near, and the country being comparatively new and sparsely settled, his rides were often quite extensive. On Sept. 2d, 1849, he was married to Miss Rosalba D. Chandler of Milan. In 1854 and 5, he was elected a Representative to the Legislature of N. Hampshire. For many years he has been a Justice of the Peace, and Notary Public. On the death of his brother, Dr. A. Twitchell, he removed to Bethel in the fall of 1859, and is now engaged in the practice of his profession.

This closes the catalogue of practising Physicians in Bethel. They have all been successful in their profession and have gained the confidence of the community. Quackery has had as little hold on this as any community with which we are acquainted. The people as a whole are too inteligent to be duped by those traveling pretenders who make great promises, great charges, and no cures.

Quite a number of Physicians were born and reared in this town who have practiced medicine elsewhere.

The first medical student who was raised in town was Dr. James Ayer. He studied medicine with Dr. Timothy Carter, and married Thirza, daughter of Moses Mason, settled in Newfield, and died Jan. 1834.

John Barker, M. D., was born in Massachusetts, but spent his early years in Bethel. He studied medicine under Dr. Carter and settled in Wilton, Me. He received an honorary degree of M. D., at Brunswick Med. College in 1846, and died in New York City where he was residing with his son, Prof. J. Fordyce Barker.

Dr. Chas. Stearns son of Chas. Stearns, studied medicine with Dr. J. Grover and settled in St. George.

Dr. Leander Gage was the son of Amos Gage, one of the first settlers in the town. Having studied medicine with Dr. Timothy Carter of Bethel he settled in Waterford where he was for many years a prominent physician and where he died.

Dr. Cullen Carter, son of Dr. T. Carter whom we have formerly noticed, settled in New York city where he still resides.

Dr. Amos Roberts was born in Bethel, now Hanover, and having graduated at Brunswick Medical College, settled in Rumford, where he now resides.

Dr. Zenas Bartlett, son of Elhanan Bartlett, was born in Bethel, now Hanover, graduated at Brunswick Medical College and is now settled in Dixfield where he has an extensive practice.

Dr. Samuel Birge Twitchell, son of Ezra Twitchell, graduated at Dartmouth College and subsequently graduated at Geneva Medical College, and commenced the practice of medicine in Wakefield, N. H. and died in Bethel in 1855.

Dr. Elias Bartlett, son of Ebenezer Bartlett, was born in Bethel, graduated at Brunswick Medical College and settled in Wilton, where he still resides.

Dr. Wm. Twitchell, son of Eli Twitchell, studied medicine with Dr. J. Lincoln of Brunswick, and graduated at Brunswick Medical College and settled in Cayuga Co., New York.

Dr. Chas. Russell, son of James Russell, studied medicine with Dr. R. G. Wiley, and settled at W. Paris, where he now resides.

Dr. J. Henry B. Frost, son of Rev. Chas. Frost, graduated at Amherst College and subsequently in a Medical College in Philadelphia and is now practicing in Bangor.

Dr. J. T. L. Kimball, son of John Kimball, graduated at Woodstock Medical College and is now practicing in Saco.

Dr. Benj. W. Kimball, son of Israel Kimball, graduated at Brunswick Medical College and has been engaged as agent for several years among the Indian Tribes in Washington Territory.

Chapter 17
Lawyers

In the early history of the town there was but little occasion for the services of the lawyer. Justices of the Peace were usually considered sufficiently competent to settle all matters of difference among the citizens. The first lawyer who came to Bethel for the purpose of a settlement was

WILLIAM FRYE

We extract from the Sermon of Rev. E. A. Buck at his funeral, his obituary record:

"The subject of the following obituary notice, William Frye, Esq., was born in Fryeburg, of this State, May 12, 1796. He was the youngest child of Richard and Sarah Frye. His grandfather, from whom the town of his nativity derived its name, was a general of distinction in the Revolutionary War. His early studies, in which, as may be inferred from his subsequent life, he was chiefly distinguished for accuracy, were prostrated in the academy of Fryeburg under preceptor Cook. As an evidence of his proficiency, he obtained the prize at the academy for a Latin Poem at the early age of fifteen. After having become fitted for an advance standing in college, eager for the active duties of life, he entered at once upon the studies of his profession, a step which in subsequent life he greatly regretted, regarding a thorough collegiate course as highly valuable for every profession and especially so for that on which he had entered. Having chosen the law for his profession, he commenced and prosecuted his studies at Fryeburg under the direction of Judge Dana and Mr. Chase. In the fall of 1820, not long after having been admitted to the bar, he decided upon settlement in Bethel, as a place whose situation gave promise of favorable circumstances for the honorable pursuit of his profession. In Sept. 1828, he was married to Miss Lois Twitchell. From the first, highly esteemed by those who were so happy as to form his acquaintance, ere many years the confidence of his fellow citizens was evinced by his election to town offices, in which he served first as one of the selectmen, and subsequently as town clerk for the period of six years. But the value of his services were known and appreciated beyond the bounds of his ordinary practice. Twice he received the appointment of County Attorney. Twice he was sent as Representative to the Legislature and twice was chosen a member of the Senate of the State. From 1852 as regularly appointed School Commissioner, he visited each town in the County laboring to promote the cause of public education. Thus for the space of eighteen years he served to general acceptance in these several stations of public life.

His interest in the cause of education was ever prominent. Viewing it as a bulwark of our free institutions, he sought not simply for the education of his own children and those in the more immediate circle of his friends, but to open facilities for the general diffusion of knowledge. As a Trustee of the Academy in Bethel, he served faithfully as Secretary of that board from the foundation of the instutution to the time of his decease.

At the age of thirteen he was drafted as a soldier in the war with Great Britain. On his arrival at Portland he was seized with a fever and returned home, probably satisfied with his experience in military life.

As a lawyer, the departed was highly and justly esteemed. He was preeminently a peace maker. He discouraged litigation, even where there were prospects of large gain to himself, if it would incite to or encourage prosecution. His clients not only looked to him with confidence for advice, but entrusted to him any and every secret with the assurance that their confidence would not be betrayed. Feeling judicious and safe, it was as a counsellor that he excelled. Possessed of that integrity and cautiousness, which though not the prominent characteristics of those who excel before the jury, are on the whole essential to a client's interests, he became one who was most highly esteemed by those to whom he was best known. Having continued his habits of study through life, and having now attained the full maturity of his mind, being possessed of an extensive experience and excelling in accuracy as a scribe, as a lawyer he held a position which another will not be able soon to fill.

As a citizen he was always interested in whatever he regarded as conductive to the public good. He even gave counsel to the town free of charge and in like manner discharged other public labors. He ever encouraged whatever was calculated to elevate society and deprecated that which was injurious. Of marked sobriety, he also preserved an equanimity of character, not always to be met with in the arena of political life, or in those harassed by the annoyances of vexed legal questions. No profane words from his lips pained the Christian's ear, or corrupted the morals of society or bespoke a spirit with in regardless of the devine claims. Pure minded and upright in his intercourse with others, he sought to cultivate the same characteristics in those around him. Courteous in all his dealings, he won the respect of strangers, confirmed the love of his friends and soon disarmed his enemies, if any such he had."

William Frye

Mr. Frye was a man of sedentary habits. He was seldom seen elsewhere than in his office or at his home. He was never seen lounging about the stores or public places of resort, but was always ready to tender his services whenever needed. This sedentary disposition probably undermined his constitution gradually, and a chronic disease of the stomach troubled him for several years, till he was suddenly taken sick and almost before his neighbors knew of his danger he was dead. This occurred Feb. 18th, 1854.

JOEL C. VIRGIN

Mr. Frye remained without a competitor till the year 1834, when he was confronted by an individual who subsequently became notorious for his thievish propensities. We would gladly omit his name from our history, but perhaps it may, by way of contrast, exhibit in clearer light the good qualities of other members of the legal profession.

Joel C. Virgin was born somewhere in New Hampshire, fitted for and entered Dartmouth College where he remained through his Sophomore year when he left and commenced the study of law. After admittance to the bar he came to Bethel in 1834. He remained here about three years and became a vagabond. His strongest propensity seemed to be that of stealing. We had the misfortune to be his room mate while in Bethel, and strangely our limited supply of money found its way out of our pockets without our consent. Still it was not for years afterwards that we mistrusted what become of it. So strong had this propensity become that he would often pilfer things that did not seem to be of any importance to him. Consequently he was frequently brought before public officers, and the last we heard of him he was in the State Prison at Charlestown, in Mass.

MOSES B. BARTLETT

Moses B. Bartlett, son of Barbour Bartlett, was born in Bethel, and after fitting for college in Gould's Academy, he graduated at Bowdoin College in 1842. After teaching a High School for a season in Brunswick, he commenced the study of Law in the office of Wm. Frye, Esq., and settled in Bethel till 1848, when he removed to Norway and subsequently to Waterford. His practice was quite lucrative, but being anxious to acquire more he removed to Wyandotte City, Kansas, where he now resides.

O'NEIL W. ROBINSON, ESQ

O'Neil W. Robinson, son of O'Neil W. Robinson, Esq., of Waterford, was born in Bethel, July 17, 1824. He graduated at Bowdoin College in

1845, and entered the office of Hon. Elbridge Gerry, of Waterford. He was admitted to the Oxford Bar and commenced the practice of his profession at Bethel in 1848. Among his other duties he practices celibacy.

RICHARD A. FRYE, ESQ

Richard A. Frye is the eldest son of the late Wm. Frye, Esq. He was born in Bethel, July 22, 1829. Having attended school at the Academy in Bethel for several years, he commenced the study of law with his father, and was admitted to the Oxford Bar in 1855, and settled at Bethel Hill where he has an extensive practice. With habits much like those of his father he can be found in his office at almost any hour of the day. He was married to Esther K. Martin, of Rumford, Dec. 19, 1854.

SAML F. GIBSON, ESQ

Samuel F. Gibson, son of Samuel Gibson, Esq., was born in Denmark. He graduated at Bowdoin College in 1844, studied law in the office of Howard and Shepley, of Portland, and was admitted to the Cumberland Bar in 1846. After spending a year in Patten and two in California, he settled in Bethel in 1851, where he now is engaged in the practice of his profession in company with David Hammons. He was married to Miss Abb Gibson, June 1, 1851.

HON. DAVID HAMMONS

David Hammons was born in Cornish, May 12, 1808. Having pursued the studies preliminary to the study of law at Limerick Academy, he entered the office of Hon. David Goodenow, of Alfred, and was admitted to the Oxford Bar and settled in Lovell, Maine. He was elected member of Congress for Oxford District in 1848. At the expiration of his term he resided a few years at Cornish, and then removed to Bethel in 1859, where he has resumed the practice of law. He was married to Miss Martha O'Brien, Sept. 29, 1839.

We believe that the duties of the legal profession are honorably discharged by the members of the profession resident here, and that they possess the confidence of the community. Their aim seems to be to become good counsellors rather than wordy pleaders; and we are not aware that they have ever been accused of falling into the habit of encouraging litigation where a difficulty could be amicably settled.

Chapter 18

Ministers

REV. DANIEL GOULD

The town had been visited by ministers of the Congregationalist, Calvinist Baptist, and Methodist denominations before the close of the last century, and it was about the year of its close that these three denominations made such organizations as enabled them to have regular preaching.

Rev. Daniel Gould was the first settled minister in town. He was born in Topsfield, Mass., Dec. 8th, 1753, and was baptized the next day. His father was Dea. Daniel Gould. He was a man of considerable property, and died when his son was fourteen years old.

Daniel was desirious of obtaining a liberal education, but his guardians opposed him in his inclinations, and refused to furnish the means, and as he was of a feeble constitution, they apprenticed him three years to a shoe maker. During his apprenticeship he spent his leisure moments in fitting for college. Like many others who have acquired an education and distinction, he regarded his minutes as golden moments to be improved as they passed along. Many, no doubt, were the discouragements that beset the student shoemaker as he stumbled over difficulties in his desire for an education. In this way he pursued his studies and his apprenticeship, till he was nearly fitted for college. Before entering college he spent a short time in completing his preparations in Byefield with Rev. Mr. Moody.

As a student he appears to have sustained a respectable rank as a linguist, and especially as a mathematician. He appears to have maintained a fondness for mathematics till late in life. We have in our possession his calculations for the great eclipse of 1806. The figures and plans are very neatly executed.

He also assisted Prof. Williams of Harvard College in calculating the Solar Eclipse of 1782, of which he left on record a written account. He also has left observations on a Lunar Eclipse in 1790. Among his text books are standard works on Astronomy and Mathematics.

He wrote a neat hand, and was fond of inserting his name in his text books with some moral precept, sometimes done in rhyme. He entered Harvard College in 1778 and graduated in 1782 in a class of thirty five. Among his classmates was Stephen Van Rensselaer, of New York.

Pursuing his course as he did during the exciting times of the Revolution, it was not a little to his credit that he should pursue and graduate without being interrupted in his studies.

Immediately after his graduation he was connected with the Continental Army, in all, about a year, till peace was declared. He was then employed as a teacher in many places for a period of twelve or fifteen years. He studied theology with his former preceptor, Rev. Mr. Moody, of Byefield. His name is not found on the church records of Topsfield. There was a vacancy in the ministry in his native town for many years, and it is probable that he united with the church during that time. There is a record of the admission of Daniel Gould and wife into the church Dec. 7, 1783, but my informant thinks that he was not married at that date, and that it must have been another.

We do not find any record of the time when or where he was licensed to preach. He came to Bethel and preached as a candidate for settlement in 1798-9. Rev. Caleb Bradbury who has outlived several generations of ministers was also a candidate for settlement. On a vote of the Parish, Mr. Gould had a majority of one vote; a division arose in the parish and several united with the Baptists. He was ordained in Massachusetts, previous to this settlement in Bethel, and was installed over the Congregationalist Church and Parish, in October 1799. The sermon was preached by Rev. Wm. Fessenden of Fryeburg.

The Church voted to give him one hundred and fifty dollars as a settlement at his installation, and to raise one hundred and sixty dollars for his safety, and that ten dollars be added each year till it reached two hundred dollars, which was afterwards to be his regular salary. His wood was also to be furnished gratutiously by the people.

Such was the apparently small beginning of ministerial effort at that time, but which was, perhaps, a greater effort on the part of the people, than is demanded of the same parish at the present time.

Mr. Gould's ministry does not appear to have been altogether a happy one. Influences that were brought to bear against him at the time of his settlement seemed to increase during his ministry in Bethel. He continued as pastor till 1809 when he was dismissed. Still the town is much indebted to Mr. Gould for its character. He opened a school for young men in his own house where they could resort and fit for college or for a profession. Many who have since distinguished themselves availed themselves of his instruction. In this way he developed the educational interests of the town, far beyond that of most towns at that time. He is represented as having indulged in good humor and wit which was

Rev. Daniel Gould

thought by some to have given him too great levity of manner for the ministry. Twenty-nine persons united with the church in Bethel during his ministry.

His college text books were all preserved by him and are now deposited in Gould's Academy. College studies and disipline were quite as severe at that time as now, as may be seen by the various annotations made by himself during that period.

He continued to reside in Bethel till 1815 when he removed to Rumford where he was installed pastor of the church there May 31, 1814. He continued pastor for several years till old age compelled him to resign. He is still remembered, holding his sermon close to his eyes, from which he never removed it till it was finished.

We have heard many anecdotes of him during his residence in Bethel, though few of them are worthy of record.

It is said that one of his hearers expostulated with him for making such long prayers in church. "Well, then, if you are tired, sit down," was his reply.

As a neighbor he was peaceable. On a certain occasion he had lost his corn, and though he had the strongest presumptive evidence who was the thief, he refused to move a step, but simply replied, "He will be his own greatest tormentor."

On a certain occasion a parishioner came to him to pay his tax, but not being able to advance the money, it was proposed that he should give his note. As Mr. Gould commenced writing "For value received," "That is not true," said the parishoner, "I have not received any value." Mr. Gould instead of being offended, laughed heartily and gave him his tax, as he belonged to another denomination.

He was neat in his personal appearance. In his cocked hat, black silk gown, and breeches, he was able to show the dignity of his position. With his chaise, the first in town, he had certainly advantages over his less fortunate people. The social element was strong in him, and his fund of anecdotes was inexhaustible. On a certain occasion he was present at a "raising," and as was the custom of the day, he made a prayer just before the broadsides were erected. After the building was up and the toddy passed round, he turned to the owner who was a young married man, and proposed a sentiment, "May you live and enjoy many years of prosperity, and, I *like* to have said, may you have a hundred children."

In making his will he made a bequest to the Academy in Bethel, on condition that it should be named after him. Unfortunately, but a part of what was supposed to belong to the Institution was ever realized. The fund so received is to be devoted to the purpose of paying the teacher for his services.

He was first married to Miss Mary Booth of Topsfield. She died previous to his coming to Bethel. He lived in Bethel in the house built by Lieut. Jonathan Clark, which is still standing. He married for his second wife, Mrs. Eunice Perley, of Boxford, Mass. She lived in Bethel during her husband's ministry, and died in Rumford. He married for his third wife Widow Anna Rawson of Paris, who still survives him and resides in Andover, Me. He never had any children. For sometime previous to his death he was totally blind. He died in Rumford, suddenly, while at dinner, and was buried at Rumford Centre, near where he resided.

As a writer we have no means of judging. The only specimen in our possession is his account of Lieut. Segar's Captivity, which was copied by him, but which could give no just clues to his powers. His theology and sermons probably were after the style of the day in which he lived.

There is an accurate portrait of him, taken when he was 82 years of age, now in possession of a nephew in Topsfield. It is to be hoped that Gould's Academy may yet come in possession of it. His nearest surviving relations are nephews and nieces residing in his native town.

I have found much difficulty in collecting all the important facts of his history but hope that this sketch will lead others to furnish the author with such information respecting him as may be inserted in an appendix at the close of the volume.

REV. CHARLES FROST

The history of every town presents the character of some men who have held a prominent position in the affairs of Church and State for many years. Such was the case in the biography of the man in this chapter.

Rev. Charles Frost was born in Limerick, Me., Jan. 12, 1796. He was the son of Moses Frost who was born June 3d, 1766, and of Sally McKenney, who was born Mar. 10th, 1766. They were united in marriage Apr. 15th, 1790. They had nine children, among whom Charles was the fourth.

Mr. Frost spent a portion of his earlier years in Gorham, Me., when he attended the Academy. He studied with reference to the ministry under the Rev. Asa Rand, Pastor of the Congregationalist Church in Gorham, and was licensed to preach by the Cumberland Association at a meeting held at Gorham, Nov. 14th, 1820.

From a diary which he kept for several years during the first part of his ministry, it appears that he preached his first sermon in Bethel, five days after he received his license, Nov. 19, 1820. His text was in Hebrews, 9th chapter, 27th verse. One who was present on that occasion described him as a young man of twenty-four years of age, youthful in appearance and exceedingly modest in demeanor, who at first sight would not have impressed strangers in his favor, but who soon obtained a strong hold upon the affections of the people with whom he had come to labor. After supplying the desk six Sabbaths he returned to Gorham where he continued to preach, and at other places, till March 25th, when he again returned to Bethel where he continued his labors till his death.

At a legal meeting of the Congregational Church in the West Parish of Bethel, held Nov. 5th, 1821, it was voted to extend an invitation to Mr. Charles Frost to become Pastor of said church. A Council was called which met at the house of Dea. Samuel Barker, consisting of the following persons: -- Rumford -- Rev. Daniel Gould, Dea. Hezekiah Hutchins. Bath -- Rev. John W. Ellingwood, Ammi R. Mitchell. Otisfield -- Rev. Josiah G. Merrill, Wm. Spurr. No. Yarmouth -- Rev. Asa Cummings, Dea. Jacob Mitchell. Waterford -- Rev. A. Douglass, Dea. Moses Treadwell. Paris -- Rev. Joseph Walker, Dea. Daniel Stowell. Turner -- Rev. Allen Greely, Dea. Martin Bradford. Gorham -- John T. Smith. Bridgton -- Aaron Beaman.

It is worthy of remark that a long journey was necessary to reach Bethel through the woods in those days. The ordination was held in the meeting house, Feb. 20th, 1822. The sermon was delivered by Rev. John W. Ellingwood of Bath.

The minister immediately entered upon his labors as pastor. He had discriminating minds among his people, and a Society that was regular in its attendance upon his ministry. With a theological library of limited size, he was compelled to draw his arguments more directly from the Bible itself, which gave a simple yet effective style to his preaching.

It was my privilege to listen to him as a preacher during the year 1835, after he had been settled over his church and people thirteen years. His congregation nearly filled the house. Among them were many who were among the oldest settlers in the town, while a large number consisted of young people, who presented a most interesting appearance at that time. It was an audience of more than ordinary intellectual character. His appearance in the desk was solemn. He arrested the attention of his hearers by a clear and argumentative exposition of his subject which he divided and subdivided so as to be easily comprehended. I remember on one occasion he commenced his sermon by introducing his peroration or close of his sermon first. This was done in the most impressive manner, and a death like stillness reigned over the house. He then proceeded with his text and argument and dismissed his audience who could not fail to be strongly impressed with his subject.

During his ministry the church received additions from year to year, but it was in the year 1839, when there was a powerful revival, and many individuals embracing a large number of intelligent and interesting young people united with the church.

During his ministry one hundred and twenty-nine persons united with the church. His relations with the church were generally pacific until the year 1843, when it was decided to build a new church in the village and form a new society on the north side of the river. Though he took but a secondary part in the matter it seriously affected him as all such transactions must do.

His health, which was never very strong, began to give way. Dyspepsia was a troublesome attendant on him. During the year 1849 he lost two of his children from ship fever which had been introduced into his family, and the other members together with himself were sufferers from it, from which he never recovered. He gradually failed in health and preached but a few times in the new church in the village. His last effort was in a few remarks which he made at the Sabbath School Convention, held at Bethel a short time before his death.

It was my lot to watch with him during the last night of his sickness. He was very feeble, though not conscious that he was so near his end. He said but little and took his medicines without any remarks. His mind appeared to wander at times. Only once he roused up during that long silent night and enquired how the railroad, then building through the town, was progressing. When I reminded him that he could not continue long, he exhibited no emotion, and as I bid him goodbye for the last time in the morning, his eye kindled up and he earnestly wished me to call again. He died Feb. 11th, 1850, after a successful ministry over the same church for twenty-eight years. His funeral was attended by a large and mourning congregation of those who had grown up under his ministry. A sermon was preached by his co-laborer for the about the same length of time, Rev. J. Douglas of Waterford, who still survives him. He was married May 11th, 1819, to Miss Lydia Fernald, who was born Feb. 22nd, 1787, and died Aug. 27th, 1825. He was again married to Miss Lucinda M. S. Smith who was born in Scarborough, Dec. 19, 1794, and died in Bethel, Nov. 12th, 1859.

Mr. Frost exerted a powerful influence for the good of his people. In the church and in the educational interests of the town he was always ready to give his time and influence. His mind was rather inclined to a mathematical exactness in everything to which he directed his attention. Geometry was with him a favorite study, and he rightly judged it a valuable study for every young person who would cultivate precision in their mental operations. In person he was of medium height. His hair had become gray, and his eye was quite expressive. His voice was slightly tremulous which rather gave effect to his public performances.

He was remarkably uniform in his whole course of life, being neither greatly elated by success or depressed by discouragements. He commenced his labors over a society that had been but little favored with a settled minister for a period of eleven years, but by his uniform course of action he left it among the largest in this part of the State. His counsel was sought after among his brethren in the ministry and respected. Cautious, though not over and above conservative, his opinion was ever valuable.

A man who has the ability to direct the spiritual interests of a church and society so long is worthy of no ordinary record, and we pass his name down to posterity as one whose name is now honored by those who best knew him.

APPENDIX

We are under great obligations to our correspondent for the following information. It fills up some important data in the biography of Mr. Gould:

"Boxford, Sept. 15th, 1860.

Mr. Editor: While persuing the very interesting columns of the *Bethel Courier* of Aug. 31st, I saw a sketch of my Grand Uncle, Daniel Gould's, life. I was sorry to learn that among his large circle of Nephews and Nieces not one could give you the desired information, correctly I mean. I have before me the history of the Gould family written by him July 1815, and presented to my Grand Father, of which I will pen you an exact copy, *ver batim*.

Daniel Gould was born Dec. 8th, 1753. He obtained a public education at Cambridge, commenced a preacher of the gospel, and was first settled in the ministry at Bethel in the District of Maine, Oct. 9th, 1799; and was settled at Rumford in the same District, May 31, 1815. He married for his first wife Mary Booth, eldest daughter of George Booth of Hillsborough, N.H. She was born July 3d, 1751, and died Oct. 1st, 1785. They were married Dec. 24, 1782; their child Molly was born Sept. 28th, 1785, and died Dec. 4th that same year, thus in a short time he was stripped of his family like his father before him. On the 25th of Dec. 1788, he was married. He married Eunise Perley, a daughter of Stephen Foster of Andover, and relict of Jeremiah Perley of Topsfield, who was mortally wounded June 3d, 1784, in assisting Thomas Emerson of Topsfield in raising a barn frame and died the next morning, aged 35. She was born Sept. 15, 1753; he had no children. He still holds the patrimony on which the Gould family first settled when they first came to this country.

I will enclose a communication which I have just received from one of his nephews:

Died, at Rumford, Maine, on the 21st inst, Rev. Daniel Gould, in the ninetieth year of his age. He was born in Topsfield, Mass. in 1753, and has relatives now living there. He was pursuing his studies at the Drummer Academy in Newbury. At the commencement of the Revolutionary War, he obeyed the call of his country, went into the service at the commencement and continued there two years. He and his brother Samuel were in a company of guards under Gen. Major Lee. Upon leaving he completed his studies at Harvard University, in Cambridge where

he graduated in 1782. He then commenced the study of Divinity, and has for most of the time since been a minister of the gospel.
By a Relative, K.G.
Yours Respectfully,
L. A. F. Gould."

Rev. John H. Leland was born in Amherst, Mass., graduated at Amherst College and at Andover Theological Seminary, and was ordained at Sherburn, Mass. Soon after the death of Mr. Frost, an invitation was extended to Mr. Leland to be his successor. He accepted and was installed pastor of the Church and Parish, July 3rd, 1850. He remained till May 10th, 1853, when he was dismissed and returned to Massachusetts. He now resides at Amherst.

Rev. Edwin A. Buck, son of James Buck, of Bucksport, was born in that town, May 31st, 1824. After fitting for College at the Academy in Andover, he graduated at Yale College in 1849 and at Bangor Theological Seminary in 1852. He was ordained in Bethel, May 20th, 1854, and settled as pastor over the 1st Congregational Church. He continued in this relation till February, 1859, when he was dismissed. He was married to Miss Elmira R., daughter of Dean Walker, who was born in Aruendel Co., Md., Dec. 9th, 1825. They were married Jan. 19th, 1853. Soon after his dismissal from Bethel he removed to Slatersville, R.I., where he resides as pastor of a church.

His successor in Bethel is Rev. J. B. Wheelwright who thus far has furnished a temporary supply.

Rev. David Garland was the first settled minister over the 2nd Congregational Church in this town. He was the fourth son of Dea. John Garland of Newfield, in this State. He was born in Newfield, March 22, 1815. He graduated at Amherst College, and subsequently at the Andover Theological Seminary. He was married to Miss Mary Elizabeth Twitchell, daughter of the late Col. Thadeus Twitchell, Sept. 17th, 1849, who was born Jan. 10th, 1821. He was ordained pastor of the 2nd Church, Aug. 15th, 1849. Mr. Garland has been settled longer over the same society than any other in the association with which he is connected.

Elder Daniel Mason was born in Stratham, N. H. in 1781. His early advantages were exceedingly limited, but possessing a good share of common sense and having experienced religion, he resolved to enter the ministry. He was ordained in Freeport, Me., Oct. 9, 1811, and preached for a time in the Calvinist Baptist Church in Bethel in 1818, and continued its pastor for seventeen years, till his death, which occurred Apr. 6th, 1835, aged 54. He had three wives. The first two were sisters by the name of Robinson. His last wife was the widow Mary Merrill, a native of England. Though an illiterate man, yet he seems to have been a man of strong common sense. He was strongly attached to the Jeffersonian School of Politics, in which he took a deep interest. Being a cooper by trade he earned his living by the labor of his hands, and by preaching on the Sabbath without any great hope of an earthly reward.

Calvinist Baptist

The first minister of this denomination was Rev. John Chadbourne, who was ordained an Evangelist at Cornish, Me., in 1798. How long he continued to preach in Bethel I do not know. He appears to have been an itinerant and the church did not increase under his ministry.

EBENEZER BRAY

Rev. Ebenezer Bray was ordained pastor of the Calvinist Baptist Church in Bethel in 1807 and continued as such till 1812, when he was dismissed and removed to Canada, where he died.

REV. ARTHUR DRINKWATER

When a licentiate, preached more or less in Bethel from 1812 till 1816, when he was ordained pastor of a church in Mt. Vernon. He is one of the most respected ministers of the denomination in the State.

ELDER DANIEL MASON

A sketch was given of Elder Mason in our last chapter. I learn from the *History of the Maine Baptists* that he was licensed to preach by the church in Fayette in 1811, and was ordained an evangelist by the same church, in 1812. He officiated as pastor of the church in Freeport from 1813 to 1816, and in the church in Bethel from 1818 till his death in 1835.

ELDER BENJAMIN DONHAM

Benjamin Donham was born in Hebron and was ordained pastor of the Baptist church in Bethel in 1836, and continued its pastor for ten years. He removed to some town in Penobscot County, where he died suddenly of cancer in the stomach.

Mr. Donham was succeeded by Elders -- Mitchell, Levi Burnham and David Holley each of whom remained but a short time, till they were succeeded by --

REV. WM. BEAVINS

Who was born in the Parish of Camerton, County of Cumberland, England, Nov. 21, 1819. He lived the most of the time in the adjoining town of Workington. His parents were engaged in a crockery store in which the son was employed. In 1837 he united with the church and at the age of 20 was licensed to preach. He labored as a licentiate for four or five years when he emigrated to America in 1843. He was first settled in the State in Waterboro where he remained two years. He came to Bethel in July 1857, where he has since been the successful pastor of the Baptist church.

In Sept. 1844, he was married to Miss Caroline Brown of Lisbon, Ct., who died in Springfield, Mass., Oct. 1847. In Sept. 1848, he was again married to Miss Mary A. Southwick of Dover, N. H.

Elder Samuel Haselton was born in Windham, N.H. Aug. 8th, 1781, and learned the trade of blacksmith. He did not enjoy the early advantages of an education, but served his time as an apprentice in Methuen, Mass. At the age of twenty he made a profession of religion and united with the Congregational church in Methuen. A few years after he united with the Freewill Baptist Church in Adams, now Jackson, N. H. He commenced preaching in Bartlett and was ordained there Nov. 23, 1819, by Elders Daniel Elkins and Joshua Quimby. He remained in Jackson and Bartlett till the year 1836, when he removed to Bethel. There were several interesting revivals during his residence there and under his preaching in other places.

One of the most interesting episodes in the life of Elder Haselton occurred at the time of the destruction of the Willey family by a slide in the White Mts., Aug. 28th, 1826. I quote the following from Willey's *Incidents in White Mountain History*. It describes the funeral services on that occasion and to those who are familiar with that event, and who know Elder Haselton, their imagination can easily shadow forth something of the scene as here quoted.

"All these bodies, after suitable time to make coffins from materials such as could be obtained there, were made ready for burial. It was decided to bury them near the house of their recent habitation, and let them remain there till they could be more conveniently moved to Conway the succeeding winter. One common wide grave was dug for them, and they were placed in its margin, to remain till the befitting and accustomed prayer at burial was performed. That prayer was made by a personal friend of my brother, and one who often ministered in holy things. The prayer was suited to the occasion, coming from a kind, sympathizing, pious heart. It was impressive as it came from the good man's lips; and then its impressiveness was greatly increased from the circumstances under which it was made. In the echoes that were awakened by his voice, the very mountains around us seemed to join with him in describing the majesty of God, and imploring his mercy on our stricken hearts. When, with slow and distinct utterance, the minister, at the commencement of his prayer, referred to the magnificence of the Deity, as described by the Prophet Isiah, saying, 'Who hath measured the waters in the hollow of his hand, and meted out heaven with a span, and comprehended the dust of the earth in a measure, and weighed the mountains in scales, and the hills in a balance,' the echo gave back every word of this sublime description in a tone equally clear and solemn with that in which they were first uttered. The effect of all this was soul stirring beyond description. I shall never forget the tears and sorrows that marked the faces of many that stood around that open grave, on that solemn occasion. The minister who made that prayer was Elder Samuel Haselton, then of Bartlett, now living in Bethel. After the prayer we buried the bodies, --

'And then, one summer evening's close,
We left them to their last repose.'

It was dark before the burial was completed, and we were compelled to spend the night in the house so lately left by the buried family."

He married for his first wife Alice Bodwell of Methuen, Mass., and for his second wife, Miss Mary Tasket of Bartlett. She died Dec. 21, 1858, aged 72. Elder Haselton, at the age of nearly fourscore, is still living with his son in Bethel.

REV. ZENAS THOMPSON

The *Gospel Banner* is publishing a series of sketches of the clergymen of its denomination, in this State. In the last issue, we find the following notice of Rev. Zenas Thompson, of Bethel:

"He was born in Auburn, Me., Dec. 30, 1804, and preached his first sermon in Unity, Me. He preached in Norway and vicinity about a year, in 1825, and then in Hampden and Frankfort, two years, and thence he removed to Farmington, where he labored five years. He then lived in Saccarappa, and preached there, and in Westbrook and in North Yarmouth, three years and a half, and he then removed to Lowell, Mass., where he labored with great success two years and a half. He accepted a call to Newmarket, N.H., where he remained two years, whence he removed to Chicopee, Mass., where he labored two years, and then he returned to Maine, and preached in Bridgton two years, then in Augusta four years, and thence he removed to Bethel, where he has been five years.

For the last two years he has preached in all the region round about Bethel, and during the whole of his life, wherever he has lived, he has answered numerous calls, for every kind of ministerial labor, and has preached as many funeral, dedication, ordination and convention sermons, and performed as much extra labor, as almost any living clergyman. At one time he was editor of a denominational paper -- the *Christian Pilot*. He is a preacher of great logical power, and deep fervor, mighty in the Scriptures, and when fully aroused, is one of the ablest extemporaneous speakers and eloquent preachers, in any denomination, and there are few places in New England where either his voice has not been heard, or where those cannot be found, who trace their conversation, under God, to his labors.

He is an ardent lover of Nature, and few are the mountains, or streams, of any note, on whose beauty his eye has not rested, and where he has not stood, and looked through Nature, up to Nature's God. The genial spirit which renders him one of the most agreeable companions in the world, has been largely nourished thus.

He is now in the prime of life, 54 years of age, healthy, more earnest and devoted than ever, with the wisdom of experience acquired, and the enthusiasm of youth not lost, and is doing as much for Temperance, Freedom, Virtue, and the highest form of Christianity, as almost any laborers in the Gospel field."

His successor in Bethel is Rev. A. G. Gaines who was settled over the society in 1857.

REV. WM. R. CHAPMAN

Quite a number of ministers have been raised in this town, whose labors have been performed elsewhere. Among these was the chapter which I copy from the *Puritan Recorder*:

"William Rogers Chapman, son of William and Abigail Chapman, was born in Bethel, Maine, February 26, 1812. He was a moral and conscientious child and youth; but while pursuing his Academical studies, he was led by the Holy Spirit who blessed an early religious training, to feel the need of something better than outward morality, or even the activity which he gave to the cause of temperance, and kindred reforms -- even an inward change of the heart, and a new and a Christian life.

He had previously prepared for College, in 1831-32, under the care of the Rev. Jonas Burnham, at Bridgton, Me. After he became a Christian, his attention was turned to a preparation for the Christian ministry. He entered Bowdoin College in 1833, where he prosecuted his studies two years. He then joined the Junior Class in Dartmouth, where he graduated in 1837. For one or two terms he was an instructor in the Academies of Wakefield and Bethel. His Theological course was begun at Andover, and was completed at New Haven in 1840.

Thus being prepared in heart and in head to enter the ministry, he became the stated preacher, for a few months, of the congregation then worshipping in the Marlboro Chapel, Boston. A number of the church afterwards formed what was termed the Garden Street Chapel Church, in this city, over which Mr. Chapman was ordained as pastor in September, 1840. The first fruits of his ministry were abundant. During the first year one hundred and fifty persons were added to the church -- mostly by profession. After five years of labor in that field, a union of this church with the Green Street Church was effected, the union being called the Messiah Church; and Mr. Chapman became the Colleague Pastor, with the venerable and reverend Dr. Jenks.

In the year 1847, Mr. Chapman received and accepted a call from the Eight Street Church in New York City, formerly under that eminent preacher and divine, the Rev. John M. Mason, D.D. There were about twenty additions during his brief ministry in that field.

In that year 1849, says an intimate friend of his, from whom the writer has gained many facts, 'the subject of this notice, with his family, visited Europe, where they spent fifteen months traveling through Great Britain, and most of the interesting countries and cities on the Continent.' He formed the acquaintance of many distinguished divines, and in the city of Calvin (Geneva) his efforts for the formation of a Sabbath School will be remembered. On sea and on land, he was ever active in disseminating the word of life, in visiting the sailor and poor emigrant with sympathy, and in distributing the religious tract wheresoever there was an opportunity.

On the return of our lamented brother to his native land, he received several invitations to re-settle in the ministry; among which was one from Cooperstown, New York, and another from a Presbyterian Church in Aurora, Cayuga County, N. Y. Over the last named he was installed, Dec. 25, 1850. His labors were accompanied with the Holy Spirit, and many were added to the Church as the seal of his ministry. He was brought low there by sickness, and his life was despaired of for some time. He however recovered his health sufficiently to labor with his people until the spring of 1854.

In August of that year, Mr. Chapman removed to Hanover in this State, where, during a ministry of five months, he received 24 persons to the communion of the Second Congregational Church. The Sabbath school was greatly increased, and the infant congregation enlarged. On the 18th of January last, he was prostrated with the disease that brought him to his grave. After lingering through the winter, spring, and summer, enfeebled with an organic affection of the brain, he was seized on the last of October, while walking in the streets of Hanover with a paralytic shock. As his goods had been removed to his native home, where he was to have gone the preceeding day to spend the winter with his kindred, he was conveyed to the nearest house where, two days afterwards, or on Thursday afternoon, the 25th ult., he fell asleep in Jesus.

Though, from the nature of his disease, he could converse but little, yet on the last two days of his life he was enabled to express his love for all communions of Christians -- to commend his wife and three children to the covenant keeping God -- to desire that the youngest should be educated for the ministry, to express his delight in the Scriptures, and in some favorite hymns, like "Rock of Ages," etc. -- to send messages to all his friends and relatives to give directions in reference to his funeral -- to make the particular request, 'Bury me with my fathers' -- and to express his peaceful trust in his Saviour, so long as he was conscious.

Four clergymen were with Mr. Chapman when he calmly yielded his spirit to God who gave it, and two of them at his request -- Rev. Mr. Cutler, of the Episcopal Church, and Rev. Mr. Freeman of the Congregational Church -- conducted his funeral services, in the presence of a large and deeply-affected congregation. Again at Bethel, on the 29th ult., there were other funeral services, which were commenced with the baptism of his infant son, William Rogers, over his coffin. The little one was dedicated to God with many tears; and a prayer of his father, that his son might enter the ministry was not forgotten. The Sermon on the occasion was preached by Rev. Mr. Sewall, of South Paris, Me., from these suggestive and striking words: -- 'All things are yours.' He was married May 16, 1842, to Miss Emily J. Bishop, of New York.

The above is but a faint outline of the life and services of an earnest minister, and warm-hearted Christian friend. If his career was not eventful, it was crowned with useful ministerial labor. Yet he expressed to the writer, in his last days, very humble views of himself and of his efforts. To him, Christ was all.

F."

Rev. Lawson Carter, son of Dr. Timothy Carter, was born in Sutton, Mass., in 1793, graduated at Dartmouth Coll., and settled in Aldensburg in the northern part of New York. He is now rector of Grace Church, in Cleveland, Ohio.

Rev. Calvin Chapman, son of Dea. Edmund Chapman, was born in Bethel, Nov. 1816. After fitting for College at Millbury, Mass., he graduated at Bowdoin College in 1839, and at the Andover Theological Seminary in 1842. He was ordained and settled in Epping, N. H. in 1843.

Alpheus Grover, son of Jedediah Grover, was born in Bethel. He fitted for college at Andover, Mass., and graduated at Bowdoin Coll. in 1839, and at Bangor Theological Seminary in 1843. He died at Lewiston on his return from Bangor in 1843, aged 34.

Rev. Nathaniel Barker, son of Samuel Barker, was born in Amesbury, Mass., in 1796, but spent his earlier years in Bethel. He graduated at Dartmouth College and studied Divinity at Andover, and was ordained and settled at South Mendon, Mass. For 20 years he has been settled at Wakefield, N. H.

Rev. Hiram C. Estes, son of John Estes, was born in Bethel, July 27, 1823. After fitting for college at N. Yarmouth Academy, he graduated at

Waterville College and having studied at the Theological School in Harvard University one year, he was settled over the Calvinist Baptist Church in Auburn in 1850 where he continued three years, and then was appointed Agent of the American Baptist Missionary Union. He afterwards was settled Pastor of the Church in Trenton, Me. In 1818 he represented that town in the Legislature, where his speeches in behalf of education attracted especial attention.

Rev. Sumner Estes was born in Bethel, and after fitting for college he commenced preaching in Sydney in this State. He has been for sometime pastor of the Calvinist Baptist Church in Thomaston.

Rev. Addison Abbot was born in Albany, but spent the most of his minority in Bethel. After pursuing his studies for several years, he was licensed to preach by the Oxford Association and died in _____.

Rev. Javan K. Mason, son of Walter Mason, was born in Bethel. He graduated at Bowdoin College and subsequently at Bangor Theological Seminary, and for several years has been pastor of the Congregational Church in Hampden, Me.

Rev. Wellington Newell, son of Seth B. Newell, was born in Pembroke, N. H. He came to Bethel with his parents in 1832. He graduated at the Bridgton State Normal School in Mass., and subsequently at the Bangor Theological Seminary in 1855. He was ordained pastor of the Congregational Church in East Orrington, Nov. 18, 1856, where he still resides.

Chapter 19

Education

The first settlers took measures to have their children enjoy the advantages of education. The first school and the first teacher of whom I have any account was about the year 1788. It was kept in a private home, by John Mason, near Capt. Samuel Barker's. About the same time a log school house, the first in town, was built at the corner of the road near Mills Brown's house, on the land now owned by J. B. Hammond. It was made of hewed spruce logs. The seats were made of slabs with legs, and served a very good purpose. Some of the oldest inhabitants are still living who attended school there. Rev. Eliphaz Chapman taught there in 1792. Sally Fessenden, dau. of Rev. Wm. Fessenden of Fryeburg, taught the summer school in 1793. Abijah Warren of Waterford taught it in the winter of 1793. In the summer of 1794, Hannah, dau. of Eliphaz Chapman, taught it. Between the years 1793 and 98, Dr. John Brickett and David Coffin taught each one or more schools.

In 1798, Rev. Caleb Badley, then a candidate for the ministry, taught a private school in Lieut. Clarke's house. This was 62 years ago, and he is still living. He had about 20 scholars. Gen. John Perley of Bridgton taught about this time.

In 1798, the town voted to erect three school-houses -- one on the north side of the river, the other near the dwelling house of Mr. Francis Barker's, and the other at Middle Intervale. The first house was erected at Mr. Barker's. The first teacher was Uriah Holt, of Albany. The first school exhibition ever held in town was had in this house on Washington's birthday the next spring after his death.

Gen. John Perley taught next. He was a "noble schoolmaster." Abigail Chapman, dau. of Eliphaz Chapman, having studied grammar with Rev. Daniel Gould, opened the first Grammar school in what is now Hanover, in 1799. The school-house at Francis Barker's was removed to Bethel Hill after three or four years, on to Honest Corner where it was burnt.

In 1799, Rev. Daniel Gould opened a boarding school at his house on the farm now owned by Aaron Cross, where, for fifteen years, he continued to board and educated youth of both sexes. Probably his school did more to give character to the town than anything else ever done for it.

He was a good linguist and mathematician, and took pleasure in teaching. Many of his pupils, as a consequence, became distinguished in subsequent life.

APPENDIX

In our last chapter, for Rev. John Barker, read Rev. Nathaniel Barker. Addendum. John Barker, M.D. Bowdoin, 1846.

About the year 1830, the town enjoyed a good degree of prosperity, and the third generation were of sufficient age to attend school, when quite a number of both sexes were desirous of obtaining an education. For this purpose a number of young men left their homes to attend some Academy or College.

In the year 1835 commenced a new order of things. A High School was set in operation in March, and the following gentlemen were Trustees: Dea. Robbins Brown -- President, Wm. Frye -- Sec., R. A. Chapman -- Treas., Rev. Chas. Frost, Jedediah Burbank, Esq., John Hastings, Jonathan A. Russell, Jesse Cross, John Harris, Ebenezer Ellingwood, Joseph Sanborn, James Walker, Esq., Timothy Chapman, Esq.

The Trustees engaged a teacher, Nath'l T. True, then member of the Sophomore class in Bowdoin College, at twenty-four dollars a month and board. The school commenced with thirty-five pupils in the old schoolhouse which stood on the spot where Mitchell's Daguerrean saloon now stands. In a week or two, the school removed into a room built for the purpose in the ell of the Bethel House and which the last year was cut up into smaller rooms. The school soon increased in numbers till there were 85 students. John P. Davis was assistant. The standing of the scholars was quite as high as at the present day, though they were much older. So encouraged were the Trustees that they again engaged Mr. True for the Summer and Fall Terms. In the summer there were 32 pupils, and in the fall 91.

Never was a happier company of pupils assembled together. Rarely has a single school so distinguished themselves. From a catalogue now in my possession published at that time, I find the names of the following students: Zenas Bartlett, M. D., an extensive practitioner in Dixfield; Moses B. Bartlett, Esq., a lawyer in Kansas; Rev. Ezekiel W. Coffin, settled in Massachusetts; Hon. John P. Davis, Senator from Cumberland Co. for two years; James Henry P. Frost, M.D.; Abernethy Grover, Representative to Legislature 184_; Talleyrand Grover, Prof. of Ancient Languages in Delaware Coll.; O'Neil W. Robinson, Esq., Bethel; Almon Twitchell, M.D., Bethel; Rev. Addison Abbott, Bethel; Samuel B. Twitchell, M.D., Wakefield, N.H.; Lawson A. Allen, M.D., Bethel; Augustus J. Burbank, Esq., Lewiston; Gideon A. Hastings, Representative to Legislature in 184_; David R. Hastings, Esq., Lovell; Moses Ingalls, M. D.; Hon. Lafayette Grover, first member of Congress from Oregon; Hon. Wm. Kimball, Paris, U. S. Marshall; Eli Wight, Principal of N. Yarmouth Academy; Hon. Robert I. Burbank, Boston; Eli. L. Kimball, M. D., Saco; Rev. Wellington Newell, Orrington; Rev. John G. Pingree; Wm. Williamson, M. D. of Bethel; Rev. Javan K. Mason, Hampden; Hiram Ellingwood, Milan, Representative to Legislature, N.H.; Hiram Bartlett, M. D.

Nearly every one in the private walks of life has become a valuable citizen, and has been successful in life.

It may not be improper to say that the young ladies of that school have very many of them married equally meritorious husbands, and that all *could* get married if they *would*.

It adds not a little to my pleasure as a place of residence to live among so many of those who were the pupils of that same Bethel High School. Some of *their* children have since graduated in College, and are now out in the world for themselves.

The success of the High School in 1835 encouraged them to obtain a charter from the Legislature for an Academy. Accordingly an act was passed to incorporate Bethel Academy, which was approved by the Governor, Hon. R. P. Dunlap, Jan. 27, 1836. The names embodied in the act of incorporation were as follows: John Grover, Moses Mason, Wm. Frye, Charles Frost, Jedediah Burbank, John Hastings, Stephen Emery, Barbour Bartlett, James Walker, Levi Whitman, Robbins Brown, Valentine Little, Geo. W. Chapman, Timothy Carter, Phineas Frost, Timothy Hastings, and Robert A. Chapman.

The first meeting of the Board under the new act was held May 2, 1836, at which time a code of By-Laws was adopted, which has been in force with but trifling changes to the present time. Dr. Timothy Carter was the first President, Dr. John Grover, Vice do., and Wm. Frye, Esq., Sec. Arrangements were made to build an Academy at this meeting. The building was erected during the summer of 1836, with the cupola in the centre, and the Academic year consisted of four terms. The first term commenced Sept., 1836.

The first Preceptor was Isaac Randall, who continued two years, and was succeeded by Wm. R. Chapman who taught one term in the spring of 1838. He was followed by Joseph Hill, who taught in the fall of the same year. Chas. M. Blake taught in 1839, Calvin Chapman 1840, Moses Soule in 1841-2-3, Moses B. Bartlett, Abernethy Grover in 1842, David H. Hastings and Talleyrand Grover in 1844, Joseph Pickard in 1846, Wm. C. Hurd in 1847, N. T. True in 1848, to the present time.

With the exception of Mr. Soule, no one had designed to make teaching a profession, consequently the school was irregular in its patronage. About the year 1842 the Rev. Daniel Gould, of Rumford, made a bequest

First Gould Academy building, 1836

to the Academy, on condition of which was that it be named after him. The Trustees petitioned the Legislature the next winter, and it was changed to Gould's Academy in Bethel. The Trustees subsequently realized about eight hundred dollars from the state. This has been made a perpetual fund, the interest of which shall go towards paying the Preceptor for his services. In 1860 the Trustees obtained from the Legislature a half township of land which they sold the next year for the sum of twenty-five hundred dollars, and the funds of the Academy were, and are now, mostly invested in the bonds of the Atlantic & St. Lawrence Railroad. Since 1848 the patronage of the Academy has been probably more uniform than that of any other Academy in the state. The school is kept the year round. The largest number of students at any one time was in the spring of 1858, when there were one hundred and forty-nine. About one thousand different pupils have attended since the present incumbent has been in office. There is now a cabinet of about 1400 mineralogical and Geological specimens mostly neatly arranged in cases, and a library of 350 volumes belonging to the United Brothers Society, which is a flourishing literary society organized in 1848, that holds weekly meetings during the year. The apparatus is increasing yearly and will soon be valuable, while maps, charts, globes and books of reference are within reach of the pupil. In 1852 the building was remodeled and otherwise improved. Though too small for the actual wants of the school, it is well planned and convenient. Its location is in one of the pleasantest spots in the State, overlooking the valley of the Androscoggin and in sight of the many mountain tips in the distance, and in a pleasant and thriving village.

In 1858 a Tree Society was formed for the purpose of ornamenting the grounds, and the students have manifested much zeal for this purpose. There is need of a few loads of manure from the Trustees to promote the growth of those already planted.

The institution has done its full share in educating the youth of our State since its incorporation and has sent forth many of both sexes who are exerting a salutary influence in society.

The following gentlemen are Trustees at the present time:

President - Hon. Moses Mason.
Vice President - Gilman Chapman.
Treasurer - Dr. John Grover.
Secretary - Richard A. Frye.
James Walker, Esq., O'Neil W. Robinson, Esq., Eber Clough, Esq., Rev. John B. Wheelwright, Rev. A. G. Gaines, Albert L. Burbank, Esq., Gideon A. Hastings, Esq.
Principal - N. T. True, M. D.
Assistant - Miss Olive C. Walker.

APPENDIX

Rev. Wellington Newell removed to Bethel in 1826, and graduated at the Bridgewater Normal School.

The following catalogue embraces all those who have received collegiate honors. This includes those who are natives of Bethel or who have had a permanent residence in town.

Rev. Daniel Gould. Harvard, 1782.
Rev. Lawson Carter. Dartmouth.
Galen Carter. Middlebury.
Rev. John Barker. Dartmouth.
Prof. John Locke, M. D. Yale.
Josh. Fanning, M. D. Columbia, 1822.
Thos. Roberts, M. D. Bowdoin, 1830.
Nahum Wight, M. D. Bowdoin, 1832.
Rev. Wm. R. Chapman. Dartmouth, 1837.
Rev. C. Chapman. Bowdoin, 1839.
Rev. Alpheus Grover. Bowdoin, 1839.
Almon Twitchell, M. D. Bowdoin, 1840.
Eli Wight. Bowdoin, 1840.
Z. W. Bartlett, M. D. Bowdoin, 1840.
Hiram Bartlett, M. D. Bowdoin, 1841.
S. P. Bartlett, M. D. Bowdoin, 1841.
Nathaniel T. True, A.M., Waterville, 1842, M. D. Bowdoin, 1846.
Moses B. Bartlett, Esq. Bowdoin, 1842.
Rev. John H. M. Leland. Amherst.
Abernathy Grover, Esq. Bowdoin, 1843.
Prof. Tal. Grover. Bowdoin, 1843.
Hon. L. Grover, Esq. Delaware, 1850.
Cuvier Grover, Capt. U.S.A. West Point, 1850.
Moses Ingalls. Bowdoin, 1843.
Sam'l F. Gibson, Esq. Bowdoin, 1844.
D'd R. Hastings, Esq. Bowdoin, 1844.
Sam'l B. Twitchell, A. M. and M. D. Dartmouth.
O'Neil W. Robinson, Esq. Bowdoin, 1845.
Rev. Javan K. Mason. Bowdoin, 1841.
Wm. Williamson, M. D. Bowdoin, 1847.
James H. P. Frost. Amherst.
J. E. L. Kimball, M. D. Woodstock.
Rev. Hiram C. Estes. Waterville, 1847.
Edwin W. Bartlett. Bowdoin.
Rev. Edwin A. Buck. Yale.

Belzaleel Kendall, Esq. Bowdoin.
Augustus J. Burbank. Bowdoin, 1850.
Oscar D. Grover. Delaware.
Benjamin W. Kimball, M. D. Dartmouth.
Harlan P. Brown. Bowdoin, 1859.
Adelbert B. Twitchell. Bowdoin, 1859.

There have been many persons engaged in professional life resident in town not included in the preceeding list. The whole number who have been residents in Bethel is not far from seventy.

APPENDIX

In Chapt. 18, read, Rev. Wm. Rogers Chapman was the son of Timothy and Betsey Chapman.

Rev. Alpheus Grover was the son of Eli and Mehitable Grover.

Javan K. Mason was born, Sept. 20th, 1817.

Chapter 20
Revolutionary Soldiers

The lands of Bethel were opened for settlement soon after the Revolutionary War, and many of the soldiers sought for themselves a home in the valley of the Androscoggin. I give here only a brief notice of them, but it will be read, no doubt, with interest by those who are familiar with the history of the town. Any additions of interest will be gratefully received.

Lieut. Jonathan Clark served as a commissary in the army. He was taken by the Indians when they came to Bethel, in 1781, but was released after going a few miles. James Mills first settled in Dublin, N. H., and subsequently in Bethel. Isaac T. York came from Westbrook and settled on the farm now occupied by Humphry Bean. He served three years. Capt. Eli Twitchell was at Bunker Hill immediately after the battle, and by carrying too heavy a gun on his shoulder contracted a disease of the bone of the arm which crippled him for life. John Kilgore lived on the farm now occupied by Chase. He came from Berwick. Zela Holt was in the French and Revolutionary wars. He was at the taking of Burguoyne. I have in my possession a leaf of a diary which he kept during the French war. He was then at Lake Champlain. Moses Mason was in the battle of Bennington. He settled on the farm now occupied by Moses A. Mason. The gun which he carried is still in possession of his son, Hon. Moses Mason. Jonathan Bean settled on the farm now occupied by Abner Brown. He came from Kingston, Mass. He served in the Revolutionary War three years. Capt. Peter Twitchell was a soldier under Gen. Lincoln in quelling Shay's Rebellion. He settled where Col. Eli Twitchell now resides. He was the last survivor among the pensioners in town. He died in 1856. Amos Gage. Daniel Gage. Jesse Dustan. Daniel B. Swan was out 9 months as a waiter to Adjutant Farrington. John Grover was at Dorchester Heights. Ebenezer Eames was born in Framingham, Mass., and died in 1832, aged 76 years. He was present at the capture of the Hessians, and at other skirmishes. Moses Bartlett lived on the farm now occupied by Milton and James Roberts. Joseph Kilgore occupied the farm now owned by Isreal Kimball. Enoch Bartlett was a teamster. He came from Newton, Mass., and occupied the farm now owned by Elias Carter, Esq. John Holt occupied the farm now occupied by Wm. Holt. Jerimiah Andrews lived on the farm now owned by Capt. Wm. Goddard. Benj. Brown was born in Lynn, Mass, and was in the army five years. He was at the battle of Lexington and Bunker Hill, and received a wound from a bullet in the top of the head. He died in 1820, aged about 60. Amos Hastings (Brigadier General) assisted in digging the trench on Bunker Hill. He was present at the taking of Fort Edward, and at the capture of Burguoyne. He resided on the farm now occupied by Israel Kimball. Absalom Farewell was a native of England, moved to Marblehead and was in the French war. He was carried to England and was in the King's service 19 years. He subsequently came back, and was present at the battle of Bunker Hill and Bennington. He came to Bethel in 1793, and died in 1820. He followed the sea 40 years. Wm. Staples. Elhanan Sprague. Samuel Ingalls. Rev. Daniel Gould was an orderly Sergeant. Ezra Twitchell was born in Sherburn, Mass. He went into Boston with the army when the British evacuated it. He was at the battle of Saratoga. John Walker was in a privateer, and was chased up the Penobscot by a British vessel. They blew up their vessel, and he was in the woods 7 days with only one seabiscuit and a frog for his subsistence. Thaddeus Bartlett occupied the farm now owned by Ball Bartlett. Jeremiah Russell. James Barker. Benj. Russell, Sen., was in the French and Revolutionary wars. He was engaged in scouting parties with the French. Nathaniel Segar was two and a half years in the Revolutionary War. He was at the retreat at Bunker Hill, and assisted in fortifying Ticonderoga. James Swan. Samuel Barker was a tailor in the army. He used to say that he had the honor of mending the clothes of Gen. Washington. Jacob Russell was born in Andover, Mass., died in 1799. He went as a privateer. Isaac Russell was a clerk in the army. He perished in a snow storm in Westbrook. Simeon Sanborn lived on the farm now owned by David Sanborn. Dea. John Holt was in the army three years. He was a waiter to a French officer. Powers. Job York. John York. Jonathan Conn. Solomon Annis was born in Hopkinton, N.H., and was the second child born in that town about 1743. He served a short time in the French war. He came to Bethel in 1799 and died in 1829.

Chapter 21

Resident Proprietors in Lower Parish

The following is a list of the resident proprietors in the lower Parish, who had settled in the town previous to 1780. It was furnished the author by Dr. Peter York, in 1858. Mr. York was born in 1777, and came to Bethel when two years old, consequently he has been a resident of Bethel 80 years, longer we believe than any other person.

Samuel Inggalls lived on the farm now occupied by Capt. Asa Kimball, and was the first person who wintered in town. This was in 1776. Jesse Dustan settled where Adam Willis now lives, in Hanover. Jonathan Bean, where Abner Brown now lives. Isaac I. York, where Humphrey Bean now lives. Nathaniel Segar, on Wm. Barker's farm. Moses Bartlett, _____ Gideon and Silas Powers on Reuben Foster's farm, now Hanover.

There were 8 families on the north side of the river, in the lower Parish, previous to 1780.

On the south side of the river, Joseph Kilgore lived on the farm of Israel Kimball. Amos Hastings on Israel Kimball's. Enoch Bartlett came from Newton, Mass., and settled on the farm of Elias Carter. Reuben Bartlett lived on Simeon Brown's farm. Benj. Russell lived on John Williamson's. James Swan lived on John Williams'. John Holt lived on William Holt's farm. Isaac Insley York lived on Humphrey Bean's. John York lived on Capt. Amos Young's. Josiah Bean lived on Edmund Bean's farm. He came to Bethel in 1780. Joseph Ayer came from Standish to Bethel, in 1786 or 7, and lived on Samuel Ayer's farm, Bean's Corner. Thaddeus Bartlett came from Newton, Mass., and lived on Ball Bartlett's farm. Jonathan Bartlett came from Newton, Mass., and lived on Elias Bartlett's farm. Amos Houghton lived on Moses Houghton's farm. Richard Estes lived on Richard Estes farm. He came from Berwick. Jeremiah Andrews lived on Capt. Wm. Goddard's. James Willis came from Sudbury, Mass., to Bethel, in 1786. He was enlisted to put down Shay's Rebellion.

Chapter 22

Politics

I am indebted to Hon. Moses Mason for the completion of the present chapter.

The first Representative from Bethel, in the Legislature of Massachusetts, was Eliphaz Chapman, in 1808, who remained 3 years; John Kilgore, 1811, 2 years; Moses Mason, 1813, 5 years; Samuel Chapman, 1818, 1 year; Moses Mason, Jr., 1 year, being the last year we were connected with Mass.; John Grover, 1821, 1 year; Barbour Bartlett, 1822, 1 year; Timothy Hastings, 1825, 2 years; Phineas Frost, 1829, 2 years; O'N. W. Robinson, 1832, 1 year; Asa Kimball, 1833, 1 year; O'N. W. Robinson, 1834, 1 year; Asa Kimball, 1835, 1 year; Ebenezer Eames, 1836, 2 years; Phineas Frost, 1838, 2 years; Timothy Hastings, 1840, 2 years; Wm. Frye, 1842, 2 years; James Walker, 1845, 1 year; Phineas Frost, 1846, 1 year; Nathan Grover, 1849, 1 year; Eliphaz C. Bean, 1851, 1 year; G. A. Hastings, 1852, 1 year; Phineas Frost, 1853, 1 year; Ira C. Kimball, 1856, 2 years; Eber Clough, 1858,_____; Jedediah T. Kimball, 1861.

The following persons have been chosen from the town of Bethel, to the Senate of the State. John Grover, 1827, 3 years; Wm. Frye, 1844, 2 years; Robert A. Chapman, 1850, 2 years; Almon A. Twitchell, 1856-7, 2 years.

The folowing persons have been chosen Councilors from the town of Bethel, to advise with the Governor. Moses Mason, 1843 and 1845, Elias M. Carter, 1849, Benjamin Freeman, 1858.

Moses Mason was appointed County Commissioner in 1830, and Wm. Frye County Attorney.

Moses Mason was elected to Congress for the years 1833-4, and re-elected for the years 1835-6.

In 1797 the town gave their votes for State officers.

The vote for Governor was, for Moses Gill, 14; Lieut. Governor, Increase Sumner, 14; Senators, Nathaniel Wells, 16, Simon Frye, 16.

The vote for Governor in 1798 stood for Increase Sumner, 20; Lieut. Gov. Moses Gill, 18.

No person could be legally a voter who had less than an annual amount of three pounds, or any estate the value of sixty Pounds. The town voted this year that there be built three school houses twenty-four feet by twenty, and to raise three hundred dollars to build the same. Voted. To raise fifty dollars to defray town charges.

The vote for State officers had been unanimous till the year 1801, when the vote stood for Governor,

Elbridge Gerry,	42.
Caleb Strong,	3.
For Lieut. Governor,	
General Heath,	39.
Judge Phillips,	2.

In 1802 the town voted to divide the Militia into two companies to be bounded by the east and west Parish.

In 1802 the vote for Governor was for

Elbridge Gerry,	24.
Caleb Stong,	16.
Lieut. Governor,	
Edward Robbins,	20.
General Heath,	16.

It was voted, that the Ferryman should receive for his trouble for carrying a man, cart and oxen 17 cts. For a man and yoke of oxen, 9 cts. Man and horse, 6 cts. Single person, 3 cts.

In 1803 the town voted to set up the sugar privilege on the school land to the highest bidder, which was bid off for $4.19.

In 1807 the vote for Governor stood for

James Sullivan,	56.
Caleb Strong,	19.
Lieut. Governor,	
Levi Lincoln,	56.
Edward H. Robbins,	18.

The question was taken this year on the separation of the District of Maine from Massachusetts. Yeas 40, Nays 17.

In 1808 the inhabitants gave in their votes for a Federal Representative to Congress,

Richard Cutts,	41.
Joseph Leland,	18.

In 1810 it was voted to choose a Committee to make arrangements for celebrating the 4th of July, and said Committee are to inspect the Oration before it is delivered in public.

In 1811, the vote for Governor stood for
Elbridge Gerry, 79.
Christopher Gore, 33.

In 1812, a committee of safety was raised in each parish, and all who were able to bear arms were ordered to equip themselves.

Chapter 23

Village of Bethel Hill

The village of Bethel Hill commenced and has ever continued to manifest a slow but steady growth, to the present time. As late as 1814 there were but four dwelling houses in what is now the village at Bethel Hill. One was situated in the rear of the Bethel House, and was owned by Capt. Eleazer Twitchell. Another was situated on the spot where Elbridge Chapman's house formerly stood at the head of the Common, and was built and partly occupied as the first store in the village by James Walker, Esq. The next was owned by Timothy Hastings, between the widow and Alphonso Hasting's dwelling houses. The frame is now in the house occupied by Alfred Twitchell. The next was built that year, 1814, by Dr. Moses Mason. It almost caused a rebellion, and a committee was raised to wait on the Doctor and remonstrate with him for setting it so high from the ground. They thought it would not stand. As was the custom, just before the broadsides were raised, a prayer was offered by the minister of the Parish, Rev. Daniel Gould, after which the liberality of the owner was tested by a generous supply of *something good to drink*. Dr. Mason is consequently the oldest proprietor in the village. The next store was situated where Albert Stiles's house now stands. It was the first painted building in the village and went by the name of Red Store. It is now owned by Phineas Stearns as Saddler's shop. The first blacksmith shop was near to W. Heywood's house. The first Carding Machine was in the grist-mill. In 1814 Joseph Twitchell and others, built a Carding and Clothing Mill where it now stands. Caleb Rowe tended the first mill. The first school house was moved from Francis Barker's on to the spot occupied by the rear store of Abner Davis. The first teacher was Dr. John Grover. The next school house was where Mitchell's saloon stands.

In 1814, 7 by 9 glass was eleven cents a square, lime 7 dollars a cask, and nails a shilling a lb. The land on which the parsonage, Timothy Barker, H. Young, and Mighill Mason's houses now stand, was sold by Dr. Mason for a clock case which still holds the best time piece the Dr. ever had.

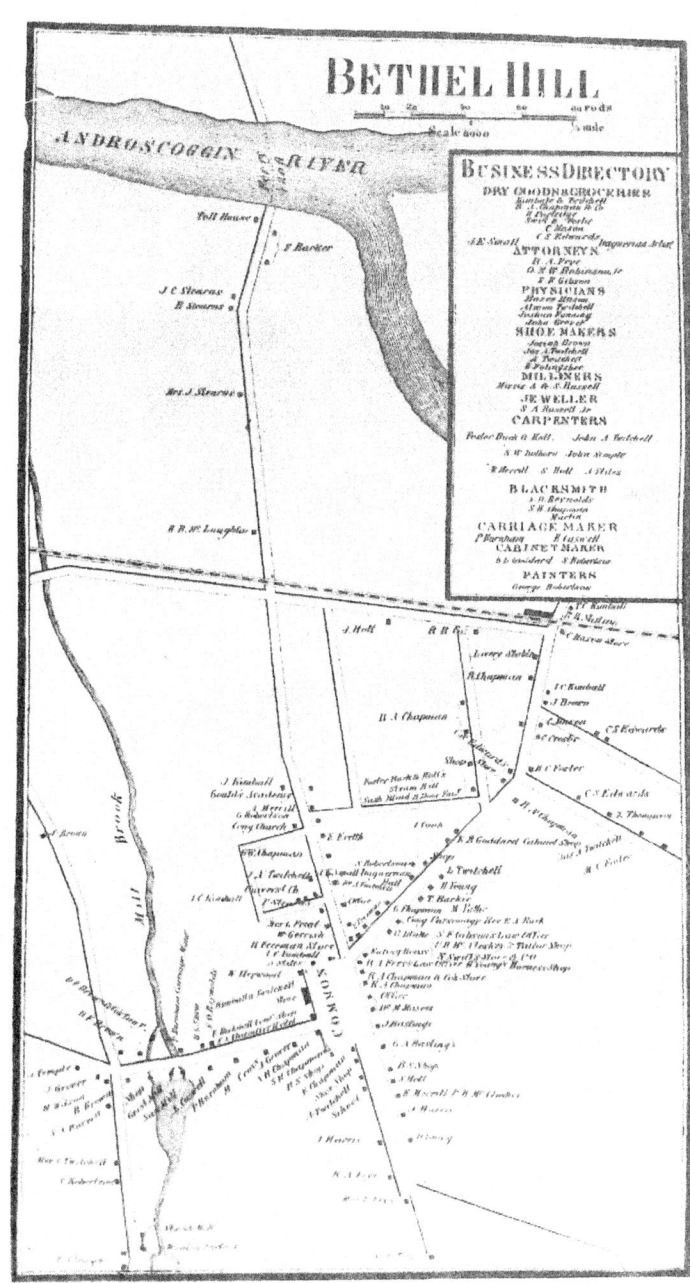

Bethel Hill Village, 1858

Swift/Wiley Block, Main Street, Bethel Hill

Dr. Moses Mason's House, 1813

Atlantic & St. Lawrence Railroad station (later Grand Trunk). Service between Portland, Me., and Montreal, Que., began in 1851.

The first Post Office was in 1814, Moses Mason, Jr., P.M. The Mail was brought by way of Waterford, Paris and Rumford, up the other side of the river to his father's. There were no newspapers taken from the office the first quarter, though several were taken in the town. Previous to this, Waterford was the nearest regular P. Office. The revenue to government the first quarter was $2.83 cts. In 1818 Mr. Crawford bought an acre in the rear of Chapman's Brick block and extending across the street including Davis's store for 65 dollars.

As late as 1835 there were scarcely any houses on Church Street, or from the Common to the Depot. From Sylvester Robertson's to Chas. Mason's house was an alder and frog swamp. On Broad Street Wm. Frye, Esq., occupied a house on the spot where his family still resides. A Methodist parsonage was in front of Capt. John Harris's. The first barrel of flour brought into town was by Capt. John Harris, in 1824. Previous to this time the inhabitants raised a surplus of flour for market. In 1848 there were 199 inhabitants in the village, in 1855, there were 404, and in 1860, 602.

When a stranger came to the town he was said to come through the woods. Everybody knew when he came, what was his business, and when he left. The first chaise was owned by Rev. Daniel Gould, in 1800. Gen. John Chandler was carried through the town in a chaise in 1814 on his return from captivity in Quebec, and caused great excitement. The first painted dwelling house was owned by Dr. M. Mason. He was thought to be very extravagant, and when he put blinds on to his house he was really becoming aristocratic. Many a boy who came to the stores from a distance surveyed it with wonder. He owned the first sofa in town in 1821. It was made in town by Mr. Bonney.

The first Meeting house in the village was the Congregational Church, built in 1847. The next on the N. side of the river was in 1848, the next the Universalist in 1853, the next the Methodist in 1860.

Chapter 24
Geology, Natural History and Botany

The surface of the town is broken up by several mountainous peaks, the highest of which is about 2500 feet above the level of the sea. This is situated in the west part of the town and has recently received the name of Anasagunticook, in commemoration of the tribe of Indians of that name on the Androscoggin river. Locke's Mt. is on the N. boundary and is 1912 feet in height. Bear Mt., situated between Locke and Anasagunticook, might with more propriety be called *Bare* Mt., for its summit to the extent of many acres is entirely destitute of vegitation. Sparrowhawk, named after one of the proprietors of the town, is in the S. W. part of the town. Walker's Mt. is E. from Walker's Mills, Mt. Farewell is N.E. from Bethel Hill about 3 miles, and is nearly in the centre of the town, while Swan's Hill is still farther East. Paradise Hill is a gradual swell of land extending from Barker's Ferry through the village till it terminates in a ledge at a distance of about 2.5 miles from the river. This is situated in the centre of an amphitheatre whose boundary is enclosed by mountains, at whose base are valleys and which forms a most interesting prospect. This Hill is a frequent resort for summer tourists, as its summit can be reached by a carriage over an excellent road. Few better views can be found in Maine.

These mountains are composed of granite, gneiss, mica, slate and an occasional patch of impure limestone. They were originally covered with a heavy growth of Pine, Spruce, Hemlock and hard wood, but a fire swept over them in 1817 which not only burnt off the wood but also the soil, so that the surface of many of them is incapable of supporting vegetation.

These elevations are a continuation of the great Appalachian chain, which extends through the central portion of the State from the White Mts. to Katahdin, and are of the same geological age and formation as the latter.

On the surface of Bear Mountain are immense grooves running along in a N. and S. direction. They are on a more extended scale than I have seen elsewhere. Good granite for building purposes is found in various parts of the town. Occasionally a large boulder is found which has been transported from a distance and which splits up into a beautiful form, and of good quality.

On the swell of land on which the village is built are frequently plowed out of the ground very curious boulders, one side of which is grooved and polished as if done by a graving tool. These boulders are unlike anything of the kind I have seen elsewhere in the State.

There is a bluff at W. Bethel composed of pyritiferous slate which is very strongly impregnated with sulphur. The action of the rains and frosts serves to decompose the rocks, by means of the sulphuric acid which is formed. Occasionally in sheltered spots, sulphate of iron, or copperas, is formed spontaneously. On a hot day in summer the odor of sulphur is very perceptible.

Between the summit of Farewell's Mt. and the Androscoggin there is a powerful vein of crystallized quartz which has forced its way through the mica slate and formed a breccia. It is several rods in width and may be traced nearly a mile. No minerals are found in it save the peroxide of iron. The only vein of trap I have seen in town is about a mile west of the village, on Sanborn's Hill. It is broken up in columnar fragments, the adjacent rock being wanting on one side so that it forms a wall. It contains augite and glassy felspar.

On the summit of Mt. Farewell there is a small quantity of limestone, but of no commercial value.

On Bear Mt. may be seen scattered over its surface globular masses of rock composed of yellow garnet cale spar, hornblende and other minerals. The gneiss has been worn away leaving these masses protruding above the surface like plums on the surface of a pudding. These globes are from a few inches to several feet in diameter. Their existence is probably coeval with the gneiss, and they were formed in accordance with the ordinary laws of crystallization.

The town is not remarkable for good specimens of minerals. In the limestone on Farewell's Mt. a few very fine specimens of cinnamon garnet have been found. One now in my possession is the finest I have seen in the State. Pargasite, Sahlite and Calcareous spar also abound there. Sphene, or the Oxide of Titanium, is frequently noticed in the gneiss. Some very fine specimens were obtained near the foot of Robertson's Hill. The deutoxide of Manganese is found on the Merrill farm near the bend of the river. Occasionally a Beryl may be seen on the mountains. Tremolite and Epidote are quite common in boulders. The manganesian and common red garnet are frequently seen. Phosphate of lime exists in the rocks on Walker's Mt. and at the Railroad cut through Robertson's Hill. I have never seen a boulder containing a fossil within the borders of the town. I obtained the last year some very good crystals of felspar in a rock in the rear of the academy. Actinolite, egeran, graphite, talc, mica, tourmaline, hornblende, iron and arsenical pyrites, jasper, hornstone, octohedral crystals of iron and apatite are common though having no special interest. Boulders of a curiously distorted mica slate are common. The drift evidently came from a great distance. In the bed of the Androscoggin river are boulders which have been brought down from the base of the White Mts. through Peabody River. They are a compact and altered granite and are worn into pebbles. Porphyritic gneiss is common in stone walls in this vicinity.

At the foot of the Anasagunticook Mt. is a chalybeate mineral spring which is fast becoming a place of resort for summer travellers. The water is impregnated with the carbonate of oxide of iron, lime, magnesia, and sulphuretted hydrogen. As the water is exposed to the air the carbonic acid escapes, and the iron is deposited in abundance. This can be collected and made use of by invalids to great advantage. A half mile east of this is another singular spring which boils up through a bed of sand, giving it the appearance of a miniature volcano. Large quantities of gas, which however, is nothing but common air, come up to the surface. Where the air comes from is a mystery, though probably through the crevices of the mountains.

The soil may be divided into high and low intervale, meadow and rocky upland. The Androscoggin river runs through the town a distance of about seventeen miles, on either bank of which are fine intervale farms. On Pleasant river in the west part of the town is intervale and meadow a distance of about three miles, and about the same distance on Mill brook and Alder river, and one mile on Sunday river. The upland is usually rocky, but when cleared it has strong and productive soil. The intervales on the other hand are overflowed annually and a fine rich sediment is left which greatly adds to the fertility of the soil.

The Androscoggin river evidently runs at a much lower level than formerly, and its channel is frequently changed. New beds of gravel are formed on one side, and banks on the other side are washed away. A marked change has taken place within a few years on the N. W. side of Barker's Island where the channel is nearly filled up. These changes frequently take place during freshets which rise suddenly and sweep down the river with great rapidity. Near the mouth of Alder river when the Androscoggin river is low, the whole geological structure of the intervales may be seen in the different strata of sand, gravel, clay of different colors, owing to the presence or absence of the oxide of iron, and some thirty or forty different strata may be counted. There is but little clay in the town. Two or three small deposits are all that are suitable for the manufacture of brick.

In 1785 occurred the greatest freshet ever known; it rose 25 feet. In 1826, the night in which the Willey family were destroyed, the river rose the highest and the most rapidly since that time. In 1838 occurred an ice freshet in the month of February, the only one, I believe, ever recorded in this vicinity. There had been a remarkably warm southerly wind for two or three days which caused the river to rise suddenly and break up

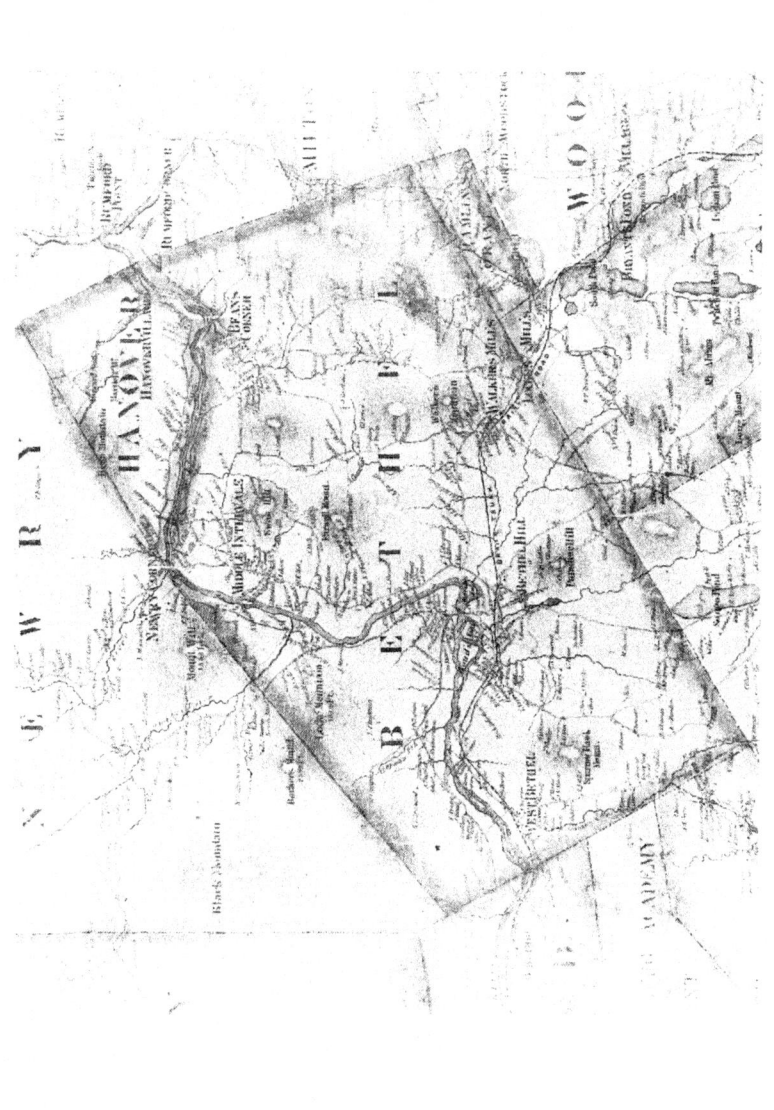

Town of Bethel, 1858

the thick ice which piled up along the banks and on the intervales, presenting a curious appearance. A bridge which had just been opened to travel at Barker's ferry was swept away, as well as all the bridges on the river as far down as Brunswick.

On the stream above Dea. Edmund Chapman's Mill there is a cascade where large potholes have been worn into the solid rock by the action of water and pebbles.

The Androscoggin falls but a few feet in its course through the town. Boats can pass the whole distance at high water.

The banks of the river are divided into high and low intervale. The high intervale is never overflowed at the present time, and it was evidently formed by the early drainage of the country during the last great geological changes of this region.

Geologically speaking, the town is composed of the Primary, or Azoic series of rocks above which the other series are entirely wanting till we arrive at the tertiary clay, diluvium and alluvium.

From this it will be perceived that the soil is wholly granitic. It is deficient in lime, which, in the form of gypsum and slaked lime, is applied to the upland with great advantage. The intervales obtain a supply from the inundation of the river which furnishes the necessary elements of a good soil.

Bethel and vicinity were fine hunting grounds previous to its settlement. The Indians and the early white hunters obtained an abundance of game. The moose was no uncommon inhabitant of the less elevated ranges of land. Two men killed sixty of these animals during one winter. The hides and tallow were usually all that were saved. The possession of a quantity of moose meat was no small addition to the bill of fare of an early settler. These animals have retreated back of the range of mountains. The last one killed in town was by Mr. Decatur Hastings.

Bears occupied the higher range of mountains and made their descent in autumn to visit the cornfield and flock of the farmer. Large numbers of these animals were killed and have occasionally been met with up to the present time. A large bear was shot by Rev. Z. Thompson, and J.S. Abbott, in 1858, I believe, a mile east of the village. Deer are only occasionally seen at the present time. Up the valley of Wild River, in Gilead, about one hundred of these animals were taken during the past winter of 1861.

Loup Cervier. This animal belongs to the cat family and receives several names. It is a singular animal. A large one was caught in 1859 by Mr. Daniel S. Hastings. They are still abundant about the lakes.

Beaver. The remains of beaver dams were very abundant on the settlement of the town. The last one caught in town was on Alder River in 1826 or 7. He probably came down the Androscoggin during a freshet, and going up the stream, built a dam and formed a pond. A trap was set and he was caught by a foot which he gnawed off and escaped. He was again caught and again gnawed off the other foot. He was caught the third time and secured.

Foxes are not very abundant. Minks and Muskrats still abound along the streams. The Sable is still occasionally caught. The fisher is also occasionally met with.

Of fowl, the duck appears to have been the most numerous. The early settlers must have had rare sport with them. A duck is rarely seen at the present time. The wild pigeon was formerly very abundant. They have ceased to be an object for the hunter. Now and then a crane or fish hawk may be seen wending their way northward to the lakes.

Among the smaller animals are the Woodchuck, Skunk, Hedgehog, Rabbit, grey, red, striped and flying Squirrels; Weasel, Rat, three or four species of the Mouse, the star nosed and ground Mole.

Of the reptiles, the different species of lizard common to all parts of the state, the water, striped, green, ring necked, and copperhead snakes are common. The rattlesnake has never, to my knowledge, been found in the town, though it exists about ten miles to the south in Albany. The adder is occasionally seen, especially on Grover Hill and vicinity.

Trout fishing has always been and still is fine sport in this vicinity. All the smaller streams are full of them. Within a few years pickerel have been introduced into the Androscoggin above Rumford Falls. The Cusk is occasionally taken in the Androscoggin. The Yellow Perch, suckers, shiners, sowfish, eels are common.

Shellfish are rare. The Unio purpuratus and U. radiatus, the Anadonta cataratac and Cyclas similis are all the bivalves we have noticed. Univalves are rare. A new species of Helix, the smallest of that genus, was discovered below Kimball's Park a few years since by Mr. Fred Morse of Portland. Quite a number of genera of shells common in other portions of the State are wanting here.

The Botany of Bethel differs essentially in some respects from that on the same meridian near the sea-coast. The original growth was that of White Pine, on the intervales, and rocky upland swells. Maple, yellow birth, and beech, on the highlands and sides of the mountains, Spruce and hemlock on the mountains, and cedar and hackmatac in the swamps.

The White Pine was very abundant, especially on the intervales, and formed one of the earliest resources of the first settlers by cutting the timber and rafting it to Brunswick. There are but few timber lots of this tree remaining in town, though the stumps still stand in many places as a witness of the past. The Norway Pine abounds sparingly. The pitch pine was quite common on the plains. Silver fir is abundant in the swamps, and frequently grows to a large size. Black spruce is still found on the sides of the mountains in large quantities, and of a great size and height. Few of the inhabitants in the town are aware of the quantity of these trees still remaining in places, at present in-accessible, among the mountains to the north of Bethel. White Spruce is less common and of little value. Hemlock grows in company with the spruces. Hacmatac grows very abundant on Alder river, and on low wet grounds generally. White Cedar was formerly very abundant, even on high grounds. Immense numbers of cedar posts and railroad sleepers have been obtained from the meadows in this town and vicinity.

The Red Maple is conspicuous in spring by its crimson flowers, and produces the *curled* maple so highly prized by cabinet makers. Rock Maple abounds in every part of the town, and is as highly prized as any other tree for the manufacture of sugar, which manufacture has much increased within a few years. The White Maple is common. The Striped Maple is beautiful as an ornamental tree. Mountain Maple is only a shrub, and of no value.

Of the Oak, we have never seen but one species, the Red Oak, and this is rare. The Butternut, I believe, is not a native, but is frequently cultivated as an ornamental tree. Of the birches -- the Canoe Birch was formerly abundant and of large size. Occasionally they may be seen on the sides of the mountains. Common White or Grey Birch, is very abundant in many places where the land has been severly burned over. Yellow birch is found associated with the rock maple, and frequently of large size. Hornbeam is found on high ranges. Hop-Hornbeam is occasionally seen. The Elm abounds on the intervales and meadows. The Beech is found somewhat sparingly on the sides of the hills. Two species of poplar are found, the American Aspen and the Large Poplar. The latter frequently grows to a large size.

The White Ash is very rarely met with. The Bass Wood is occasionally found of large size. Black Alder grows everywere on low grounds. Cherry trees, black, choke, and red, are abundant. Dogwood is the only poisonous tree in this vicinity. The Mountain Ash is quite abundant, and is frequently transplanted as an ornamental tree, but the frequent attacks of the borer of late years have rendered them less desirable for this purpose. Swamp Willow is abundant on low grounds.

The foregoing list embraces all the native trees found in this town. Several species have been introduced here as elsewhere, and may be regarded as naturalized, such as the Locust, Lombardy Poplar, Balm of Gilead, Yellow Willow, and perhaps some others. The second growth is abundant in the town, and will furnish all the necessary fuel for the inhabitants. The mountains were burned over in 1817, and much of the rest of the town, in 1825.

INDEX

ABBOT, Addison 181
ABBOTT, Addison 183 J S 199
ABINGTON, E 104
ADAMS, G E 103 104 J Q 120
   John F 114 Sam'l 98
ALDEN, Capt 44
ALLEN, Capt 15 Lawson A 183
AMHERST, Gen 49
ANDRAS, Jermiah 80
ANDREWS, Capt 46 Jeremiah
   19 190 Jerimiah 189 Robert
   103
ANNIS, Solomon 189
ARNOLD, Gen 47
ASTIN, Petter 80
AUSTIN, Hope 52 53 Mrs 53
   Peter 21 23 51
AVERY, John 98
AYER, James 93 119 162 Joseph
   190 Sam'l 190 Thirza 93 162
AYERS, Eunice 93 William 93
BAKER, Joseph 115 Joshua 114
BALLARD, E 29
BALDWIN, Isaac 8 Jeduthan 8
BARBOUR, Dorcas 84 Miss 85
BARKER, Benjamin 60 Daniel
   78 Esther 93 Francis 182 194
   J Fordyce 162 James 189
   John 93 113 119 162 183 186
   Nathaniel 180 183 Samuel 21
   23 104 171 182 189 Timothy
   194 Wm 23 190
BARLTETT, Lucia 89 Moses B
   184

BARNARD, Benj 44
BARRE, Isaac 83
BARTLET, Jonathan 17 79
   Moses 79 Thaddeus 17
   Thadeas 79
BARTLETT, Ball 189 190
   Barbour 113 165 184 191
   Curatio 68 86 88 Delenda 89
   Dorcas 84 Ebenezer 162
   Edwin W 186 Elhanan 85 162
   Elias 162 190 Enoch 188 190
   Hiram 184 186 Jonathan 83
   84 99 190 Julia 89 Lucy 89
   Moses 83 84 188 190 Moses B
   165 183 186 Mr 85 Mrs 84
   Mrs Moses 84 Reuben 190
   Rhoda 88 S P 186 Stephen 83
   84 85 Thaddeus 83 189 190 Z
   W 186 Zenas 162 183
BARTON, Aaron 17
BATES, George 116
BEAMAN, Aaron 171
BEAMER, Aaron 103
BEAN, Anna 93 Edmund 190
   Eliphaz C 191 Humphrey 190
   Humphry 188 Jonathan 188
   190 Josiah 190
BEARCE, Lt 62
BEAVINS, Caroline 176 Mary A
   176 Wm 114 176
BECKER, Bro 114
BEEN, Daniel 79 Jonathan 79
   Josiah 79
BELKNAP, Nath'l 8

BENT, Elijah 8
BETH, Peter 10
BIGELOW, Professor 126
BISHOP, Emily J 180
BIXBY, Martha 6 Nathan 6
BLAKE, Chas M 184 Ebenezer 114
BODWELL, Alice 177
BOLSTER, O C 113
BOND, Col 15 Lt Col 13
BONNEY, Mr 195
BOOTH, Geo 173 Mary 170 173
BRACKET, Anthony 44
BRADBURY, Caleb 168 Nathan 113
BRADFORD, Abigail 85 Betsey 85 Edmund 85 Eliphaz 85 Geo W 85 Hannah 85 Jonathan 85 Martin 103 171 Moses 85 Samuel 85 Sarah 85 Timothy 85
BRADLEY, 77 Caleb 20 101 182
BRAY, Ebenezer 114 175
BRECKENRIDGE, 131
BREWSTER, David 145
BRICKETT, Dr 20 John 117 182
BROWN, Abner 188 190 Benj 189 Caroline 176 Col 15 David 7 Harlan P 187 Josiah 6 113 Mills 22 182 Robbins 77 104 112 183 184 Simeon 190
BUCHANAN, R 153
BUCK, E A 6 103 163 Edwin A 174 186 Elmira R 174 James 174 Mr 104
BULLARD, Sarah 87
BURBANK, A L 22 23 65 81 86 Albert L 185 Augustus J 183 187 Jed 22 Jedediah 79 112 121 183 184 Robert I 184
BURGOYNE, 188 189 Gen 16
BURNET, William 135
BURNHAM, 77 Betsey 23 Jonas 178 Levi 175 Pinkney 23
BURTT, Richard 8

CALLIAOS, 47
CARLEY, Mr 135
CARRUTHERS, J J 113
CARTER, Benjamin 119 Cullen 162 Dr 118 Elias 188 190 Elias M 118 191 Fanny 117 122 Frances 119 Galen 118 186 James T 118 Lawson 118 180 186 Luther C 118 Lydia A 118 T 162 Theodore R 119 Timothy 104 112 117 121 162 180 184 Timothy J 118
CARTIER, 31
CHADBOURNE, John 114 175
CHAMBERLAIN, Ephraim 103 John 36
CHANDLER, John 195 Rosalba D 161
CHANEY, Jonathan 114
CHAPMAN, 6 195 Abigail 178 182 Algernon 23 Algernon S 12 Betsey 187 C 186 Calvin 113 180 184 D W 86 Edmund 113 180 199 Elbridge 104 194 Elias M 119 Eliphaz 64 68 85 86 182 191 Geo 86 Geo W 184 George W 20 Gilman 12 23 78 185 Hannah 182 Lydia D 119 Mr 87 179 180 Mrs 86 R A 183 Robert A 119 184 191 Samuel 112 Sarah W 119 Timothy 64 85 86 183 187 Vincint 12 William 178 William Rogers 178 Wm R 184 186 Wm Rogers 187
CHASE, 188 Mr 163 Seth B 116
CHICKERING, J W 103 John W 113
CHILD, Geo 114
CHOATE, Mr 29
CHURCH, 64 Benj 46 Capt 37 39 Col 42 Nathan 102
CLAP, Edward 8
CLARK, 64 69 Benj 80 Benjamin 50 52 57 59 60 93 Betsey 61

CLARK (Continued)
 Betty 93 Col 68 69 John 22
 Jonathan 8 17 23 50 77 79 99
 100 170 188 Lt 23 53 63 65 86
 182 Mr 58 Mrs 23 50 51 81
CLARKE, Lt 81 82
CLAY, 120
CLOUGH, Eber 6 185 191
COBB, Allen H 114 Dr 133
 Stephen 113
COFFIN, David 182 Ezekiel W
 183 Rev Dr 101
COLE, Benj 114
CONN, Jonathan 189
CONNYERES, Capt 46
COOK, 163
CORNWALLIS, Lord 59
CRAWFORD, Mr 195
CRESSEY, Noah 103
CROSS, Aaron 92 182 Abigail 92
 Caroline 92 Dr 133 Frances
 92 Isaac 96 Jesse 91 183
 Jonathan 92 Lydia 91 92
 Moses 92 Mr 92 Samuel 117
CUMMINGS, Asa 103 171
CUMNER, John 114
CURATIO, Bartlett 89
CUSHMAN, B 123
CUTLER, Rev Mr 180
CUTTS, Richard 192
DANA, Judge 163
DAVIES, E 116 Rev Mr 114
DAVIS, 78 195 Abner 194 John
 P 183
DAWSON, W W 136
DEVAUDREUIL, M 47
DEWITT, Prof 161
DIKE, Nathaniel 8
DODD, I 113 John 113
DODGE, Mr 62
DONHAM, Benjamin 114 175
DOUGLAS, J 172
DOUGLASS, A 171 John A 103
 113
DOW, Huse 114

DOWNING, Isaac 114
DOWS, Lodwick 8
DRAKE, 42
DRESSER, Levi 78
DRINKWATER, Arthur 114 175
DUDLEY, Gen 46
DUNLAP, R P 184
DUNNELLS, Richard 93 Suza
 93
DUPONCEAU, 31
DUSTAN, Jesse 11 12 188 190
 Peregrine 12
DUSTEN, Jesse 79
DUSTIN, Jesse 17 23
DWIGHT, Wm T 103
EAMES, Ebenezer 191 Ebenzer
 188 Nathaniel 8
EBERLE, Dr 133
EIDENBROTT, L E 161
ELINWOOD, Jacob 91
ELKINS, Daniel 176
ELLINGWOOD, Ebenezer 183
 Hiram 184 J 90 John W 103
 171
ELLINWOOD, Jacob 90
EMERSON, Thomas 173
EMERY, Stephen 184
ENGALLS, Samuel 80
ESTES, Hiram C 180 186 Richard 190 Sumner 181
FAIRBANKS, C 114 Deborah 5
 Jonathan 114 Joseph 5
FANNING, Dr 91 James 161
 Josh 186 Joshua 104 161
FAREWELL, Absalom 189
 Josiah 35 Mr 48
FARRINGTON, Adjutant 188
 Capt 64 Lt 77 Stephen 63 77
 W T 114
FARWELL, Absalom 92 Foster
 11
FASSET, Deborah 6
FAY, John 8 Jonathan 8
FENNO, 65
FERNALD, Lydia 172

FESSENDEN, Sally 182 Wm 101 102 168 182
FISK, Mr 19
FLOID, Capt 46
FOSTER, J P 113 James 146 John 113 Reuben 190 Stephen 173
FRANCIS, J W 161
FRANKLIN, 138
FREELAND, Fanny 117 James 117
FREEMAN, Rev Mr 180
FROST, Charles 103 104 112 113 170 171 184 Chas 162 183 Henry B 162 James H P 186 James Henry P 183 Lucinda M S 172 Lydia 172 Moses 170 Mr 103 172 174 Phineas 184 191 Salley 170
FRY, Simon 79
FRYE, 6 36 Esther K 166 Joseph 2 Lois 163 Mr 35 165 Richard 163 Richard A 166 185 Sarah 163 Simeon 191 William 163 Wm 112 165 166 183 184 191 195
FULLER, Aaron 114 Caleb 114 Isaac 3 Joseph 15 Nathan 13
GAGE, Amos 101 113 162 188 Daniel 188 Leander 162
GAINES, A G 116 178 185
GALVANI, 124
GARDNER, Col 13
GARLAND, D 103 David 104 113 174 John 113 174 Mary Elizabeth 174
GATES, Gen 16
GERRY, Elbridge 166 192 193 Joseph 116
GIBSON, Abb 166 Sam'l F 186 Saml F 166 Samuel 166 Samuel F 166
GIDEON, 190
GILL, Moses 191
GODDARD, Wm 189 190

GOODENOW, David 166
GOODHUE, D 104
GORE, Christopher 193
GORGE, Wm 40
GOULD, Daniel 50 101 102 121 167 168 171 173 182 184 186 189 194 195 Eunise 173 L A F 174 Mark 104 119 Mary 173 Molly 173 Moses 113 Mr 168 169 173 Samuel 173
GRAHAM, George 135
GRANVILLE, 83
GRAY, 92 J S 103
GREELY, Allen 103 171 Joseph 12 Rev 42
GREEN, John 8
GREENWOOD, Joseph 101 102 Mary 93 102 Nathaniel 93 Sarah 102
GREGORY, 124
GROUT, 86
GROVER, Abernathy 122 Abernethy 183 184 186 Alpheus 180 186 187 Andrew 93 Cuvier 122 186 Dr 121 Eli 21 93 187 Elijah 21 89 93 Elmira 93 Esther 93 Hannah 93 J 162 James 21 102 104 Jedediah 21 99 180 John 19 21 47 63 79 119 120 159 160 184 185 188 191 194 L 186 Lafayette 21 122 184 Leonard 104 112 Mehitable 187 Moses 22 Mr 22 Naoma 21 Nathan 191 Olive 21 Oscar D 187 Peter 93 Philophrene 122 Rachel 93 Sarah 21 Tal 186 Talleyrand 183 184
HACKETT, Simeon 113
HAMMOND, J B 182
HAMMONS, David 166 Martha 166
HARD, Carlton 113
HARRIS, John 183 195 L W 113 Thaddeus M 123

HASELTON, Alice 177 Elder
  176 177 Mary 177 Samuel
  176 177
HASKIN, Robert 44
HASTING, John 6
HASTINGS, Alphonso 194 Amos
  98 99 189 190 D'd R 186
  Daniel S 199 David H 184
  David R 184 Decatur 199 G A
  191 Gen 12 21 Gideon A 183
  185 John 21 183 184 Joseph
  116 Timothy 184 191 194
HATCH, Capt 15
HATHORNE, 39
HAWKINS, John 46
HEARD, Ann 44
HEATH, Gen 192
HEYWOOD, W 194
HILL, Joseph 184
HILLIARD, Timothy 103
HINKLEY, 42
HINMAN, Wm 114
HITCHCOCK, 20
HOLLAND, Cornelius 119
HOLLEY, David 175
HOLT, John 188-190 Uriah 182
  William 189 190 Zela 102 188
HOPKINS, E S 103 113
HOUGHTON, Amos 190 Bethiah 93 James H 93 Moses 190
HOW, Cyprian 10
HOZACK, David 161
HOZAK, David 161
HUNNIWELL, Lt 45
HURD, Wm C 184
HUTCHINS, Hezekiah 103 171
  Sarah 85
HUTCHINSON, 77
INDIAN, Adewando 46 Assabeel
  75 Assacumbuit 33 Ausado
  47 Bagerson 39 Black Susup
  75 Capt Phillip 75 Capt
  Swarson 67 75 Chocorua 33
  Damhegan 40 Darumkine 40
  41 Dumhegan 41

INDIAN (Continued)
  Edgar Emet 42 Hegan 46
  John Hogkins 38 Joseph
  Traske 39 Kancamagus 38 39
  Lewey 75 Lewis Annance 72
  Madokawando 42 Matalluc
  71 Matalluck 71 72 73
  Mataluck 72 Mesambomwtt
  46 Metolic 71 Mohawk Susup
  75 Mollocket 28 65 Mollockett
  69 Mollylockett 69 Mollynockett 70 Mollyocket 34 38
  Mollyockett 69 117 Mollyrocket 69 Mollysusup 67 75
  Moxus 42 Mugg 42 Nanamacomuck 33 Nanamocomuck
  38 Natalluc 71 Nataluc 72
  Natanis 47 Neanongasett 40
  Neonongassett 41 Nimbatsett
  41 Nonannocomuck 39
  Numbenewett 40 Oorumby
  42 Pagus 34 35 Parmagimmet 71 Paseel 75 Passaconnaasoay 38 Passaconnaway
  31 33 Paugus 36 37 Peol 75
  Philip 34 Polan 33 Quallimosit 75 Rosalluc 74 Sabatis 29
  63 64 Sabattis 34 67 75
  Sabbattis 47 Sassacus 27
  Sauquish 47 Sawloo 75
  Sawwaramet 47 Squando 33
  Swarson 34 Tom Hegan 68
  Tomhegan 50 53 75 Tumtumhegan 75 Waaununga 47
  Warcedeen 47 Warrumbee 41
  Warumbee 40 Wattanummon
  46 Wawah 34 36 Wawawnunka 47 Wedon 41 Weedon
  40 Wehickermett 40 Wexar
  46 Whihhermete 41 Wilumpi
  71 Wonnalancet 38 Worombo
  38 39 Worumbee 42
INGALLS, Elijah 53 Moses 184
  186 Samuel 12 17 23 189
INGGALLS, Samuel 190

JACKMAN, Hannah 85
JACKSON, 62 Andrew 120
JENKS, Rev Dr 179
JEWETT, Leander 113 Stephen 103
JOBIN, Mr 121
JONES, Benj 114 Dan 114 T 116
JOSSELYN, 33
KENDALL, Belzaleel 187
KENNEY, Stephen Bartlett 83
KEYES, Esq 85 Jonathan 12
KIBBY, Joshua 8 9
KILGORE, Jno 188 191 Jos 188 190
KILLGORE, John 99
KIMBALL, 11 Asa 12 102 190 191 Benj W 162 Benjamin W 187 Charlotte 93 Eli L 184 I C 91 Ira 91 Ira C 191 Israel 162 189 190 Isreal 188 J E L 186 J T L 162 Jedediah T 191 John 68 162 Peter 23 Wm 184
KIRKLAND, Dr 126
KNAP, Javan 93 Jesse 92 Lydia 92 Mary 92
KNIGHTS, P 9
LARY, Fanny 122
LEE, Gen Maj 173
LELAND, John H 174 John H M 103 186 Joseph 192 Rhoda 88
LINCOLN, Gen 87 188 Gov 71-73 J 162 Levi 192
LITTLE, Valentine 103 184
LIVERMORE, Elijah 8
LOCKE, 124 126 Dr 127 129-137 139 141-152 154-159 John 122 123 148 152 186 Prof 145 Samuel Barron 122
LORING, A S 104
LOVEJOY, I H 113
LOVEWELL, 65 69 Capt 35 John 34
MARSHALL, 61 David 61 63 92 Lucy 61 63 92 Moses 63 Mr 62 Mrs 62

MARTIN, Dr 117 Esther K 166 John 114
MASON, Aaron 93 Agnes 119 Amos Jr 91 Anna 93 Ayers 12 13 82 86 89 93 Bethiah 93 Betsey 19 60 Betty 93 Catherine 93 Charles 93 Charlotte 93 Chas 195 Daniel 92 114 174 Dr 93 120 Elder 175 Elmira 93 Esther 92 93 Eunice 93 Experience 92 Hannah 89 93 Hugh 92 Javan K 181 184 186 187 John 93 182 John M 179 John Y 148 Lawson 93 Louisana 93 Lucy 61 92 Lydia 92 93 M 195 Martha 18 92 Mary 93 174 Meghill 194 Moses 6 18 31 63 73 89 92 93 119 160 162 184 185 188 191 194 Moses A 19 81 85 86 93 119 188 Moses Jr 91 191 195 Rachel 93 Suza 93 Thirza 93 94 162 Walter 89 93 181
MAURY, Lt 148
MAYNARD, Deborah 6 Joseph 6
MCKENNEY, Sally 170
MERION, Joseph 8
MERRICK, Bro 114
MERRILL, John 121 Josiah G 103 171 Mary 174 Rev Mr 103
MERRITT, Bro 114
MILLS, Hannah 89 93 James 89 93 188
MINUITS, Peter 6
MITCHELL, 183 Ammi R 103 171 Elder 175 Jacob 103 171 S T 161
MOHR, Christopher 13
MOODY, Rev Mr 167 168
MORE, Isaac W 114
MORRISON, John 92 Lydia 92
MORSE, Dr 148 Fred 200 Jos 8 Nath'l 8 9 Nathaniel 8

MORSHAALL, David 80
MOTT, Valentine 161
MOULTON, 71
MULVEY, B C 160
NEWELL, Ebenezer T 114 Seth B 181 Wellington 181 184 186
NEWTON, Abner 8
NOYES, John 8 10 Moses 8
NUTTALL, Mr 128
O'BRIEN, Martha 166
OAKMAN, Tobias 42
OCKETT, Molly 1 67-69
OWEN, David D 136
PACKARD, C 113 Charles 113
PAGE, Benjamin R 113 True 114
PAIN, John 114
PARKER, Clement 114 Esther 22 Thomas 8
PATERSON, James 8
PEASE, Hannah 93 John 93
PENN, Wm 30
PEOL, Molly 67
PERKINS, John 95
PERLEY, Eunice 170 Eunise 173 Jeremiah 173 John 182
PERRY, Amy 87 Dan 114 Edward West 87 Jos 4
PETTENGILL, 64 James 51 Mr 52 54 Mrs 52
PHILLIPS, Judge 192 Sam'l 98
PICKARD, Joseph 184
PIKE, Maj 43 46
PINGREE, John G 184
POOR, Peter 53
PORTER, Nath'l 102
POST, W 161
POTTER, C E 39 Judge 38
POWERS, 189 Amos 17 23 79 Gideon 19 80 99 Hiram 147 Paul 19 Silas 19 100 190
PRATT, Job 114
PROCTOR, Mary 11
PURCHASE, Mr 40 41 Thomas 39

QUIMBY, Joshua 176
RAND, Asa 170
RANDALL, Isaac 184 Joshua 114
RAWSON, Anna 170 E 49
REDINGTON, Judge 20 Samuel 20
RICE, Susanna 89
RICH, J G 73
RICHARDS, Aaron 8
RICHARDSON, Aaron 8 Ebenezer 92 Josiah 2 3 8-10 Thaddeus 8
RIDER, Mary 6 Moses 6
RINDGE, Capt 53 58
RIPLEY, Lincoln 102 Wm 103
ROBBINS, Edw 98 Edward 192 Edward H 192
ROBERTS, Amos 162 James 188 Milton 188 Thomas 186
ROBERTSON, Sylvester 195
ROBEY, Joseph 102
ROBINSON, 174 O'N W 191 O'Neil W 91 165 183 185 186
ROGER, 31
ROGERS, Col 50 67 Isaac 113 Maj 34 Robert 49 William 180
ROI, Mr 121
ROOD, L 104
ROSS, 138
ROWE, Caleb 6 20 194 Martha 18 19 23 29 67 77 Mrs 63
RUSEL, A Braham 80 Benj 79
RUSH, Dr 128
RUSSEL, Benj 99
RUSSELL, 101 Abbott 11 23 Abraham 11 17 23 86 B 96 Benj 12 81 99 100 102 189 190 Benjamin 11 17 23 78 95 97 98 Chas 162 Eunice 93 Isaac 189 Jacob 189 James 78 95 162 Jeremiah 189 John 12 Jonathan A 183 Lydia A 118 Mary 11 60 102 Mr 61 Stephen A 93

RUTER, Dr 132 Rev Dr 131
SABINE, Col 142 143
SADDLER, 194
SANBORN, David 61 189
  Joseph 183 Simeon 189
SANGER, Deborah 6
SEGAR, 64 75 77 Josiah 85 Lt
  16 18 50 71 170 Lucy 89
  Nath'l 12 Nathaniel 13 23 50
  189 190
SEPOY, Lt 143
SEWALL, D 104 Henry 103
  Jotham 113 Rev Mr 180
  Samuel 103
SHAPLEIGH, Nichols 40
SHAW, John 114
SILLIMAN, 129 Prof 141
SLAVE, Plato 53 57 58
SMALL, 44
SMITH, 127 Dr 133 John 28
  John T 103 171 Joseph 113
  Lucinda M S 172 Nathan 124
  Solon 125
SOULE, Moses 184
SOUTHWICK, Mary A 176
SOUTHWORTH, Capt 46
SPARROK, Nath'l 8
SPEAR, Elijah 114
SPRAGUE, Elhanan 189
SPURR, Wm 103 171
STAPLES, Wm 189
STARK, Gen 92
STEARNS, Chas 162 Dr 118
  John 100 Phineas 91 194
STEUBEN, Baron 117
STEVENS, W C 116
STILES, Albert 194 Valentine 6
STINSON, David 114
STONE, D 131 Ethan 131 Josiah
  8 9 10
STOWELL, Daniel 103 171
STRAW, Agnes 119
STRICKLAND, Rev Mr 69
STRONG, Caleb 192
SULLIVAN, James 192

SUMMERSIDES, W 116
SUMNER, Increase 191
SUSUP, Molly 67
SWAN, Betsey 85 Daniel B 188
  Elijah 12 Greely 81 86 James
  12 17 23 34 80 95 100 189
  190 John 85 Joseph G 99
  Joseph Greely 52 Mr 82 Mrs
  68 Nathaniel 12 67
SYLL, Capt 39
TAFT, 101
TALLEYRAND, Prof 122
TASKET, Mary 177
TAYLOR, 49 Joseph 48 Joshua
  114
TEUKSBURY, G F 103
TEWKSBURY, C F 113
THOMPSON, Z 199 Zenas 116
  177
THURSTON, David 103 Wm 103
TILMORE, Daniel 114
TINKER, John 38
TOWLE, Ira 159
TREADWELL, Moses 103 171
TRIPP, Elder 114
TRUE, Dr 73 N T 6 184 185
  Nath'l T 183 Nathaniel T 186
TRUMBULL, Joseph 8
TUCHILL, Joseph 5
TUCKER, Julia 6 Wm 6
TUTTLE, Alma 161
TWICHELL, Ebenezer 3 Joseph
  6 10
TWITCHEL, Abijah 4 Ebenezer
  4 Eleazer 80 Eli 80 Ezra 86
  Jo 80 Joseph 9 80 90
TWITCHELL, Abel 6 Abigail B
  160 Adelbert B 187 Adeline
  21 Alfred 194 Almon 87 161
  183 186 Almon A 191 Alphin
  86 87 89 Amos 6 21 Amy 87
  Anna 89 Asa 21 Benj 5
  Calvin 89 Capt 6 19 20-22 63
  64 88-90 92 Cynthia 21
  Deborah 6 21 Dr 124 E 81 91

TWITCHELL (Continued)
Ebenezer 8 Edward 8 Eleazer 6 17 18 21 23 50 75 81 86 87 89 90-93 95 102 194 Eli 6 86-91 99 162 188 Elizabeth 6 Ezra 6 87 89 101 102 104 162 189 Hannah 89 Harriet 87 John A 2 87 112 Jonathan 87 Joseph 3 5 6 8 12 17 18 21 77 87 88 90 91 116 161 194 Julia 6 87 Lois 163 Lydia 21 91 93 Martha 6 18 21 92 Mary 6 Mary E 113 Mary Elizabeth 174 Molly 6 Moses 18 21 Mrs 20 75 Nathan 23 89 Nathan F 113 Ozmon M 161 Peter 5 6 87 188 Rosabla 161 Sam'l B 186 Sam'l F 186 Samuel 6 Samuel B 183 Samuel Birge 162 Sarah 87 Sarah J 23 Simeon 18 21 75 76 Susanna 89 102 Sylvanus 21 Thaddeus 89 160 Thadeus 174 Wm 162
VANRENSSELAER, Stephen 168
VETROMILE, 28
VIRGIN, Joel C 165
VOLTA, 124
WAKEFIELD, Ms 125
WALDRON, Maj 39
WALKER, Abigail 85 Daniel 8 Dean 174 Elmira R 174 Ezekiel 91 Gardiner 91 H D 104 James 85 90 91 112 183-185 191 194 John 189 Joseph 103 171 Nathaniel 63 Olive C 185 Sears C 148
WALLS, James 13
WALTON, Capt 46
WARD, Richard 8

WARREN, Abijah 182
WASHINGTON, 87 Gen 59 189
WEBSTER, 120 Baker 93 Louisana 93
WELLS, Dr 147 Mr 146 Nathaniel 191
WENTWORTH, Daniel 114
WHARTON, Richard 40 41
WHEATSTONE, Prof 145
WHEELRIGHT, J B 104
WHEELWRIGHT, J B 174 John B 185
WHITE, 101
WHITEHOUSE, Daniel 114
WHITMAN, Levi 184
WIGHT, Eli 184 186 Elizabeth 6 Joel 6 Marcus 114 Nahum 186
WILEY, Abigail B 160 Dr 160 Jerusha 21 R G 162 Robert G 159
WILLEY, 68 81 176
WILLIAMS, John 190 Prof 167
WILLIAMSON, 48 49 John 160 190 Wm 160 184 186
WILLIS, 44 Adam 11 23 190 James 190
WILSON, John M 71 72 Rev Dr 131
WOOD, Cornelius 8 9 10
WRIGHT, 120 M B 122 135 152 Nathaniel 123
WYMAN, Ensign 35
YORK, Isaac 80 Isaac I 190 Isaac Insley 190 Isaac T 188 Job 189 John 11 17 23 79 100 189 190 Peter 23 190
YOUNG, Amos 11 12 23 78 190 H 194

www.ingramcontent.com/pod-product-compliance
Lightning Source LLC
Chambersburg PA
CBHW050136170426
43197CB00011B/1862